Scale of map: one inch to 78 miles

The Heartland

TIME-LIFE Library of America

The Heartland

**Illinois Indiana Michigan
Ohio Wisconsin**

By Robert McLaughlin
and the Editors of
TIME-LIFE BOOKS

Time Incorporated, New York

The Author: An associate editor of TIME, Robert McLaughlin was born in Chicago. He received his primary and secondary education in that city and attended the University of Illinois. In the 1930s, after working as a reporter for the Denver, Colorado, *Rocky Mountain News,* he returned to Chicago and began contributing short stories to national magazines. During World War II he served in the Chemical Warfare Service, and after the war became a TIME writer. Mr. McLaughlin has also written articles for a number of other national publications. He is the author of four novels and the co-author, with his wife Mignon, of *Gayden,* a play produced on Broadway in 1949.

The Consulting Editor: Oscar Handlin, Winthrop Professor of History at Harvard University and chairman of the university's Charles Warren Center for Studies in American History, is one of America's foremost social historians. His work on U.S. immigrants, *The Uprooted,* won the Pulitzer Prize in 1952.

The Cover: Testimony to the Heartland's industrial might, smoke pours at dusk from the tall stacks of the U.S. Steel works in Gary, Indiana.

TIME-LIFE BOOKS

Editor
Maitland A. Edey

Text Director   **Art Director**
Jerry Korn   Sheldon Cotler

Chief of Research
Beatrice T. Dobie

Assistant Text Directors:
Harold C. Field, Ogden Tanner

Assistant Art Director:
Arnold C. Holeywell

Assistant Chiefs of Research:
Monica O. Horne, Martha Turner

Publisher
Rhett Austell

General Manager: Joseph C. Hazen Jr.
Circulation Director: Joan D. Manley
Marketing Director: Carter Smith
Business Manager: John D. McSweeney
Publishing Board: Nicholas Benton,
Louis Bronzo, James Wendell Forbes

TIME-LIFE Library of America

Series Editor: Oliver E. Allen

Editorial Staff for *The Heartland:*

Assistant Editor: Jay Brennan
Picture Editor: Grace M. Brynolson
Designer: Ben Schultz
Assistant Designer: John Newcomb
Staff Writers: Simon Johnson, Jonathan Kastner
Chief Researcher: Clara E. Nicolai
Text Research: Don Nelson,
Louise Samuels, Sondra Albert
Picture Research: Judy Gurovitz,
Nancy J. Jacobsen, Diane Wynne,
Elizabeth McClintock, Ruth Silva,
Tony Chiu

Editorial Production

Color Director: Robert L. Young
Assistant: James J. Cox
Copy Staff: Marian Gordon Goldman,
Patricia Miller, Dolores A. Littles
Picture Bureau: Margaret K. Goldsmith,
Barbara Sullivan
Traffic: Douglas B. Graham
Art Assistants: Carol Iselin, Virginia Wells

The text for the chapters of this book was written by Robert McLaughlin, the picture essays by Simon Johnson and Jonathan Kastner. Valuable help was provided by these individuals and departments of Time Inc.: the Chief of the LIFE Picture Library, Doris O'Neil; the Chief of the Bureau of Editorial Reference, Peter Draz; the Chief of the TIME-LIFE News Service, Richard M. Clurman; Bureau Chief Mark Sullivan (Detroit), Correspondents Ron Berquist (Chicago), Roger Rowand (Cleveland), Dick Rawe (Cincinnati), Ray Kenney (Milwaukee) and Gordon Englehart (Indianapolis).

Contents

Introduction

The little town of Pekin, Illinois, in which I was born in the last decade of the 19th Century, was named for the city of Peking, China, the capital of the Chinese Empire—the domain over which Kublai Khan reigned and from which many centuries ago came the discovery of printing and gunpowder.

The choice of the town's name occurred, I am told, in an odd but charmingly innocent way. In the 1840s the citizens of the recently settled town on the Illinois River had been unable to agree on a name and had finally asked the ranking Army officer of the area to pick one. Being a prudent man, he delegated the choice to his wife, who upon examining their location on the family globe and finding it to be near the 40th parallel ran her finger along that line until she came to the great Chinese city. And so the name of my hometown became, in slightly simplified form, Pekin.

The town of Pekin has changed considerably since that time and has grown apace. Many other cities have developed in that area, and today the entire Heartland flourishes. Here are the farms and the cities, the steel mills and the auto assembly lines, the rail terminals and the airports that nourish and give vitality to the nation and the far corners of the world. Mail-order houses located here have supplied the needs of distant customers for many years.

Earth-moving equipment from Peoria has chewed up jungles and laced them with roads; these powerful machines have created cities in previously inaccessible interiors and built dams to make possible the irrigation of former deserts. The earth has been encouraged to yield up its fruits in increasing abundance through the use of farm machinery, chemical fertilizers and techniques developed here.

The five Midwestern states forming the Heartland contain more than 38 million people, or about 20 per cent of the total population of the United States. In the early 1960s the region accounted for 29 per cent of the value added by manufacture in the entire nation, for 27 per cent of the total investment for new plants and equipment in the U.S., and for 26 per cent of the nation's total value of exported manufactured products.

The people of the Heartland have been blessed with a soil unusual in its richness and abundance, with a plentiful supply of fresh water and with superb mineral resources. The minerals are especially significant, for it is here that they are fashioned and fabricated into almost everything used anywhere in the world. The people do not take such riches for granted, however, but accept a responsibility to use them in trust, as it were, for the benefit of the brotherhood of mankind.

Their feeling of brotherhood comes naturally. Brothers they are, these men and women, for there is no remote corner of the earth whose people are not represented here. In one Illinois voting ward some years ago, I counted no less than 50 national and racial groups. They are an adventuresome people, never content to stop at the threshold but always seeking to press on. Challenge dismays them not; adversity has been no stranger; hardship has toughened and molded them. They are workers and achievers and they are proud of themselves and of their country.

The area's will to progress is exemplified by one of the most popular of its many attractions, the Museum of Science and Industry, in Chicago on the shore of Lake Michigan. Here are exhibits that work. There are no "Do Not Touch" signs. Visitors can play ticktacktoe with a computer, walk inside a 16-foot model of a human heart, clamber through a captured German submarine, descend an elevator to tour an operating coal mine, or watch chickens hatch in an incubator. The emphasis of the Heartland is on work, research and doing it better. The entire region crackles with creative optimism.

Not many years ago the earth was shaken in the Heartland, in a way that irrevocably and in one instant changed the course of mankind and opened to us the challenge of space—and eventually perhaps even that of the solar system. This happened on a snowy day, the 2nd of December, 1942, in a laboratory at 57th and Greenwood Avenue in Chicago. There, under the plank board seats of an abandoned football stadium, Dr. Enrico Fermi and his colleagues announced that sustained controlled production of atomic energy had been accomplished. Mankind was thus given a new tool—a tool that was also a weapon of awesome proportions. The crucible of war furnished the means by which that weapon was produced for military use, and the war was ended through its use. But the weapon was so formidable it has remained sheathed ever since.

Tools forged and powered by nuclear energy have in the intervening years spread out from the Heartland to make the earth more fruitful and to alleviate human suffering. Nor is the region's nuclear potential even now developed to its fullest extent. The Atomic Energy Commission in 1966 selected a Heartland site, Weston, Illinois, as the most suitable in the nation for the location of its proposed 200-billion-electron-volt proton accelerator. This will be the largest and most complex machine ever built for fundamental scientific research. The knowledge gained as a result of the work done here will bring about a broader understanding of the basic building blocks of matter and the forces that govern the operation of the universe.

Such knowledge is an essential prerequisite for the journey into an entirely new era. We can expect this Heartland base to be the launching site for many a successful breakthrough, piercing the barriers to our knowledge and enlarging our comprehension of the enormous sources of power available to mankind. These reservoirs of energy have always surrounded us, but we are just now beginning to understand them. Scientists have reported promising experiments in cancer treatment through the use of electron and proton machines. The growth of our nation appears certain to be spurred, and the world's standard of living enhanced, through the work done in the Heartland.

The motto of Chicago is "I Will." In its early days the infant city was refused a development loan by the bank of Shawneetown, whose officers considered the area uninhabitable and worthless. The Chicagoans were not easily deterred, however, and the city grew anyway. Midwesterners make no little plans. They will and they do. Chicagoans just before the Civil War raised the entire city several feet above Lake Michigan and later reversed the direction of the Chicago River so that it flowed out of the lake instead of into it. Recently Midwesterners helped open up the St. Lawrence Seaway linking the ports of the Great Lakes with those of the outside world. As world trade enriched the cultures of Venice and the ancient Phoenicians, so there permeates the Heartland a sensitivity to the community of mankind.

From this region have come many men whose names and deeds are history. They were men who had to struggle. Underprivileged they were. Quenchable of spirit they were not. Such a person was Abraham Lincoln. Sorely used by ill-fortune and a man who knew well the effects of poverty, this son of Illinois was neither embittered nor vanquished. The dark nights of the soul through which he must have lived reinforced his determination to light a candle of freedom and hope for millions of others.

Hopelessness is alien to the people of the Heartland. They are a rugged lot and they work and persevere and then they work some more. Vitality is everywhere. People of diverse cultures have brought here their customs and have distilled from a cosmopolitan chemistry an essence that is pure Midwest.

Friendliness abounds here, as this book points out so accurately. The Midwestern Rip van Winkle in Chapter 8 might not recognize the people around him, but he would almost certainly find them to be neighborly, and friendly too.

The people of the world today know more about themselves and their planet than they did one hundred years ago. Man's ability to communicate each with another has accelerated with astonishing velocity. O'Hare Field in Chicago is not many more hours by air from Tokyo than it is from Athens. Midwestern television is connected by satellite to distant world capitals. Such communication augurs well. Dialogue between faiths and nations contains an enormous potential for good.

I am glad that the TIME-LIFE Library of America is doing this book. Although we live in an age of high-speed transportation, this is not an unmixed blessing. Jet airliners soar above the clouds, and interstate expressways antiseptically insulate the traveler from any but minimal contact with the people and the country through which he speeds on ribbons of concrete. We need a sense of history, together with a better knowledge of our country and of the people of all its parts who made it great and who continue to build it. This book will stimulate an awareness that the Heartland's history is neither dull nor dead but an exciting tribute to the people of the region—a people who are a little less than the angels but always trying to do better.

—Everett McKinley Dirksen
U.S. Senator from Illinois

Drifted by the biting winter prairie wind, light snow marks off the furrows between seemingly endless rows of stubble on a farm near Champaign, Illinois. In the distance, farm buildings huddle together awaiting the inevitable surge of another springtime.

1

The Heartland Mood

The Heartland, that sprawling region of the United States comprising Illinois, Indiana, Michigan, Ohio and Wisconsin, is a land of space and speed, progress and plenty. Above all, it is a land of paradox. The rich farmlands stretching from horizon to horizon grow grain enough to meet half the nation's needs, yet the Heartland is one of the most urban regions of the United States. The Midwestern cities are landlocked in the center of the continent, yet the Great Lakes and the great rivers give easy access to the Gulf of Mexico and the Atlantic Ocean. Michigan touches no ocean, yet it has, after Alaska, the longest coastline in the Union—2,250 miles.

Although it normally holds much the same opinions as the rest of the country, the Heartland frequently sounds far more extreme on great national issues. The voice of the Midwest, said Woodrow Wilson, "is a voice of protest," and the Heartland is often more against something than in favor of something else. As a home of native radicalism of the Left and Right it has had little inclination to follow foreign "isms." The Heartland's Progressives and Greenbackers were forever charging into battle against plutocracy and "vested interests."

It is impossible to discover who speaks for the Heartland. The same soil that nurtured such Right-Wingers as Mayor "Big Bill" Thompson of Chicago, Colonel Robert R. McCormick, publisher of the *Chicago Tribune*, and Senator Joseph R. McCarthy of Wisconsin also produced a long line of volubly liberal governors: John Peter Altgeld of Illinois, Hazen Pingree of Michigan and "Fighting Bob" La Follette of Wisconsin, among others. The Heartland eternally creates opposites. The agnostic

Names and nicknames of the Heartland states

The Prairie State

Settlers in the early 1800s, who trekked through the tall grass of the prairie *(left)* that covers much of Illinois, gave the state the nickname by which it is still most widely known. The state's name, Illinois, is derived from Illiniwek, the name by which the Algonquian Indians of the area referred to themselves. It meant "the superior men."

The Hoosier State

Indiana's principal nickname may be a corruption of "hoozer," a term used by Indiana settlers from Cumberland County, England, to mean "hill dweller" or "highlander." At the right a Hoosier tills his uphill farm. The state's name, formed from "Indian," is Neo-Latin, meaning "the land of the Indians."

The Buckeye State

Ohio's principal nickname comes from the once-plentiful buckeye tree *(Aesculus glabra),* a variety of chestnut, whose nut *(left)* has a spot that looks like the eye of a buck deer. The state was named after the Ohio River, whose name in turn may have come from Iroquois words meaning "beautiful" or "beautiful river."

The Badger State

Lead miners in the 1820s in Wisconsin were called badgers because many of them dug holes, much like badger burrows, for winter homes *(right)*. In time "Badger" came to be used as the state's nickname. "Wisconsin" derives from the Chippewa name for the river of the same name, meaning "the gathering of the waters."

The Wolverine State

According to a popular story, Michigan's nickname grew up about 1800 because a famous tavernkeeper, Conrad Ten Eyck, enjoyed telling diners they had just finished a wolf steak—to which one girl replied, "Then I suppose I am a Wolverine?" The state was named after Lake Michigan, whose name meant "a great lake."

advocate Clarence Darrow and his sometime opponent, the fundamentalist politician William Jennings Bryan, were both products of the region. In the same year—1905—and in the same city—Chicago—Paul Harris founded the businessmen's organization known as Rotary International and Eugene Victor Debs organized the militant Industrial Workers of the World, a group better known as "Wobblies." And that, in a sense, is the Heartland: a bizarre and uniquely American mixture of Rotarians and Wobblies.

A geographical region as large in size as France, the Heartland has more industrial muscle than that country and the United Kingdom put together. Along the Great Lakes, from Superior to Cleveland, stretches a thousand-mile belt of factories, mills, refineries, blast furnaces and machine-tool plants. You name it—tractors or traveling cranes, copper or ketchup, limestone or light bulbs, pork or plate glass—the region produces it or grows it or claws it from the earth. The Chicago-Gary metropolitan area alone pours more steel than all of France. The Detroit area builds a third of the nation's autos. Elkhart, Indiana, makes 60 per cent of the world's band instruments. All told, the region produces more than three quarters of the nation's construction machinery and iron and steel forgings, more than half of its radio and TV sets, refrigerators and power-transmission equipment, half of its steel ingots and farm machinery, and a third of its soap and detergents, sporting goods, house trailers, paints, soybeans, corn, coke and tires.

As the transportation hub of the country, the Heartland launches string after endless string of freight cars to every point of the compass. A single one of these trains can carry enough wheat to feed Algeria for two days, enough autos to form a five-mile motorcade, enough coal to fuel the generating plants of a sizable city for a sizable period of time. Toll roads and freeways tremble to the hurtling weight of huge trucking rigs—silvery juggernauts by day, and by night festooned with more lights than a luxury yacht. Overhead sounds the whistling roar of the jets that make Chicago's O'Hare Airport the busiest commercial field in the world, handling 20 million passengers a year. On the vast network of inland waterways, towboats move lines of 20 and more barges loaded with oil and sand, coal and cement. Through the blue, sun-glinting waters of the Great Lakes travel freighters from Israel and Ghana, Britain and Japan, as well as the majestic 700-foot ore boats of the lake fleet.

The Heartland sky seems higher and wider than the East's, and it is surely more filled with drama.

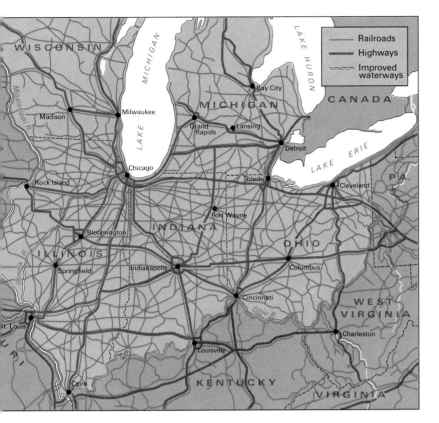

Routes on land and water

A key factor in the Heartland's economic health is the region's superb transportation network. The map shows the principal improved waterways, the railroads and the major highways. Unlike some other regions, the Heartland has no mountain barriers between large settlements. In the entire area the only real impediments to overland travel are the rivers and lakes. In fact, Chicago became a great national transportation hub partly because the transcontinental routes had to detour around the southern tip of Lake Michigan. But the rivers and lakes happen also to serve as excellent paths for shipping. The early settlers traveled by water and built the first towns on the water's edge, where they became junctions between water and land transportation routes. In time, Chicago, Cincinnati, St. Louis and other cities on the lakes or rivers grew to be major terminals for railroads as well as for shipping and road traffic. And as the airlines took on a significant role in transportation—today almost 6 per cent of all passenger traffic moves by air —it was natural that principal airports would be located in or near these cities.

Swirling black thunderheads lock in Manichaean combat with fleecy white cumulus. Heat lightning walks along the horizon and waterspouts spin across the lakes. Tornadoes suck up dust—and sometimes rooftops—from the prairie. Thunder sounds like whole nations of giants falling downstairs.

Winter is unconditional war between man and weather. Spring is brief but beautiful, arriving on a booming wind and departing from a land filled with greenery counterpointed by pink and white as the great orchards lining Lake Michigan burst into flower. In summer the sun is king and the land throbs with heat—farmers swear they can hear the corn growing in August. The Heartland will match its autumn against any in the world. Mrs. Frances Trollope, mother of the British novelist Anthony Trollope, who spent some time in Cincinnati in the late 1820s, was dumfounded by fall when "the whole country goes to glory!" The silent explosion of color is a last pledge of allegiance by the leaves of the Heartland's trees. The leaves turn yellow on hickories, beeches and ironwoods; wine-red on white oaks; red, yellow or orange on maples; royal purple or mauve on white ashes; shimmering, bright orange on sassafras. Just as the riot of color seems ended, scarlet oaks throw their light across the land. Children run scuffling through leaf piles as through

surf. The crisp, clean air is spangled with haze and threaded with the heartbreak scent of burning leaves. From a thousand towns each autumnal Saturday rises an exultant roar as crowds urge on Massillon High or Earlham College or one of the behemoth elevens of the Big Ten.

It is a man's country. Contemplative anglers wade hip-deep in trout streams or troll for northern pike or muskellunge in tens of thousands of lakes. In Indiana it is a tradition to hunt rabbits on Thanksgiving. Business virtually closes down in Wisconsin and Michigan during the deer season. Along the wide, misty rivers and the mirrored lakes the first light of dawn finds hunters in their blinds, decoys set out, awaiting the flyover of migrating geese and ducks. The North Woods trails of northern Wisconsin and Michigan are fragrant with balsam. All night long treetops sough gently in the wind and the heavy silence can be broken by the inquisitive snuffling of an occasional bear.

Much of the landscape has a pleasant intimacy, hemmed in on all sides by groves, wood lots and tree lines. Flights of ballet-minded starlings curvet, swoop, and change direction with bewildering speed and precision. Hawks hover on outstretched wings, crows wrangle in the bare branches, grouse rise with a whir. Driving to town or coming home,

A famous evocation of autumn

"Injun Summer," the two-panel cartoon shown here, was drawn by John T. McCutcheon in 1907 for the *Chicago Tribune*. McCutcheon, who later won a Pulitzer Prize for a biting Depression-era cartoon, considered "Injun Summer" to be "just a day's work," but the nostalgic drawing with its accompanying text was so popular that the *Tribune* has reprinted it every fall since 1912. In the text the old man says:

"Yep, sonny, this is sure enough Injun summer. Don't know what that is, I reckon, do you?

"Well, that's when all the homesick Injuns come back to play . . . Don't be skeered—hain't none around here

now, leastways no live ones. They been gone this many a year. They all went away and died . . .

"But every year, 'long about now, they all come back, leastways their sperrits do. They're here now. You can see 'em off across the fields. Look real hard. See that kind o' hazy . . . look out yonder? Well, them's Injuns— Injun sperrits marchin' along an' dancin' in the sunlight . . .

"See off yonder; see them tepees? They kind o' look like corn shocks from here, but them's Injun tents, sure as you're a foot high. See 'em now? Sure, I knowed you could. Smell that smoky sort o' smell in the air? That's the campfires a-burnin' and their pipes a-goin' . . .

"You jest come out here tonight when the moon is hangin' over the hill off yonder an' the harvest fields is all swimmin' in th' moonlight, an' you can see the Injuns and the tepees jest as plain as kin be. You can, eh? . . .

"Jever notice how the leaves turn red 'bout this time o' year? . . . That's when an old Injun sperrit gits tired dancin' an' goes up and squats on a leaf t' rest . . . an' ever' once'n a while a leaf gives way under some fat old Injun ghost and comes floatin' down to the ground. See —here's one now. See how red it is? That's the war paint rubbed off'n an Injun ghost, sure's you're born.

"Purty soon all the Injuns'll go marchin' away agin, back to the happy huntin' ground, but next year you'll see 'em troopin' back—th' sky jest hazy with 'em and their campfires smolderin' away jest like they are now."

a man can glimpse chipmunks, rabbits, a pheasant. Awakening early one morning he may see from his window a deer standing motionless and alert.

Most of the Heartland's country towns lie flat against the earth and are announced from a distance by water towers, each with a name stenciled big: here comes Paw Paw, there goes Coloma. Some of them dream of a remoter time. Frame houses, with front porches as ample as a grandmother's lap, are set back on wide lawns and hold memories of a creaking swing, the tinkle of a ukulele, the gleam of white dresses moving in and out of screen doors. Stately trees make a leafy tunnel of each street. A lamp glimmers at a distant corner, moths bump blindly against the glass, and stars, seen through the moving leaves, tremble in the heavens.

The past is well remembered. Old locomotives of the Nickel Plate Line are finally at rest behind neat picket fences; Civil War soldiers stand at parade rest in town squares; the Indian and his artifacts are given ironic tender loving care in a hundred museums. In Sandusky, Ohio, and in Milwaukee, Wisconsin, children crowd around gilt-and-glass wagons just as their parents did before them to buy the delights of hot buttered popcorn and roasted peanuts. This Heartland evokes the fabled Golden Age, the time "when the frost is on the punkin and the fodder's in the shock," recalled by John T. McCutcheon's nostalgic cartoon "Injun Summer," which is still printed annually in the *Chicago Tribune*.

Like the rest of the nation, the Heartland is on a cultural binge. The major cities have long had their symphonies, little-theater groups, art museums and block-long, block-wide public libraries. Even such smaller cities as Evanston, Illinois, have had local symphony orchestras for a quarter of a century or more. But the passion for the arts has become so deep and so widespread that Sears, Roebuck sells paintings today as it formerly sold horse collars and kerosene lamps. At the Occidental Hotel in Muskegon a Michigan artist-entrepreneur offers paintings on a "60-Day Lay-a-Way Plan." In rural Clark County in Wisconsin the first Beaux Arts festival ever held there realized $850 from the sale of local paintings. Wisconsin towns as remote as Rhinelander and Fish Creek hold annual art festivals. Music also covers the state, from band concerts in Two Rivers to Johann Schiller's *Wilhelm Tell* presented in German and English versions by the citizens of New Glarus, most of whom are of Swiss descent. There are now so many lovers of dance, drama, painting and sculpture, both from within and without the state, that Wisconsin issues a quarterly listing of coming cultural events—a publication that would have been inconceivable only a generation ago. The president of the Wisconsin Arts Foundation and Council in the mid-1960s was no estranged intellectual—he was also secretary of the Board of Trustees of the Northwestern Mutual Life Insurance Company.

The cities have developed their own styles. Chicago has been blessed by architects and has returned the compliment by welcoming innovation and displaying a foresight remarkable in a city so young, raw and impatient. D. H. Burnham, architect for Chicago's first planning commission, was fond of repeating the slogan, "Make no little plans!" The result is one of the world's finest man-made waterfronts, and the architectural historian Leonard Eaton of the University of Michigan says, "If you want to see what the city of the future could look like, walk down Chicago's North Dearborn Street from Monroe to the river." Detroit has made a beginning on its own neglected waterfront with a new Civic Center and has also drawn up an ambitious master plan to renew other large sections of the city. Cincinnati has swept away many of the decaying tenements and buildings of its downtown in an effort to revitalize the area.

The mill towns of the Heartland, bleak by day, compensate at night by detonating a neon fury. Motels and gas stations, used-car lots and eateries proclaim their excellence with sunbursts, star shells and caracoles of leaping light. Geometric eye-catchers switch on and off, spotlights play on fluttering pennons, twirling disks and rippling banners. Great batteries of stop-and-go signals flash from red to green—it seems every evening as if block parties were beginning. The only sedative note is supplied by the subdued indirect lighting of colonial-style funeral homes.

There is great variety but it can be found only if one is willing to stray from the superhighways. The towns in the western part of Michigan's Upper Peninsula have a mountainy air and retain some of the brash and cocky aspect of early mining days. To pass at night through the industrial cities of the Calumet area southeast of Chicago, or those of Steel Valley in Ohio, is to tread the circles of hell amid spurts of flame, the clangor of anvils, the brimstone billowing of smoke. Along the Mississippi and the Ohio and their tributaries lie the river towns, reaching in a broad arc from bustling La Crosse, Wisconsin, to tree-shaded Marietta, Ohio. Many of these are the Heartland's oldest cities and some, like the Wabash River town of Vincennes, Indiana, were thriving communities

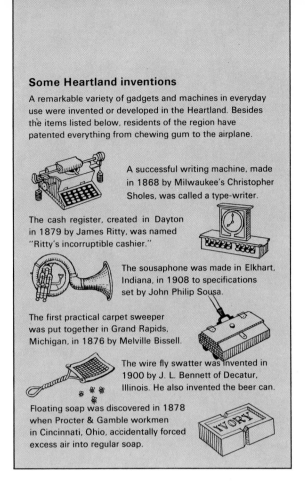

Some Heartland inventions

A remarkable variety of gadgets and machines in everyday use were invented or developed in the Heartland. Besides the items listed below, residents of the region have patented everything from chewing gum to the airplane.

A successful writing machine, made in 1868 by Milwaukee's Christopher Sholes, was called a type-writer.

The cash register, created in Dayton in 1879 by James Ritty, was named "Ritty's incorruptible cashier."

The sousaphone was made in Elkhart, Indiana, in 1908 to specifications set by John Philip Sousa.

The first practical carpet sweeper was put together in Grand Rapids, Michigan, in 1876 by Melville Bissell.

The wire fly swatter was invented in 1900 by J. L. Bennett of Decatur, Illinois. He also invented the beer can.

Floating soap was discovered in 1878 when Procter & Gamble workmen in Cincinnati, Ohio, accidentally forced excess air into regular soap.

when much of Pennsylvania was still a wilderness. A few have a rare beauty, with houses built in Steamboat Gothic and trimmed with carpenter's lace. Galena, Illinois, which once had reason to believe that it would eclipse Chicago, now dreams away its days above the Galena River, largely unchanged since Civil War times. Not far to the southeast lies Oregon, on the Rock River, so scenic that it has been host to generations of artists, as have Saugatuck, Michigan, and Brown County, Indiana.

In the veins of the Heartland's 38 million people flows the blood of virtually every nation on earth. Chicago has half as many Poles as Warsaw. A Detroit radio station broadcasts in Arabic, Maltese, Lithuanian and Armenian. Frankenmuth, Michigan, celebrates its annual Bavarian Festival. Hancock, on Michigan's Upper Peninsula, is renowned for its Finnish choirs. Along with this myriad of ethnic strains exists an intense, high-octane Americanism. To some the chauvinism on occasion seems excessive, but it has perhaps constituted a unifying influence among peoples of great diversity. Many polysyllabic surnames have been anglicized, but even when the family name remains Kowalski or Garofalo, Lopez or Jankovich, Rabinowitz or Paulavicius, the man is a Midwestern American—and defiantly proud of it. From the beginning,

Heartland settlers had the sense of being an elite who had chosen their own land and built their own communities with their own hands. Discussing some of the freewheeling practices of pioneer days, Thomas Ford, an early governor of Illinois, expressed the sentiment: "A large crowd of strangers, as it were, had met here for adventure."

While the Heartland was long a stronghold of isolationism and pacifist sentiment, it has always responded lustily to war, and its regimental flags carry honors from virtually every major American battle. The region outdid itself in the Civil War, producing some of the North's most distinguished fighting units and three of its most successful generals—Ulysses S. Grant, William T. Sherman and Philip Sheridan—as well as the wartime President, Abraham Lincoln, and the man who was his major opponent for the Presidency, Stephen A. Douglas. The Confederacy even borrowed its anthem, "Dixie," from a Heartland composer—it was written for a minstrel show by Daniel Decatur Emmett of Ohio.

The people of the Heartland resemble the French in their passionate attachment to their land, but many of them leave it frequently and with great readiness. Always a restless people, they have traditionally moved from farm to town, town to city, city to suburb, state to state. Entire generations are often on the wing—retired oldsters to the sun cities of Florida and California, the young to the East and South, the middle-aged in all directions.

With all its vitality, the Heartland has always had a sense of being under siege. That feeling was much more pronounced in the past but considerable traces of it are evident even today. Deep in the regional memory remains a fear that a potent "They" are out to get the Midwest, to spoil and defraud it, and to thwart all its honest efforts. "They" have been identified at various times as Wall Street, the East, the Pope, That Man in the White House, the Federal Government, Creeping Socialism or World Communism. At the heart of this suspicion lies the Heartland conviction that all problems are capable of solution and that, given willing Midwestern hearts and hands, even the impossible can be speedily accomplished. If it is not, then the fault must obviously lie elsewhere.

There are historical reasons for this attitude. The Heartland has always been a home of conspiracies. The earliest settlers learned to play profitably on the rivalries of France, Spain and England. The Indians banded together in a secret alliance in 1763 under the great Ottawa chief Pontiac, and did so again nearly 50 years later under the Shawnee

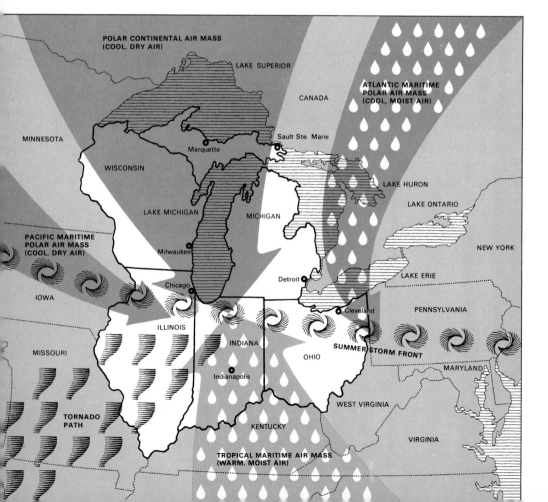

Winds of change

The violently changeable weather of the Heartland is the result of continuing clashes of four of the main air masses that dominate the North American climate. The two larger masses—the Polar Continental from northern Canada and the Tropical Maritime from the Gulf of Mexico—collide over the region in the summertime, creating storms along a constantly shifting front. In the winter the polar air forces the tropical mass far south, but occasional warm spearheads break through, creating sudden balmy spells. The two other major air masses—the Pacific Maritime and the Atlantic Maritime—spill into the region at random intervals. An additional complication is added by the tornadoes that sweep up through the Heartland with insane fury, sometimes reaching as far north as Michigan's Upper Peninsula. The Great Lakes moderate the air passing over them. In the summer this gives Michigan a long, mild growing season. In the winter, however, moisture from the lakes precipitates as snow, giving cities on the lee shore, like Marquette and Sault Ste. Marie, some of the nation's heaviest snowfalls.

leader Tecumseh. One of the first American commanders in the Heartland, General James Wilkinson, is known to have been on the payroll of Spain. Involved with Wilkinson, although ignorant of his connections with Spain, was Aaron Burr, who formulated a plan to seize Spanish territory and in 1806 used an island in the Ohio River as a rallying point for prospective "colonists." Subsequently tried for treason, Burr was acquitted, but suspicions about his intentions persisted. The record is clear in regard to Clement Vallandigham of Ohio: a former congressman, he unquestionably engaged in treason during the Civil War and found support for his ambition of taking all of the Heartland states out of the Union. The Mormons, who lived for a time in the Heartland in the 1830s and 1840s before undertaking their trek to Utah, reinforced the region's worries over conspiracies.

Thomas Ford, who was Governor of Illinois at the time, wrote that "it was believed by vast numbers of the people that [the Mormons] entertained the treasonable design, when they got strong enough, of overturning the government, driving out the old population, and taking possession of the country." Of more recent date is the Negro Black Muslim movement, which regards all whites as devils incarnate. Founded in Detroit in 1930, it now has its headquarters in Chicago.

The threat of real and imaginary dangers encouraged the formation of secret societies to protect hearth and home. The Know-Nothings, who enjoyed great strength in the nation in the 1840s and 1850s, and who once elected a mayor of Chicago, were antiforeign as well as anti-Roman Catholic, as was the American Protective Association, an organization that flourished in the early 1890s. Members of the Knights of the Golden Circle and a successor group, the Sons of Liberty, tried to get Illinois, Ohio and Indiana out of the Civil War, just as the Union Leaguers tried, with greater success, to keep them in. During the 1920s, the Ku Klux Klan briefly flourished within the region on an all-embracing program of opposition to Catholics, Jews, Negroes, foreigners, Bolsheviks, bootleggers, pacifists, Darwinians and anyone it considered immoral. Grand Dragon David C. Stephenson could accurately boast, "I am the law in Indiana!" Yet there was perhaps a good deal less danger in these various plots, subplots and conspiracies than there appeared to be at the time. The historian John Higham has observed that antiforeign movements have "surged and subsided time and again in American history. Each time the stresses that fostered them had eased in a few years . . . and the people

The grass of prairie and plain

Two types of grassland that are often confused are depicted in the drawings above. On the left is the tall-grass prairie that once spread like a sea over much of the western Heartland. On the right is the short-grass plain that extended west of the Heartland. In the prairie areas—where rainfall reaches 20 to 40 inches a year, the soil is rich humus, and there is considerable sun —the grass rose as high as nine feet. On the plains —where rainfall varies from 10 to 20 inches, the soil is poorer, and the sun shines even more frequently—the grass grew only one to three feet tall. Today corn, a relative of the tall grass, thrives in the prairie region. Wheat, itself a short grass, grows on the plains.

had recovered their temper and their aplomb."

The Heartland, nevertheless, has strong opinions, strongly voiced. A fuel dealer in Michigan says, "Don't talk to me about farmers. I know a fellow raises onions down south of here. I treat my dog better'n he treats his help." In a small office in a cavernous building on North Third Street, a former mayor of Milwaukee concludes that there is a Right-Wing madness abroad in the land and sees hope primarily "in the clergy and the colleges." A Community Chest chairman in Illinois muses about teenagers: "I'm damned if I know what we could provide for them. They're just in a bad age group— too young for the taverns and too old for the Youth Centers, which they regard as kid stuff." A steelworker in East Chicago explodes, "With all the tax income from industry, we have just about the lowest property taxes in the country. This town should be a garden spot but, instead, it's a cesspool." A Chicago housing expert says flatly that once the Negro population of a neighborhood reaches 25 per cent, white families flee en masse. He adds, "Negro leaders hate to hear about a white 'level of tolerance,' but it's a fact of life, and the sooner it's accepted the sooner we'll get truly integrated cities."

By turn the Heartland character is derisive and sentimental, conservative and eager for new things, litigious and group-minded, boosterish and skeptical. It was a Heartland judge who called the automobile "a house of prostitution on wheels." When Michigan City won the All-America city award, Mayor Randall Miller was told by a local citizen, "If we won it, then the rest of the country must be in terrible shape." The historian Charles Beard explained Marxism to his banker father back home in Indiana, and his father replied, "Yes, yes, I follow you. The workers rise and take over the property. Now what I want to know is, how soon do the smarties get it back?"

Signs and billboards proclaim both the Heartland style and its passion to communicate. Near Grand Haven, Michigan, one reads: "Caution—friendly area ahead." Another says, "You're only a stranger until you stop." A sign near Hillsboro, Indiana, announces that the town is the "Home of 600 happy people and a few old soreheads." One such sorehead erected a billboard beside Route 31 in Michigan, announcing, "Welcome to Muskegon County, where the taxes are going higher and higher." Printed on the rear of a bakery truck is, "Hit me easy, I'm full of pie." Williamston, Michigan, says plaintively, "Stop—or smile as you go by."

The Heartland is still home to the oldtime religion. Fundamentalist preachments line the back roads, from the admonitory, "Stop serving Satan!" to the apocalyptic, "America! Repent or Perish! Christ died for our sins!" Frequently seen is a string of Burma Shave-style signs reading: "Future Farmers"–"Turn the sod"–"And never once"–"Forget their God." New churches take their places beside the old but a number seem to have been designed by the same man: instead of boxes topped by a steeple, the new houses of worship are free-form structures of angled masonry slabs.

While there is probably not a distinct Heartland culture, a visitor will often encounter words, turns of phrase and expressions foreign to him. No one but a Cornishman or a resident of northern Wisconsin or upper Michigan would know that pasties (rhymes with "nasties") are tasty meat pies originally brought to the U.S. by Cornish miners. It would take a Midwestern oldster to define a "peanut cruise"—a lake cruise so short that it lasted scarcely longer than the time required to eat a bag of peanuts. And only Clevelanders would comprehend, "It was so cold last night that Tom L. Johnson put his hands in his pockets" (Johnson is a former mayor remembered by a sedentary statue in Public Square). In Michigan's Upper Peninsula the word "camp" describes any recreational structure built outside a town, whether it cost $600 or $60,000.

A visitor may well be baffled by "pony keg" and "jack salmon," but Cincinnatians know that the first is a store where beer may be purchased and the second is deep-fried pike. Unwary travelers who ask for a Scotch and soda may get a gagging drink made with white soda, a popular, sweet-flavored beverage. (The proper order is "Scotch and Seltzer.") Quite frequently in Heartland restaurants the first drink served at lunch or dinner is coffee and the first food a salad—usually excellent.

The Heartland is no respecter of foreign tongues. The name of the Illinois village of Bourbonnais is pronounced "Burr-BO-nus." The river that early French settlers called the Febvre became the Fever. Versailles emerges as "Ver-SALES." The final word in Prairie du Chien emerges as "Sheen" and both "s's" in Des Plaines are sounded. Midwesterners pronounce Chevrolet after the French fashion but sound the "t" in Joliet. Terre Haute becomes "Terra HOTE." Chicagoans insist that Devon Avenue is "De-VAHN" and what they do to Goethe Street is a caution. Mackinac Island is "Mackinaw."

It is a land both senselessly violent and eminently reasonable. A man thrown out of a Chicago bar returns with a can of gasoline, sets the place on fire and then goes home to bed while 13 people die in the holocaust and 21 are seriously injured. One can find motorists who think it a sporting proposition to try to beat a railroad train to a crossing—an off-duty suburban policeman even drove around the lowered gates in his effort to cross ahead of an oncoming diesel locomotive, and lost the race and his life. Yet men like Bishop Richard Emrich of Detroit will go anywhere anytime and talk or listen to anyone if there seems the slightest chance that community good will result.

The Heartland, indeed, is repeatedly described as the most American region of the U.S., possibly because it contains many parts of the whole. A Southerner would be at ease amid the pillared mansions and magnolias of southern Indiana and the southern tip of Illinois. New Englanders can find another Connecticut in the quiet commons and steepled churches of Ohio's Western Reserve. For visitors from upstate New York there is a haunting familiarity in the rolling green hills and blue lakes of Wisconsin.

Ever since the region was settled, the Heartland has been the hub around which the nation turns. Had any of America's other regions been detached over the course of history, the United States would not be the nation as we know it—but it would still exist. Without the Heartland, however, the United States would be inconceivable.

Checking the harvest, Clarence Garriott examines oats grown on his 239-acre Valparaiso, Indiana, farm. Oats, the third-largest grain crop in the Heartland, take up most of the Garriott land. The remainder is devoted to corn and pasturage for pigs.

An unmatched diversity

Night and day, ships, trains, planes and trucks hasten through the Heartland, carrying into, across, above and out of it an extraordinary variety of products and raw materials. Agriculture, employing one million people who turn out almost four billion dollars' worth of grain, vegetable, fruit and dairy products each year, is a major force in the economy; so is heavy industry as it produces steel, aluminum and other metals that are in turn used in the manufacture of goods of every size and use. Factories are not confined to one choked area; nearly every city and town has at least one plant turning out one or more of the Heartland's thousands of products. The diversity of its output, the efficiency of its transportation system and the skills of its 38 million people combine to give the Heartland one of the best-balanced economies in the world.

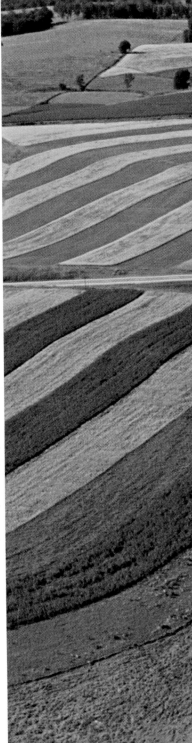

Swirling furrows, contour-plowed across the gently rolling landscape of southwestern Wisconsin, surround the tidy rectangle of a fa and its outbuildings. Although it is the leading dairy state, Wisconsin also produces vast quantities of corn and hay.

Topped with golden tassels, cornstalks packe 15,000 to the acre, stretch to the horizon on an Illinois farm. Modern farming techniques allow twice the yield per acre possible only 2(years ago, and place Illinois second only to Iowa in United States corn production.

Plentiful harvests
from well-tended fields

Despite increasing industrialization and urbanization, more than half the Heartland is still given to agriculture. The Corn Belt, 260,000 square miles of flat or rolling farmland, covers nearly all of Illinois and parts of Indiana, Ohio, Michigan and Wisconsin—as well as most of Iowa and northern Missouri and parts of other states outside the Heartland.

Although the major crop in this area is corn, the term "Corn Belt" is misleading, for large amounts of soybeans and hay, plus wheat, rye, potatoes and tobacco, are grown in the belt. Most of Wisconsin and parts of Michigan are dairy country. The two states' farms have helped make the region a leader in dairy production. In fact, Wisconsin, which calls itself "America's Dairyland," ranks first in the U.S. in the output of milk and cheese. Because the dairy industry is so important to the state's economy, it is protected by law wherever possible. Up to the mid-1960s, for example, Wisconsin was the only remaining state that attempted to safeguard butter sales by outlawing artificially colored margarine.

Enshrouded in the smoke and dust that are by-products of its tremendous output, the Gary Steel Works of the United States Steel Corporation sprawls along the Indiana shore of Lake Michigan. Its furnaces are seldom cold; tended by an 18,000-to-19,000-man army of workers, the steelworks, which covers some 1,500 acres, operates around the clock every day of the year. Forty thousand different sizes and shapes of steel are turned out at this plant alone, one of four maintained by U.S. Steel in Gary.

The glow cast
by heavy industry

Everywhere the factories appear—rising starkly next to the neat rows of cornfields, sitting squat and gray beside the rivers and along the Great Lakes. These are the giants of industry, housed in mammoth installations that may extend over more than a thousand acres. They provide employment for almost a million men and women—8 per cent of the Heartland's nonagricultural labor force. The heavy industries supply a substantial part of the nation's iron and steel, but a good portion of it stays in the Heartland. Much of the metal goes to manufacturers within the region—to the producers of railroad cars and automobiles, of power shovels and cranes for construction, and of huge electrical generators and turbines to light cities across the United States.

An efficient network of transportation

The huge railroad yards of Chicago, focal point of the nation's rail lines, are only one cog in the Heartland's mammoth transportation machine. The wharves of Detroit, Chicago, Toledo and other Great Lakes ports are crowded with deepwater vessels as well as Great Lakes ore and grain boats. In Terre Haute, Indiana, two major trucking roads— east-west Route 40, which spans the continent, and Route 41, which links Chicago with the South— intersect. Aircraft crowd the skies above Chicago's O'Hare Airport night and day. This transportation web benefits the entire region, and especially Chicago. No other city can move as many people and tons of goods in so little time and at such low cost.

Jets in profusion jam the passenger area at O'Hare Airport. The busiest civil field in the world, O'Hare, whose extensive facilities are spread over 7,200 acres, handled 520,000 flights in 1965—one take-off or landing every 20 seconds in peak periods.

Miles of freight cars line the tracks of Chicago's Cicero switching yard. The terminal, with a total capacity of 3,000, is never filled: so quickly are the freight cars shuffled and reshuffled that the average length of stay is only 15.5 hours.

An outpouring of goods from a single city

In the middle of Illinois, surrounded by the endless fields of the Corn Belt, lies the state's second-largest metropolitan area; at its center is Peoria. The area is a veritable Heartland in miniature, with more than 300 factories turning out some 900 products. In the 1950s Peoria was not so well off. The city government was spotted with corruption; streets were filthy; the downtown area was disintegrating; businesses were threatening to depart. But a group of reformers won control of city hall and launched a vast renewal program. By 1966 much of the downtown area had been renovated, and many firms had decided to stay and to expand. Caterpillar Tractor, for years the major employer and taxpayer in the metropolitan district, moved its national headquarters into the city proper, and other firms were eying reborn Peoria with interest.

Muirson Label manufactures labels for the canned-food industry.

Caterpillar sells $1.5 billion worth of bulldozers and other heavy equipment a year.

Princess Peggy's factory c

Keystone Steel and Wire can produce 800 miles of barbed wire a day.

Bemis Company's plant yearly makes more than 100 million shipping bags.

Peoria Colonial bakes and de 35,000 loaves of bread a da

Peoria's new face *(left)* presents itself to visitors entering the city from the east on Interstate 74. The new highway supplements an outdated two-lane road that had been clogged with traffic for years. Modernizing and rebuilding, Peoria is now keeping pace with the continuing industrial growth and ever-widening output of the rest of the metropolitan district. The sampling of products shown on these pages accounts for only about 1 per cent of the types of goods produced in and around Peoria, but it indicates the breadth of the area's economic diversity—and the sheer volume of its production. Peoria manufactures more tractors, distills more whiskey and produces more fly swatters than any other place in the world.

s 432,000 dresses a year.

Hiram Walker produces up to 1.5 million bottles of liquor each day.

Peoria Casket makes up to 3,000 caskets annually.

Laidlaw Wire produces 10 million fly swatters a year.

Armour's Peoria plant packages 420 frankfurters per minute.   25

Glowing cheerfully, TV receivers at the Niles, Illinois, research center of the Zenith Radio Corporation, the nation's leading producer of television sets, are checked in long-run, off-on tests. The punishing treatment simulates home viewing conditions.

Masters of the art of mass production

At the root of the region's productivity is its mastery of technological skills and its pursuit of ever-better methods of mass production. Scarcely an item produced in the Heartland is not subject to assembly-line techniques. Fleets of reapers and combines work the fields almost 24 hours a day to bring in the crops at their peak of freshness. Hens sit row upon row depositing their eggs on conveyor belts. Heavy industry, long dependent on mechanized processes, has added automation to mass production. The light industries, such as electronics, also use assembly-line techniques to achieve not only greater output but stricter quality control.

Gleaming soundlessly, French horns await final inspection at Conn, Ltd. in Elkhart, Indiana. Each week Conn's 18 assembly lines turn out thousands of French horns and other instruments, including mellophoniums, euphoniums, sousaphones and saxophones.

2

Wealth Wrung from the Fertile Soil

New settlers in the Heartland proudly display the bounty of their farm near Washburn, Wisconsin, in 1895. Cheap land lured many settlers eager to improve their life. Farmland, sold for $1.25 an acre in the early 1800s, was by this date worth $12.50 an acre.

A tremendous wall of ice thousands of feet high crunched down over the Heartland, leveling mountains, shearing off forests, bringing icy death to mastodons and other fearsome predators. Four times the glaciers advanced from the arctic, reaching as far south as the future sites of Cincinnati and St. Louis, and four times they slowly withdrew. The last glacier, called the Wisconsin, departed some 12,000 years ago, and its irregular southern edge is still marked by moraines—humps of dirt, gravel and debris brought down from the north.

The forest came back like an advancing army, throwing out over the bare land a skirmish line of birch, aspen and alder, supported by such conifers as tamarack, spruce and fir. Next came companies of blueberries and other thickets, and, finally, the massed battalions of the deciduous forest—tall hardwood trees that each fall dropped two tons of leaves per acre. The forest found its way blocked by hundreds of thousands of lakes and ponds, glacial puddles left by the melting ice. Many of these were gradually converted to forest floor.

The great American forest was like none the world has ever seen. Conifers occupied the north, and their evergreen density was splashed with the lively white of canoe birches and the gold of larches. The hardwood forests of Ohio, Indiana and southern Michigan came in two kinds: the maple-beech woodland had a cathedral grandeur, with trunks soaring upward like pillars to a leafy canopy so thick that it limited undergrowth to occasional dogwood and witch hazel, while the oak-hickory was a more open forest, mottled with sunlight and thickstrewn with smaller trees and bushes—hazelnut,

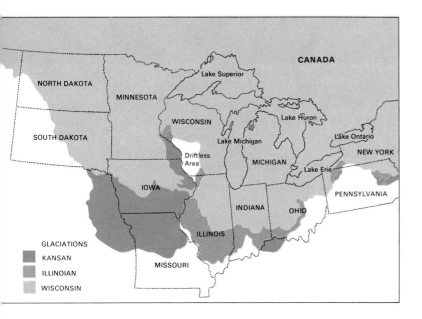

Sculpting of a region

Starting about a million years ago, four successive waves
of glaciers advanced and retreated across much of the
Heartland, modifying the physical character of the region.
Traces of the first wave were almost obliterated during
the later glaciations—the Kansan, Illinoian and Wisconsin
—whose dimensions are shown above. As the vast ice
sheets retreated, they deposited rock debris, or "drift,"
which in various locations took different forms known as
moraines, kames, eskers and drumlins, or left steep-sided
depressions called kettles. These formations are grouped
together in the artist's conception below. Wisconsin's
Driftless Area was virtually untouched—and today
stands out abruptly from the countryside surrounding it.

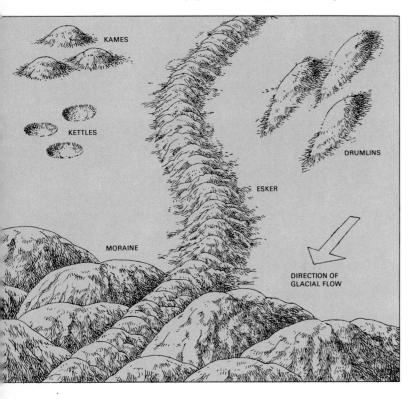

redbud, blackberry. The green wilderness was intensely alive, from the trees themselves to the birds
that nested in them to the predators padding below
to the deep humus swarming with insects. It was
the scene of constant carnage, for, as always in nature, the larger forms of life found the smaller ones
appetizing.

The forest halted at the western edge of Indiana
and gave way to the prairie, which flowed on to the
Mississippi like an ocean of grass. Summer after
summer the grasses grew to a man's height and
blossomed with wild roses, bluebells, cornflowers,
shooting stars and sunflowers. Now and again an
early frost killed the grass and only a flash of lightning was needed to ignite the dead grass and spread
destruction in a wide circle. Prairie fires roared on
with tornado force and lighted up the sky at night.
For days after, charred bits of grass hung in the air
like a curtain. The annual grass growth and the
periodic fires created a thick, black soil containing
just the nutrients needed for growing grain.

This marvelously fertile soil was ideal for farming and it fixed forever the essential character of
the Heartland. It drew to the region its first settlers, mostly farmers weary of New England's rocky
hillsides, and determined the region's agrarian politics. And despite heavy industrialization in the last
century, the land and its farms continue to be of
great importance, not just in the region's economy,
but in the very tone and tenor of its life.

The Heartland's earliest inhabitants, however,
were not primarily farmers. They were seminomad-
ic peoples who came from Asia, crossing a land
bridge now drowned by the Bering Strait. Some of
these ancient peoples were skilled craftsmen, able
to work copper mines on Isle Royale and the Keweenaw Peninsula of upper Michigan. A somewhat
later Indian people, called the Mississippi, built
conical earthen structures in southern Wisconsin.
Other prehistoric Indians who belonged to what
scholars call the Adena-Hopewell culture displayed an almost Egyptian talent for constructing
durable monuments. They built thousands of burial mounds and other structures that remain visible
throughout southern Illinois, Indiana and Ohio.
One of their citadels, known as Fort Ancient, still
stands on a plateau above the Little Miami River.
Its massive walls are 20 feet high in some places,
extend for three and a half miles, and enclose an
area of 100 acres.

We know what these ancient builders looked like:
in one grave has been found a statuette of a man
with unmistakably Indian features, and with his
ears slit into loops that held ornaments. Since this

was also a practice of the Shawnee Indians, they are thought by some to be descendants of this prehistoric people.

Most Heartland tribes were of the Algonquian family. Although the tribes were frequently at war with one another, they were more ready than most Indians to form defensive alliances against outsiders. The Cahokia, Peoria, Kaskaskia, Michigamea, Moingwena and Tamaroa belonged to a federation known as the Illinois, or "the superior men." The Chippewa, Ottawa and Potawatomi formed a similar league, and the other major Heartland tribes—Sauk, Fox, Kickapoo, Winnebago, Menominee, Miami and Shawnee—established combinations as needed. The traditional enemies of the Heartland tribes were the Iroquois to the east, the Cherokee to the south, and the Sioux and Osage to the west.

The Algonquian Indians were animists who saw a spirit in every rock and tree, although they also worshiped a single, all-powerful god who, they believed, had created the world. A number of the tribes thought this divine being took the shape of an enormous rabbit.

The Heartland tribes were semisedentary, and squaws cultivated small fields of beans, squash, tobacco and corn. Each fall the Indians turned

loose their ponies to drift south ahead of winter for recapture in the spring. The braves and some selected boys moved north to winter camps that were used as bases for hunting, trapping and fishing. In summer an Indian came to fulfillment—it was the time for war parties.

The land was a delight to the eye. One visitor wrote, "No man will ever forget his first view of the Ohio." Another conceded that the Hudson had some highly scenic views but felt that no other river in the world was so beautiful along its entire length as the Ohio. "What a country this is!" cried the New York journalist Charles Fenno Hoffman, delighted by Michigan's oak openings—parklike woods where deer grazed in herds and so free of undergrowth that a carriage could be driven through them for miles. Lakes studded the woods like silver mirrors, and one observer recalled that they were "so beautifully transparent that the canoe suspended on their bosom seems to float in mid air!"

Beauty lay everywhere. It resided in the river bottoms, with their tall pecans, hickories and cottonwoods draped with grapevines; along the prairie edges thick with plum, persimmon and crab-apple trees; in the meadows bright with cowslips, Johnny-jump-ups, cyclamens and Indian paintbrushes. The land was dazzling in the spring when the swamps

The mysterious mound builders

Among the earliest Heartlanders were a prehistoric Indian people called Hopewell, who between 300 B.C. and 600 A.D. built large burial mounds, evidences of which can still be seen in the Ohio River Valley. In the artist's reconstruction above, a high priest *(in face mask)* officiates over a cremation and a burial. As soon as the house was filled with covered graves, it was destroyed and the site was heaped high with earth to form a mound *(right)*. In such mounds modern archeologists have found many skillfully designed artifacts.

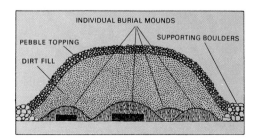

INDIVIDUAL BURIAL MOUNDS

PEBBLE TOPPING

SUPPORTING BOULDERS

DIRT FILL

and woods were lavishly lighted by crimson daisies, purple foxgloves, red columbines, snowy lilies of the valley, mauve adder's-tongues and brilliant fireweeds. The French observer Alexis de Tocqueville, visiting the Heartland in 1831, wrote: "It is difficult to imagine the charm which surrounds these beautiful places where man has not yet made his abode and where a profound peace and uninterrupted silence still prevail." He regretted "that soon this delightful solitude will have ceased to exist."

The white settlers began their move in the decades after the American Revolution. They came not singly but in groups, their household goods piled in gaudily painted red and blue Conestoga wagons pulled by slow-paced teams of horses, or floated down the Ohio in keelboats and on rafts. Some chose the so-called National Road across southern Ohio and Indiana. The first settlements were made at the mouths of rivers or at portages, and each new Ohio village had its fort. Marietta, named for France's Queen Marie Antoinette, who was soon to lose her head under the guillotine, was founded by veterans of the Revolution. So was Losantiville, which was renamed Cincinnati in honor of the Society of the Cincinnati, an organization of Revolutionary officers.

The westward movement began each autumn after a last harvest had been gathered from fields about to be left forever. Then the roads would be full of wagons, cattle, horses, hogs, sheep and families "all joyously wending their way to their new habitations." Yankee emigrants rode west singing:

> *'Tis I can delve and plough, love*
> *And you can spin and sew;*
> *And we'll settle on the banks*
> *Of the pleasant Ohio.*

A typical group of early settlers consisted of a half-dozen families from Vergennes, Vermont, who established the tiny Illinois community of Bluffdale in 1820. Traveling by land, the Vermonters took two months to reach their destination near the banks of the Illinois River, and in the final stages they had to cut their way through a ravine, felling trees that stood in their way and bridging shallow creeks. The big lure was the inexpensive land that could be bought from the government for as little as $1.25 an acre. Many settlers took over land that had not yet been surveyed or offered for sale, and these squatters took pledges among themselves to defend the land against all comers. Even George Washington had been unable to force squatters off some of his Western property.

The settlers generally trusted only themselves and their neighbors. When Bluffdale was swept in 1821 by "the ager" (ague), which made the victim's teeth chatter and his body vibrate "like a harp with a hundred strings," the citizens devised a system under which each cabin was visited daily to make certain that at least one member of the family was up and about. In the absence of doctors, cures were found on the land itself—holly bark for ague, feverbush to reduce temperatures, swamp laurel for diarrhea, slippery elm for sore throat, aspen bark for malaria, sulfur for the "Illinois mange." Other illnesses common on the border were yellow jaundice and the often fatal "milksick," a disease possibly contracted by drinking the milk of cows that had eaten poisonous plants. It was the milksick that killed Abraham Lincoln's mother.

Only the sturdiest babies survived infancy, and every few years cholera raged through the river towns. During the Black Hawk War of 1832, regular troops who were rushed to Buffalo from Fortress Monroe in Virginia brought cholera with them. Their transports became plague ships and carried death and terror to Detroit and Chicago as dying soldiers were put ashore. One aspect of settler life is summed up by an Indiana headstone:

> *Thirteen years I was a virgin,*
> *Two years I was a wife,*
> *One year I was a mother,*
> *The next year took my life.*

If the land was unbelievably fertile, the climate was awesome—and still is. Most major U.S. storms pass through the Heartland. The region is swept by cold dry air from the arctic, which often clashes head on with warm moist air moving northward from the Gulf of Mexico. The area is also hit by cold air from the Great Plains, and even moist air from Labrador can give the Heartland an icy swipe. In summer, hot air masses from the Gulf of Mexico, superheated by travel over the South, can lie like a damp summer blanket on the Heartland.

This competitive air traffic accounts for the frequent, violent changes in weather. In a 10-day period in January the temperature can go from 17 degrees below zero to 70 above. A weatherman once described a typical April day as being "warm and sunny in the morning, cluttered with fast-moving clouds, followed by a heavy shower, followed by strong north winds, rapidly falling temperature and 24 hours of rain splatters, overcast skies and exasperated Midwesterners. It's tough on the old and the ill, but great for crops."

The Heartland weather made a deep impression

on early settlers, especially newcomers from across the Atlantic. Rebecca Burlend, a sturdy Yorkshire-woman, wrote in the 1840s that winter nights in Illinois "are at once inexpressibly cold and poetically fine. The sky is almost invariably clear, and the stars shine with a brilliancy entirely unknown in the humid atmosphere of England. Cold as it was, I often stood at the door of our cabin, admiring their luster and listening to the wolves, whose howlings among the leafless woods at this season, are almost unceasing."

It was a strange land—vast, storm-ridden and filled with wonders. Rebecca and her husband were terrified by their first sight of fireflies, which seemed to them the work of the devil. It was equally dismaying to come upon the footprint of a raccoon, so like that of a tiny, barefoot child as to waken memories of elves and fairies. There were days when passenger pigeons filled the skies in such numbers that they hid the sun. One stunned observer of the pigeons in flight wrote, "It was an endless hurricane on wings" with "such an uproar as seemed to be prostrating the forests!" Once so numerous, the passenger pigeons are all gone now, driven into extinction by the fire of shotguns and the settlers' destruction of their forest habitat.

For boys the Heartland provided a happy round of fishing, swimming and excursions to gather wild grapes and nuts. They went coon hunting when the corn was in roasting ear, and set out box traps with figure-four springs to catch quail and prairie hen. Their games were competitive: bull pen, prisoner's base, foot racing, high and "far" jumping, and wrestling in all the frontier styles—the square hold, the side hold, breeches hold, catch-as-catch-can and Indian hug.

And there were the Indians themselves, making their forlorn way in small groups to the promised land beyond the Mississippi that they sensed would be the graveyard of their race. They had by now been thoroughly beaten and seldom caused trouble, but one settler recalled that "their appearance, enveloped in their gaudy blankets, porcupine-quill embroidered leggings with moccasins to match, long unkempt hair and tomahawk in belt, caused alarm, especially to lone women and children when the men folks were away." The Indians gave the Heartland a final fright and then passed on. Of all the area's tribes only three remain in any numbers —the Potawatomi, the Chippewa and the Menominee, who live mainly in Michigan and Wisconsin, the first two on sizable reservations.

The settler's first and toughest job was the "clearing away of surplus wood." It was done with such a

Patron saint of orchardmen

The story of Johnny Appleseed wandering barefoot through the forests, planting apple trees, is one of the enduring legends of the Heartland. Like many legends, this one is based partly on fact. The 1863 drawing at the left, which is traditionally associated with the legendary Johnny Appleseed, is derived from a sketch made in the 1850s by a man who had known the real human being. Behind the myth was a man named John Chapman, who was born in Leominster, Massachusetts, in 1774. Chapman actually did wander through Pennsylvania, Ohio and Indiana and acquired land at a number of sites between 1797 and 1838. He helped many pioneer families to establish orchards by selling them young trees from the nurseries he had established in the wilderness. This, coupled with his befriending of pioneers, caught the popular imagination. Even before Chapman died in 1845, stories about him were giving rise to the legend that has made him the patron saint of orchardmen.

will that an English visitor thought Americans had a special hatred of trees. As many as six axmen would attack a forest giant, and the rhythmic tattoo of their axes was greatly admired. When a settler had cleared his first acres, leaving the stumps to be dealt with later, his neighbors turned out to help in "log rolling" the felled trunks into piles for burning. For years the settlements were permeated by the eye-stinging, pungent smoke of burning woodpiles. Other communal occasions were muster days (when the militia drilled), house-raisings, quilting bees, cornhuskings and weddings.

Many parts of the Heartland have changed little since the early decades of the 19th Century. This is particularly true in the southern areas. Below Orleans, Indiana, back-country roads meander through wooded hills where rude cabins fall in on themselves and rail fences enclose stony deserted fields. A motorist may be briefly slowed by a herd of Black Angus being turned into a meadow by a shouting, arm-waving farmer or by the approach to narrow, one-lane bridges spanning creeks with names like Little Muddy or Lost River. From each hilltop unfolds a vista of hill after rolling hill, timbered as of old, each looking just as it did to the Piankashaw Indians and the first pioneers.

Evangelism swept in waves through the Heartland

in the decades before the Civil War when wandering preachers strove for "a world reclaimed and converted to Christ." Enormous crowds gathered for camp meetings; scores would be "seized" by God and rushed to the "penitents' ring," where they would shriek and shout and be so shaken by convulsive jerks and quiverings that posts were driven into the ground for them to cling to. The preachers hoped that evangelism would surge through the land as "fires spread and roar through the parched forests." The metaphor was apt—after the tumult of a week-long camp meeting a community would fall into a collective daze that was described as being "burned out."

Education was rudimentary. A teacher could often be hired for room and board and would move each month from the cabin of one pupil's parents to another. As a child, Lincoln attended a "blab school" at Dale, Indiana, where students studied aloud—they could be heard half a mile away. Teachers were encouraged to "spread the word with the bark on," but the use of the switch did not noticeably tame the pupils. There were tough schools then, as now, in which the biggest student's ability to lick the teacher was rated high.

Some of the early colleges required 20 hours of manual labor a week, both as an aid to poor students and as a means of building character. In 1804 the Ohio legislature incorporated Ohio University, the Heartland's oldest, but for decades it and other new colleges lived on short rations and their libraries would be disdained by many grammar schools of today. One of the early colleges, Oberlin, scandalized the Midwest with its heretical policies. It was the first coeducational college, admitted Negroes in considerable numbers and combined liberal views with a particularly enthusiastic brand of Calvinism. From this distance it is hard to say whether it was because the rules were so strict or the students so rambunctious, but the early Heartland colleges were frequently swept by student "revolts," usually over a question of free speech rather than a panty raid or a poor athletic record. Most professional men in the Heartland were self-taught or had learned through apprenticeship. This was especially true of doctors, who were said to have "killed quick but cured slow."

Governor Thomas Ford of Illinois noted in 1847 that "a few settlers would fix the character of a settlement for many years after its commencement. If bad men began the settlement, bad men would be attracted to them. Rogues will find each other out and so will honest men." Each Heartland state had communities where desperadoes could not be

brought to justice because they were in league with local officials. Farmers taking produce down the Ohio traveled in convoys to hold off forays by river pirates lurking at Cave-in-Rock. Illinois long had a bad reputation: its southern Massac County was regarded as beyond the law; horse thieves and counterfeiters hid out in the trackless Kankakee swamps and "Prairie Pirates" infested the Rock River country. Illinois was said to be the hiding place for "villains from every part of the U.S."

Local vigilante groups, often called Regulators, waged war on the desperadoes, frequently obtaining evidence from reluctant prisoners by holding their heads under water until they showed a willingness to talk. When a prisoner was reported "gone to Arkansas," it meant that his body had been thrown into the river to drift south with the current. Ultimately the Regulators became as great a burden as the original bad men, because the vigilantes used their power to work off private grudges and whipped or tarred and feathered anyone who spoke out against them. Governor Ford was not alone in concluding that the people of the Heartland "were neither capable of governing themselves nor of being governed by others."

But the spirit of freedom was highly contagious. Letters home from immigrants would often empty whole villages in Germany and Ireland as they had earlier emptied them in New England. In the 1850s Francis Hulman wrote his brother in Germany: "Oh, Herman, Herman, follow my advice, get mother's consent and hurry here. Here you will have a different life and be an altogether different person." An Englishman named Morris Birkbeck, who persuaded a number of English families to immigrate to the Heartland in 1818, hoped "to transplant, into these boundless regions of freedom, the millions grovelling in ignorance and want."

The prairie was long regarded as useless for farmland because the complex networks of grassroots were too strong for existing plows. John Deere, a blacksmith in Grand Detour, Illinois, solved the problem with his mill-saw blade, which was self-scouring and kept turning over the black, sticky soil that was so rich it "could grease your fingers."

The fertility of the prairie farmland was beyond belief, but a steady prosperity continually eluded the Heartland farmer. Like farmers everywhere, he faced the perils of drought, insect pests, flood and frost. But he had other troubles as well. Before the Civil War, Heartland farmers were hampered by the lack of transportation. Some built or bought flatboats to carry their produce downriver to New Orleans, but, as one pioneer noted, "one crop was lost by absence and another by taking it to market and [a man] often returned to a farm gone to ruin in his absence."

The farmer was further bedeviled by the bizarre banking practices of the time. Almost anyone could start a wildcat bank and issue as much paper money as he pleased with no backing other than his good name. The banks were supposed to redeem their paper in gold or silver on demand, but many were unable to do so. The paper currency issued by these wildcat banks became a national joke and was rarely exchanged at par value. With the serious shortage of U.S. coins, the Spanish dollar was greatly in demand and was often cut up like a cake into quarters, bits (eighths) and fips (sixteenths). Two bits, of course, made a quarter—thus the still-current American slang for a 25-cent piece. "Shinplasters" were small bills issued by business firms, counties and even individuals.

The repeated failures of banks and the worthlessness of their paper made "banking" a dirty word to Heartland farmers. The conviction took hold that bankers, and especially Eastern financial interests, were of dubious probity and were certainly bent on ruining the farmer. This view carried over into the post-Civil War period when the farmer felt squeezed by everyone. His basic problem was the need to raise a cash crop in order to buy staples and luxuries from the East. The high tariffs established by Congress to protect the nation's growing industry meant in effect that the farmer had to buy at seller's prices and to sell at buyer's prices. He was further trapped by high freight rates on the railroads—it cost as much to ship wheat from Minneapolis to Milwaukee by rail as to ship the same amount of wheat via the Great Lakes, the Erie Canal and the Hudson from Milwaukee to England. This sense of being victimized by "the interests" made the farm region a fertile seedbed of political radicalism.

The Heartland has always had difficulty finding its political voice and has therefore had a weakness for third parties. The Republicans began as a Heartland third party—the birthplace is still in dispute between Ripon, Wisconsin, and Jackson, Michigan. The Civil War for a time assured Republican dominance in the Heartland because few veterans could resist the slogan, "Vote the way you shot!" Since it was unthinkable to support a Democrat and since the Republican Party could not be budged from its high-tariff position, disgruntled farmers turned to a succession of third parties—Greenbackers, Populists, Progressives. They all had roughly similar platforms, calling for cheap money,

Machines that eased farming

Until the invention of devices like the three shown here, Heartland farms remained small and limited to ground that could be tilled easily. Then in 1837, in Grand Detour, Illinois, John Deere developed a steel plow that could cut through the tangled prairie-grass roots that had stymied wooden plows. In Chicago in the 1840s, Cyrus McCormick perfected the mechanical reaper, replacing scores of men at harvesttime, and in Racine, Wisconsin, Jerome Increase Case put together a threshing machine. With them, farmers could begin to release the tremendous potential of the region's rich, loamy earth.

JOHN DEERE'S
SELF-SCOURING PLOW

CYRUS McCORMICK'S REAPER

JEROME INCREASE CASE'S THRESHER

tax reforms, economy and honesty in government, and federal ownership and regulation of railroads. The Greenbacker program also demanded a "free ballot, a fair count, and equality for all classes." Led by such tub thumpers as "Roaring Bill" Allen of Ohio and "Blue Jeans" Williams of Indiana, the Greenback Party in 1878 polled more than a million votes and helped put 15 representatives in Congress.

During the 1870s and 1880s, the farmer's plight became increasingly severe. Caught between generally low commodity prices and the exorbitant rates charged to handle and ship his grain by the operators of grain elevators and by the railroads, he turned to an organization called the Patrons of Husbandry, or the Grange. The Grange movement was stronger west of the Mississippi, where the farmers were worse off, but it also enjoyed widespread support in the Heartland, especially in Illinois and Indiana. The Grange energetically fought the farmers' battles and succeeded in getting several state legislatures to pass profarmer "granger laws." The Eastern newspapers promptly concluded that the Grange was "under the red flag of Communism." Adopting the slogan, "Raise less corn and more hell," the massed farmers sang:

> *I once was a tool of oppression,*
> *As green as a sucker could be,*
> *And monopolies banded together*
> *To beat a poor hayseed like me.*

This Western insurgency puzzled and frightened the East. Newspapers and magazines fulminated against the "dangerous characters of the inflammable and covetous West." The West replied in kind as a farm-journal editor wrote: "I cannot recall another conspiracy in the history of mankind quite equal in colossal and criminal splendor to the profound and universal plot of Wall Street." The Midwestern author Hamlin Garland reflected that the war of East and West was now beginning on the battlefield of politics.

One result of the long, bitter war was a change in the national image of the farmer from Jeffersonian hero and backbone of the country to a comic rube wearing chin whiskers and funny boots. The ridicule of the Eastern press concealed a deepening fear that the Heartland meant to change the rules of the game. When it became apparent that Heartland farmers were at last deserting the Republican Party in large numbers to support the Democrat William Jennings Bryan for President, editorials warned that Bryan's election would mean "the end of capitalism." Millowners told their workers that if Bryan became President the factory whistle would not blow on the morning after the election.

Bryan, in turn, labeled the East "enemy territory," and drew enormous crowds as he stumped the Heartland. The historian Russel Nye has written: "They gathered in the small towns of the Midwest, farmers in overalls and their wives in faded sunbonnets and calico, people with hard, tired faces and worn hands, come by wagon team to fight the devil—plutocracy in a checkered vest, gold watch chain and silk hat." Nye and other historians have noted that, despite the scare headlines and harsh words, the two sides shared the same convictions. Clinton Rossiter of Cornell has observed that the Heartland farmers, "however fearsome they may have appeared to Eastern capitalists . . . were solid Americans crying out for justice from an America they knew and loved far better than many of their enemies. Never in their most desperate moments did they challenge seriously the institutions of private property and capitalist enterprise." To author John Chamberlain, Bryan's campaigns were "not stirrings of red revolution, but merely a struggle between small and large capitalists."

In fact the force that beat back the rebellion came not from the East but from the Heartland itself. Mark Hanna of Cleveland, a tough political realist, had captured the Republican Party from the Eastern bosses in the 1890s. Hanna's Presidential candidate was the handsome, pliable William McKinley of Canton, Ohio, a man who kept his ear so close to the ground, said Joseph Cannon, Speaker of the U.S. House of Representatives, that it was full of grasshoppers. In a fiercely partisan election, McKinley triumphed by only 609,687 votes.

Bryan ran twice more for the Presidency but never again came close to winning. Although a silver-tongued orator, he was notably deficient in ideas. After hearing the "Cross of Gold" speech that won Bryan the 1896 Democratic nomination in Chicago, Governor John Peter Altgeld of Illinois said to Clarence Darrow, "I've been thinking over Bryan's speech. What did he say anyhow?" Another observer said that you could drive a prairie schooner through a Bryan speech "without scraping a hub on a solid thought."

With the coming of the new century, and especially during World War I and the boom times of the 1920s, the farmers' militancy diminished. But when the nation plunged into the Great Depression the farmers were once more on the barricades. Prices fell so low that milk was dumped on the ground and corn was burned as fuel rather than taken to market. When the courts ordered farms sold for delinquent taxes or unpaid mortgages, the farmers at first stood

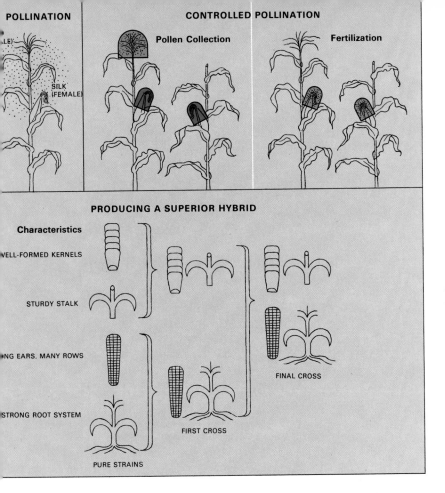

POLLINATION

SILK (FEMALE)

CONTROLLED POLLINATION

Pollen Collection

Fertilization

PRODUCING A SUPERIOR HYBRID

Characteristics

WELL-FORMED KERNELS

STURDY STALK

LONG EARS, MANY ROWS

STRONG ROOT SYSTEM

PURE STRAINS

FIRST CROSS

FINAL CROSS

How hybridization works

The huge yields—particularly of corn —from Heartland farms are largely the result of scientific crossbreeding to produce hybrid varieties. The diagrams show how this process is accomplished. Before corn kernels can develop, pollen—produced by the tassel, or male part of the plant— must fertilize the silk, or female part. In nature, this takes place at random *(top left)*. In the controlled process, tassels and silks are covered *(top center)* to prevent random fertilization, and pollen produced by plants with specially selected traits is collected *(blue bag)* to be transferred to the silks of plants with other desired qualities *(blue bags, top right)*. The kernels thus produced are used as seed for the next crop. The lower diagrams show how several specially selected traits may be combined. A plant with large kernels is crossbred with one that possesses a sturdy stalk, and a plant with even rows of kernels is crossed with another that has a strong root system. The plants produced from these crossings are in turn crossbred, creating a single new variety that boasts large kernels, even rows, sturdy stalks and deep roots.

off the deputies with shotguns. Later they used more sophisticated methods: they would assemble, armed, at a sheriff's sale and see to it that the dispossessed farmer was the only bidder. Near Howard City, Michigan, a grand piano was sold for four cents, a hay loader for 11 cents. Total proceeds of the sale came to $2.40. The purchasers returned all the items to the farmer.

Yet it was during these hardship years that the future of Heartland agriculture was being shaped in a dozen agricultural testing stations and laboratories. The most important development to emerge was hybrid corn. The goal of the researchers had been to produce, by selective breeding of different strains of corn, plants both more vigorous and fruitful which would at the same time be more resistant to insect blights and violent weather. They succeeded so well that the new strains of corn increased yields per acre by as much as 40 per cent.

Before this discovery farmers had saved the best ears of their crop to use as seed the next season, and many were deaf to news of the benefits of hybrid corn. Lloyd Graham, country agricultural agent in Kankakee, Illinois, says, "They had seldom paid for seed corn before and they weren't going to start now. It was the same as when we tried to introduce limestone as fertilizer. Farmers said, 'My God, I

broke my back getting rocks out of my fields and now you want me to put rocks back in!'"

Farmers resisted hybrids until they could no longer explain away the massive yields obtained by the few adventurous men using them. By 1948 fully 75 per cent of all U.S. corn was of the hybrid strain, and today its use is nearly universal. Each year, as elsewhere in the nation, a farmer sends a sample of his soil to the nearest land-grant university and gets a report on what fertilizer he should use and how much. The yields would be even more enormous than they are if many farmers did not succumb to the human impulse to cut corners. Lyman McKee, who farms 1,100 Wisconsin acres, says, "Few if any farmers apply to the land all the fertilizer the university recommends. Being farmers, they always skimp a bit."

Hybrids have not been alone in creating the farm bonanza. Artificial insemination of cows has resulted in a vast improvement in herds and greater production of milk. If a cow does not become pregnant it is culled from the herd and sold—such culls provide much of the nation's hamburger. Some of the calves are also sold to specialist farmers who fatten them for market.

Even with increased mechanization, dairy farming is still hard work. Bob Gulcynski owns a typical farm near Thorp, Wisconsin, and is on the job 15 hours a day. He milks his herd of 50 cows twice a day, using four Surge buckets, automatic milkers that cut the hand-labor time from eight or nine hours to two. The cows are milked at the same time and in the same order each day since, as Gulcynski puts it, "Cows are creatures of habit." A tank truck stops by every second day and takes aboard an average of 1,300 quarts. Some tank trucks also service the farms, dropping off bottles of pasteurized milk, butter and eggs.

The dairy barn must be ready at all times to pass inspection: there must be sufficient filtered light, correctly spaced, the floor must be limed regularly, and all doors must be closed when not in use. Each cow has to be properly washed before milking and must bear a card setting forth its name or number, proper registration and birth cycle. Milk must be covered from the time it is poured into buckets until it is dumped into the cooler tank, and all equipment is required to be clean and disinfected. All this is hard work for Gulcynski and for his family.

Gulcynski's pretty wife, Arnoldine, does her best to "keep the barn out of the home," but, like most farm wives, she is pressed into service when needed during harvesting. The Gulcynskis have five young sons and two daughters, and all the children do more than ordinary farm chores by helping to load or unload hay, or even driving the tractor when an extra hand is needed. Equipment is the biggest continuing expense: tractors cost $5,000; a single big silo can run to $22,000. Management is probably the biggest dairying headache, and Bob Gulcynski now regrets his failure to go on to college. As it is, each Wednesday he attends night school, where he learns how to get better milk at a lower cost and how properly to manage his time and his work.

Mechanization has turned some farms into virtual factories. Peter Dillon's farm, near Sterling, Illinois, has 800 pigs that have never wallowed comfortably in mud or even been outdoors. The pigs are divided among three buildings. The first, called the gestation house, is where the boars and the sows are bred. The second is the "farrow-nursery," where the young pigs are born and nursed and kept with their dams until weaned. A third houses the young pigs while they are being fattened for market. Experiment has proved the surprising fact that pigs not only are intelligent but have a flair for cleanliness. A pig soon learns to get a drink of water by pushing a button with its snout. When nature calls, the pig retires to the toilet—a portion of the barn with a slotted floor that empties into a water-filled concrete ditch that feeds into an underground

tank. The liquid manure is used as fertilizer. When the fattened pigs are about six months old and weigh about 210 pounds they are given their first glimpse of the outside world—on their way by truck to the slaughterhouse.

Indoor stock raising frees land for crops, keeps costs low, and makes for pleasanter working conditions. Indoor farming was pioneered by poultrymen; some broiler "factories" house more than 100,000 chickens. In fact, the mixture of farm and factory is very common in the Midwest, and farmer and factory worker are often in sight of each other. On the outskirts of the northern Illinois city of Belvidere there is a Chrysler assembly plant that looks about a mile long—yet at each end there is a dairy farm. Peter Dillon's indoor pig farm is run by a manager while Dillon himself drives into Sterling to his job at the Northwestern Steel & Wire Company, which his family controls.

Farm mechanization has caused a sharp rise in the accident rate. Many farmers have lost a finger or a hand to either the corn picker or the bar cutter. Clifford Erikson, who owns a 600-acre Ohio farm, says, "If either of those machines were put into a factory, the place would be immediately shut down by the state inspectors as too dangerous for continual use."

The corn picker is normally operated in the fall when the weather is often cold enough for a farmer to wear gloves. Erikson says, "Every now and then an ear of corn will get jammed in the machine and the farmer will reach in to free it. If he's not fast enough—and he has to be damned fast—the corn picker will snatch his glove and take off his hand with it. That's what the machine is supposed to do —it's just the same as stripping ears of corn from the stalk." Cliff Erikson still has both his hands and all his fingers, but that is probably because he spends his time in another building on his farm that houses the Eastern Specialty Varnish Company, of which he is president. One of his products is a yellow-dye concentrate that is used to give oranges a uniform color and is exported as far as Spain and South America.

The marriage between university scientists and farmers and the development of hybrids, artificial insemination, new machines, fertilizers and new methods of operation have all contributed to the vast amounts of food that pour from the cornucopia of the Heartland. When these techniques and skills are adopted in underdeveloped lands, there is a possibility that the earth may one day be able to feed properly the uncounted millions destined to be born in the years ahead.

Grain feed, tailored to hogs' meat-building requirements, pours into controlled-environment pens on the Don Stoller farm near Gridley, Illinois. Amenities to improve production include automatic radiant floor heating and a water-spray cooling system.

Food processor to the nation

Food-processing plants dot the Heartland landscape, turning crops, crop-fed animals and dairy produce into a cornucopia of marketable goods, from breakfast cereals to packaged hams to after-dinner liqueurs. For the region is not only one of the world's most bountiful farming areas but a remarkably busy food-processing center. To keep their factories supplied, processors import raw crops from many other areas of the U.S. as well as from all parts of the Heartland. In complicated techniques, processors may treat the foodstuffs with chemicals; wash, slice, grind, pound or pulverize them; and then boil, bake, fry or roast them before freezing, canning, bottling or bagging them for market. And their methods become ever more exotic as scientists in Heartland laboratories continue their search for new ways to convert crops into salable foods.

Kernels of recently picked corn shoot onto a waiting truck on the farm of Joe Hinkle near Walton, Indiana. Hinkle guides the tube from his four-row combine, which automatically picks, husks and shells the ears, and stores the kernels until the truck arrives.

Corn: a wealth of uses for the country's dominant crop

Corn—America's largest crop at more than three billion bushels annually in recent years—is of critical importance to the Heartland. It dominates the agriculture of the Corn Belt and sustains a tremendous number of Heartland food-processing concerns. The major processors of corn include the alcohol and alcoholic-beverage industry, animal-feed manufacturers, wet millers and dry millers. The dry-milling industry makes corn meal, hominy and breakfast cereals. The wet-milling industry—so called because it uses water to break the corn kernel into its component parts—is the primary refiner of corn for food products. From the corn germ the wet millers extract oil used in margarine and mayonnaise, in salad dressing and cooking oils. From the starch they derive products used in desserts, chewing gum, baking powder, canned vegetables, candies, soups, baby foods and yeast. They also refine the starch into corn syrup or corn sugar, used in ice cream, jams, jellies, licorice, syrup, and frozen or dried eggs. However, despite the many human foods that utilize corn products, the crop's single most important use is as feed for farm animals—hogs, cattle, sheep and poultry. Thus most of America's corn crop actually reaches the consumer in the form of ham, bacon, beef, mutton and chicken.

40

A technician at the A. E. Staley Company in Decatur, Illinois, examines the thickness and moisture of a sheet of cornstarch as it is washed to remove salts and carbohydrates.

Corn syrup cools in a vast tank at the Staley Company. The syrup is made by a hydrolysis process, which if continued to completion would turn the syrup into dextrose.

Corn flakes, a cereal made by a dry-milling process, cascade from a hopper at the Kellogg Company in Battle Creek, Michigan. Kellogg uses more corn than any other grain.

Corn oil fills Mazola bottles at Corn Products Company, Argo, Illinois. Manufactured in a wet-milling process, the oil is extracted from the corn-germ part of the kernel.

Holstein cattle bred specifically for greater milk production graze outside a barn on a Wisconsin farm. Improved stock and special feeds have increased the average daily production of a good milk cow from about six quarts in 1940 to 10 quarts today.

Dairy products: volume and variety from farm and factory

Four of the five Heartland states rank among the top nine states in cash receipts from dairy products. Each year food processors in the region turn out vast quantities of milk and milk products. They do so even though many dairymen are leaving the business—in Wisconsin alone an average of 10 a day quit in the 1960s. To keep production high, many of the remaining dairymen operate their farms like factories, installing feeding machines and mechanical barn cleaners for greater efficiency. Some dairymen are turning to computers to determine which cows are producing poorly and are thus due for replacement.

Checking milk flow, Earl Ufken, a dairy farmer near Juda, Wisconsin, examines the pipeline system that carries milk direct from cow to cooling tank. Automation has doubled the average dairyman's productive capability since 1950.

Making cheddar cheese, workers in the Lake to Lake Dairy Cooperative plant at Kiel, Wisconsin, comb the curds and the whey, causing them to separate. The settled curds are then cheddared (cut and turned) and finally salted and cured.

Dripping their chocolate covering, ice-cream bars rise from a coating bath before going to the sacker at the Borden Company plant in West Allis, Wisconsin. The machine makes a continuous supply of bars, working on 1,183 at a time.

Fruit: science and machines for the growers

Thanks to moderating winds that sweep in from the Great Lakes, parts of Michigan, Wisconsin and Ohio possess a climate ideally suited for growing fruit. The result is an unending supply of sweet and sour cherries, blueberries, apples, peaches, plums, pears, grapes and strawberries, among others. Although all the fruits are delicate, they have responded favorably to the Heartlander's penchant for mechanization and scientific experimentation. In factories, carefully devised production methods are combined with controlled freezing and storing to make seasonal fruit available all year long in the form of pies, sauces, juices and preserves. On the farms, improved plant varieties developed in the region's laboratories produce even larger harvests, and new picking machines give promise of ending the tedium of hand labor in the fields and orchards.

Testing blueberries for texture, a worker in a Pillsbury Company research-and-development laboratory readies the fruit for a press that will "bite" the berries to determine their tenderness. The test aids the company's search for berries best suited for food mixes.

Liquid cherry jelly flows into 10-ounce jars (back row) at The J. M. Smucker Company plant in Orrville, Ohio. The jars then move in rows to capping machines. Fruit for jelly is compressed and the resulting juice is frozen and stored until needed on the production lines.

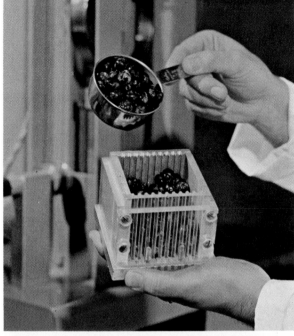

Blueberry preserves, capped and ready for labeling, are weighed by a quality-control worker at Smucker's Orrville plant. The fruit for preserves is generally frozen near the field by packing concerns who in turn sell it to processors like Smucker.

Cherry pie shells are filled automatically at Chef Pierre, Inc., in Traverse City, Michigan, as workers check the amount of fill. After the shells are filled, they move along the line to receive their top crust and thence to be frozen, packaged and cartoned for market.

An experimental picker straddles a row of blueberry bushes on a Michigan plantation and its mechanical arms shake the berries onto a conveyor belt that carries them to boxes. The average height of the bushes is six or seven feet, but some grow as high as 12 feet.

Soybeans: farm bonanza with a glowing future

The efforts of Heartlanders to find additional uses for their crops have had their most dramatic success with the soybean. This plant, cultivated for at least 4,000 years by the Chinese, was largely ignored outside the Orient until some 40 years ago. As late as 1940 soybeans were the nation's 11th money crop; by 1964 they had reached third place, after corn and cotton—and first place in dollar value among export crops. This remarkable increase has been spurred by the wide range of uses discovered for the soybean. Today great quantities of soybeans are used in livestock feed and in cooking oil, in health foods and as meat substitutes. For the future, scientists look to new soybean-based foods to help alleviate the world's deepening food shortage.

Soybeans grow in long rows on a farm near Sheldon, Illinois. The beans are generally yellowish and are borne on plants that may grow three feet high and yield an average of 24 bushels per acre. Illinois is the nation's leading soybean-producing state.

Freshly made margarine flows into half-pound tubs at the Lever Brothers' plant in Hammond, Indiana. In recent years about 25 per cent of the soybean oil produced in the United States has gone into margarines, which also contain many other vegetable oils.

Meatless frankfurters, one of many kinds of simulated meats made from soy protein fiber, are hung on racks at the Worthington Foods company in Worthington, Ohio.

Soy sauce pours into bottles at La Choy Food Products in Archbold, Ohio. La Choy makes the sauce by a process lasting a year and by newer methods taking only a few weeks.

An ice-cream-like dessert made from soy protein fills a cone in a Central Soya Chemurgy laboratory in Chicago. This test product is one of many being studied.

3

Turbulent Years of Growth

The Heartland is bloody ground and has known many allegiances. A dozen Indian tribes and three great nations have struggled to gain primacy over it. In turn the Heartland has seen the fleur-de-lis of France, Britain's Union Jack and the Stars and Stripes. It even briefly knew the Confederate Stars and Bars—when John Hunt Morgan's cavalry raided into Indiana and Ohio in 1863. To many men the Heartland has been well worth fighting and dying for.

With French help the Heartland tribes were strong enough for more than a century to confine the English and American settlers east of the Appalachian Mountains. During the French and Indian War the tribes even took the offensive, striking into western Pennsylvania, where they forced George Washington to surrender Fort Necessity and butchered General Edward Braddock's army of British regulars and American militia. After France's power was broken with the capture of Quebec and Montreal, Britain obtained title to the Heartland. But the region had yet to be

conquered, and Pontiac, chief of the Ottawa, was determined to keep it that way. Uniting the tribes, Pontiac struck in May 1763, destroying eight English forts and laying siege to Detroit. The British fought with guns, and with a particularly nasty version of germ warfare—blankets infected with smallpox were sent to the Indians, ostensibly as placating gifts. The British finally raised the siege of Detroit and pacified the tribes by proclaiming the Heartland closed to white settlement and reserved for the use of the Indians "under [the] sovereignty, protection, and dominion" of the Crown. For administrative purposes the region was made a part of the Colony of Quebec, an act that infuriated the American colonists and helped bring on the Revolutionary War.

The big and decisive battles of the Revolution were fought east of the Appalachians, but a vitally important, though small, campaign took place in the Heartland. Virginia, which laid claim to most of the region, supplied George Rogers Clark with an "army" of 175 men, who floated down the Ohio River in keelboats and captured the settlements of Kaskaskia and Cahokia in what is now Illinois and Vincennes in Indiana with scarcely a shot. The French *habitants* of those towns had no love for the British and cheerfully swore

49

His flagship *Lawrence* battered into little more than a floating hulk during the crucial Battle of Lake Erie in the War of 1812, the American commander Oliver Hazard Perry directs his men to their sister ship, *Niagara,* in this romanticized lithograph. After reaching the *Niagara,* Perry rallied his remaining vessels and defeated the superior British squadron. Since the waterways of the region were the chief routes over which supplies and men moved, the American victory helped secure the Northwest Territory, which is today the Heartland. Perry also took part, with General William Henry Harrison, in the capture of Detroit and assisted in the defeat of the British and their Indian allies in the Battle of the Thames, the war's final encounter in the Heartland.

allegiance to the rebellious American colonies. The English commander in the Heartland was Captain Henry Hamilton, dubbed the "Hair Buyer" because of the bounties he paid Indians for American scalps. He set out from Detroit with his own modest army—36 English regulars, 60 Indians and 124 militiamen—and quickly recaptured Vincennes. Francis Vigo, a fur trader, presently brought word to Clark in Kaskaskia that Hamilton had overconfidently released most of his troops and had gone into winter quarters at Vincennes with a garrison of only 80 men. Clark led a small band of American and French volunteers on a harrowing 180-mile march in mid-February. They labored through snow and mud for 17 days, often without food, but Vincennes fell and the "Hair Buyer" was taken prisoner. The loss of Vincennes, their most important post after Detroit in the Heartland, was a psychological blow from which the British in the area never recovered.

With the end of the war and the Treaty of Paris of 1782, England ceded all its possessions south of Canada and east of the Mississippi to the United States. It was a staggering acquisition. The Heartland alone added 245,000 square miles to the new nation and was potentially so rich that several of the 13 states claimed all or parts of it on the basis of their original charters from the British Crown. Maryland, whose royal charter had granted it no rights in the west, feared that it would be overwhelmed by mammoth neighbors if the western claims were upheld, and refused to sign the Articles of Confederation unless the lands were surrendered to the federal government. The other states finally gave in, although Virginia retained lands in southern Ohio for distribution to veterans of the Revolution and Connecticut kept a reserve of some four million acres (the so-called Western Reserve) in an area surrounding present-day Cleveland on the understanding that the land would be sold and the money received spent on schools—in Connecticut, of course. Another Ohio strip near Sandusky Bay was designated the Firelands and sold to compensate families whose homes had been burned or destroyed during the Revolution.

George Washington, Benjamin Franklin and others among the Founding Fathers owned large tracts of land in the Heartland. Even so, in drawing up the ordinances for the "Northwest Territory"—the "territory of the United States northwest of the river Ohio"—they displayed as much wisdom as they did in writing the Constitution.

The ordinances of 1785 and 1787 provided that

the entire area be surveyed and divided into the gridiron pattern it retains to this day. Within this grid a township consisted of 36 sections of 640 acres each (640 acres is a square mile), with one section set aside for schools. Once a territory had 60,000 inhabitants it could petition Congress for admittance to the Union "on an equal footing with the original States, in all respects whatever." Finally, the ordinances guaranteed freedom of religion and trial by jury, and forbade slavery.

But the Heartland had still to be cleared of the Indians, who had so briefly enjoyed the protection of the British Crown. The first struggle was for the Ohio country, then home of the Miami, the "Lords of the Forest." Most of the new settlements were protected by forts, and any pioneers who were rash enough to settle in unprotected communities were burned out or murdered by the Miami and their allies. Starting in 1790 three U.S. armies fought for four years to defeat the tribes—in one battle General Arthur St. Clair lost 630 of the 3,000 men in his command. Finally in 1794 at Fallen Timbers, near present-day Toledo, two hours of fighting ended 40 years of frontier war, when the Miami and their allies ignored the advice of their leading strategist, Chief Little Turtle, and attacked a vastly superior force of Americans under General Anthony Wayne, losing scores of braves and a number of chiefs in hopeless combat. After this decisive defeat the beaten Indians surrendered millions of acres of land and sullenly retired to the Indiana Territory.

The victory opened a floodgate of immigration. Within eight years of Fallen Timbers, Ohio had enough inhabitants to become a state. Cincinnati grew from a forest clearing on the Ohio River to a thriving city. New Englanders poured into the Western Reserve; Pennsylvanians settled in the Seven Ranges area near Steubenville, Virginians in the Scioto Valley and Kentuckians in western Ohio. An English visitor reported: "Old America seems to be breaking up and moving westward." New York newspapers complained of "plots to drain the East of its best blood."

There were advantages to states as well as people in establishing themselves early in the region. Congress had decreed that an east-west line be drawn through the "southerly bend or extreme of Lake Michigan" to mark the northern boundary of the three lower states to be formed from the Northwest Territory. As Ohio was petitioning for statehood it discovered that Congress had used a faulty map and that Lake Michigan ran 50 miles farther south than Congress imagined. A line

The Indian chief Tecumseh meets in 1810 with General William Henry Harrison at an unsuccessful peace conference. Harrison in 1811 defeated some of Tecumseh's forces near the Tippecanoe River. He later used the victory to help him and his running mate, John Tyler, win the Presidential election of 1840 with the slogan "Tippecanoe and Tyler too."

drawn through the southerly bend would rob Ohio of part of its Lake Erie coastline. The Ohioans simply drew a new line from a point slightly north of the southern extremity of the lake and canted it northeast to award themselves the mouth of the Maumee River and the future site of Toledo. The slice of land thus removed from the Michigan Territory came to be known as the Toledo Strip.

As the next state to be formed, Indiana was even more land hungry: it pushed the line another 10 miles north to gain a longer coastline on Lake Michigan. Illinois was slower off the mark. Its scanty population was concentrated in the south and it paid little attention to its northern boundary. To obtain the total of 60,000 inhabitants required by law, many citizens were counted twice. When that proved insufficient, even travelers passing through were included in the count. But Illinois blithely accepted the northern line as drawn by Congress, which would have given the site of Chicago and 14 northern Illinois counties to the Wisconsin Territory. The state's future was saved by its territorial representative in Washington, Judge Nathaniel Pope, who warned Northern congressmen that Illinois would become a Southern, proslavery state if it were not tied to the North by a harbor and a Lake Michigan coastline, and he won permission to advance the line north to its present position.

The people of Wisconsin and Michigan loudly protested the rape of their lands, but in vain. The three new states had representatives in Congress and votes in national elections; the territories had neither. The historian Milo Quaife wrote: "Ohio, Indiana and Illinois took what they wanted because they had the political power to enforce their grabs; the Michigan and Wisconsin Territories submitted because they had to."

Congress made an effort to atone by awarding Michigan the Upper Peninsula, a region considered so barren and worthless that Wisconsin did not mind losing it. To pacify Wisconsin for the loss of Chicago and 14 counties, Congress promised federal aid in building roads, lighthouses and harbors. The bitterness remained. Michigan and Ohio mobilized and nearly went to war over the Toledo Strip. There were even a few skirmishes, but the total casualties amounted to a deputy with a flesh wound and a stray dog shot dead. The historian R. Carlyle Buley observed: "The so-called 'Toledo War,' in proportion to the forces involved and the casualties suffered, was one of the wordiest wars in history."

The two states are still verbally at war. In 1965 Ohio demanded the cession by Michigan of a 140-acre splinter of land north of Toledo known as the Lost Peninsula, which had been inadvertently overlooked when Ohio seized the Toledo Strip. Even though the tiny peninsula is attached to Ohio, has only about 130 residents and nowhere abuts on Michigan, Michigan's attorney general, Frank Kelley, bellicosely declared that the state would never surrender "one inch" of its land to Ohio.

The new, land-hungry states of the Heartland welcomed the approach of the War of 1812, regarding it as a God-given opportunity to drive the English from Canada and to seize land from the Indians —whom they suspected the English of arming in an effort to block American expansion. John Quincy Adams noted that opposition to the war was "marked and virulent" in New England and the East generally, but that in the Heartland "there was only one sentiment; love of country sparkled in every eye and animated every heart."

Once again the Heartland was to feel the weight of gun and tomahawk. As the war neared, Tecumseh, the Shawnee leader, was hard at work organizing a great alliance of all the tribes from the Great Lakes to the Gulf of Mexico. Tecumseh traveled south, winning support from the powerful Creeks

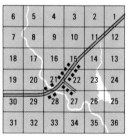

THE TOWNSHIP GRID

A pattern for new lands

In 1785 the first Congress enacted one of its most enduring laws. In the East, land division had been haphazard. The new law called for a grid system to be used in the western lands, beginning with seven ranges, or rows of townships, in eastern Ohio *(left)*. Later, meridian (north-south) and base (east-west) lines were staked out as the nation expanded westward. In 1796 the township grid *(above)*, a six-by-six-mile square, was standardized. From the Appalachians west, surveyors laid down the mile-square checkerboard pattern that is so readily visible a feature of the American landscape.

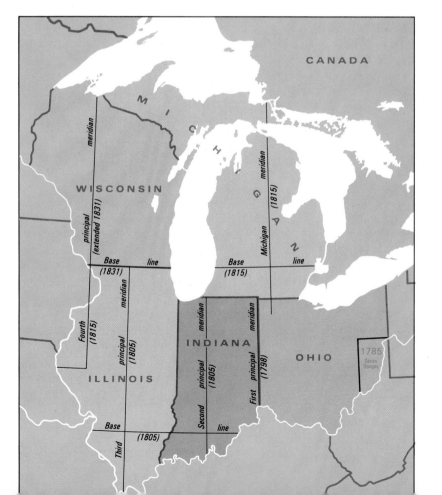

and being rebuffed by the slaveholding Choctaw. His one-eyed brother, Tenskwatawa, the Prophet, carried his potent medicine fire and his sacred white beans to the north and west. The Chippewa listened in their birch-bark wigwams in the North Woods and joined the alliance. Chief Black Hawk brought his Sauk and Foxes into the conspiracy in all their finery of feather-trimmed lances, bear-claw necklaces and nodding crests of red-dyed deer tails. Their Kickapoo kinsmen and the vengeful Miami followed suit, as did the Winnebago and the Delawares. Even the peaceful Menominee laid aside their "courting flutes" for war clubs.

Hoping to gain an advantage over the Indians during Tecumseh's absence in the South, General William Henry Harrison marched in the autumn of 1811 on Prophetstown, the Shawnee stronghold in northwestern Indiana. The Shawnee attacked his camp before dawn, swarming up a bluff above the Tippecanoe River, and the result was a minor victory for the Americans—although it was magnified into a glorious triumph in Harrison's Presidential campaign 29 years later. The battle also gave encouragement to the western "war hawks" in the U.S. Congress, helping them to override Eastern opposition to the declaration of war against Britain, which came on June 18, 1812.

The war that the Heartland had so eagerly welcomed began with a succession of disasters. Fort Mackinac fell to the British without a shot fired. Tecumseh and 2,000 Indian braves joined the British at Detroit, and General William Hull, commander of the U.S. garrison, meekly surrendered his 2,000 troops. When the garrison at Fort Dearborn, the future site of Chicago, tried to escape along the Lake Michigan shore, it was ambushed by a band of Potawatomi. General Harrison launched an assault on Detroit from Ohio, hoping to capture the fort and press on to conquer Canada. Against his orders 1,000 of his men precipitately attempted to take Frenchtown, a small settlement on the Raisin River. Surprised by a British-Indian war party, 250 of them were killed and 500 taken prisoner. "Remember the River Raisin!" became the American battle cry. Harrison and the remainder of his men retreated to the newly established post of Fort Meigs, where they were besieged by Tecumseh.

With Michigan already lost to the enemy, the last Heartland hope rested on Captain Oliver Hazard Perry. His flotilla, manned by Ohio militiamen and Negro sailors from the East Coast, defeated the British squadron in the Battle of Lake Erie in September 1813, and Perry sent back the triumphant message, "We have met the enemy and they are ours." With command of Lake Erie secured, the balance shifted to the Americans. Detroit was retaken and the British began to lose heart.

The northwestern frontier was finally secured in October 1813 when Harrison defeated a force of British and Indians at the Battle of the Thames in what is now the Canadian province of Ontario. The victory had other repercussions as well; Tecumseh was slain during the battle, and his dream of a huge Indian confederation collapsed. Black Hawk and his Sauk and Foxes returned to their homeland on the beautiful Rock River in Illinois, where later, in 1832, Black Hawk was to lead the last, futile Indian uprising in the Heartland. After the end of the War of 1812 the Indians were gradually rounded up and escorted across the Mississippi, where, they were assured, the land would be forever theirs. Some, like the Delawares, who had already been pushed all the way from the Atlantic Coast, listened cynically. Ravaged by war, smallpox and whiskey, the Heartland Indians lamented, as Tecumseh had said, that they were losing "the whole of our hunting grounds, from the rising to the setting sun."

In the postwar prosperity that swept the Heartland, everything moved, even the state capitals. Ohio's went from Chillicothe to Zanesville to Columbus, Indiana's from Vincennes to Corydon to

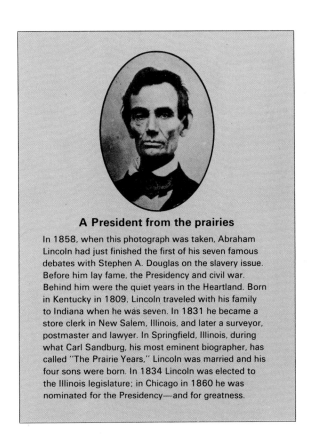

A President from the prairies

In 1858, when this photograph was taken, Abraham Lincoln had just finished the first of his seven famous debates with Stephen A. Douglas on the slavery issue. Before him lay fame, the Presidency and civil war. Behind him were the quiet years in the Heartland. Born in Kentucky in 1809, Lincoln traveled with his family to Indiana when he was seven. In 1831 he became a store clerk in New Salem, Illinois, and later a surveyor, postmaster and lawyer. In Springfield, Illinois, during what Carl Sandburg, his most eminent biographer, has called "The Prairie Years," Lincoln was married and his four sons were born. In 1834 Lincoln was elected to the Illinois legislature; in Chicago in 1860 he was nominated for the Presidency—and for greatness.

Indianapolis, Illinois' from Kaskaskia to Vandalia to Springfield. Emigrants came in wave on wave from Germany and Ireland. Swiss settled Vevay in Indiana and New Glarus and Monroe in Wisconsin. Almost the entire village of Colebrook, New Hampshire, moved to Wisconsin to settle Beloit.

The early decades of the 19th Century were a time of visions, when idealists dreamed of the City Beautiful where men would live without social strife in true brotherhood. At Harmony, in southern Indiana, the night watchman made his rounds calling, "Again a day is passed and a step made nearer to our end. Our time runs away and the joys of Heaven are our reward." Harmony's leader, George Rapp, believed that the end of the world was at hand. He had brought 800 German followers to the Heartland and put them to work clearing the forest and building a town as something to occupy their hands and thoughts while awaiting Judgment Day. The Harmonists prospered so greatly that Rapp feared they might turn to materialism. He had a chat with the archangel Gabriel, whose giant footprint may still be seen in the town, and then sold out to a wealthy British idealist, Robert Owen, moving his colony to a new site in Pennsylvania to await the Last Trumpet.

The Owenites changed the name of the town to New Harmony and set out to establish a model community on socialist principles in which learning and the arts would flourish. The colony failed when the cultured Owenites fell to quarreling among themselves and neglected their fields and livestock. Some utopians, however, had better luck. German Separatists in Zoar, Ohio, acquired 7,000 fertile acres and built their own sawmill, machine shop, tannery, dye works and flour mills. The Shakers, originally a New York sect, set up several communities in the Heartland, including one on what is now the site of the prosperous Cleveland suburb of Shaker Heights. They produced the best garden seeds in the nation, and their excellently made wooden boxes and furniture often outlasted metal. Since they practiced celibacy, the Shakers were forced to keep up their numbers through conversion and by adopting orphans. Eventually, however, the Heartland Shakers disappeared.

The Mormons, who attempted to establish a new Zion in the Heartland, fared no better there than other utopians. Joseph Smith, who had founded the Church of Jesus Christ of Latter-day Saints after the Book of Mormon had been revealed to him in upstate New York, set up a Mormon colony in Missouri in 1831 and another in Kirtland, Ohio, in that same year. The Mormons rapidly became unpopular in both Ohio and Missouri. They were a close-knit and frequently standoffish group of whom neighbors were understandably suspicious. Eighteen of them were killed in a massacre in Caldwell County in Missouri and the Mormons were hounded out of the state; they aroused antagonism in Ohio when their Kirtland bank, following a practice of the time, issued thousands of dollars in paper money despite the state's refusal to issue them a bank charter. In 1839 Smith and his followers established a new settlement in Illinois which they called Nauvoo. There, as converts poured in, they built a magnificent million-dollar temple.

By 1845 Nauvoo had 20,000 inhabitants and had become the largest city in Illinois. Courted by both Whigs and Democrats, the Mormons acquired enormous political power. Neighboring townspeople and farmers were made nervous by the Mormon army, the Nauvoo Legion, and especially feared a Mormon land mine so devastating that it was called a "hell's half acre." Mormon popularity did not increase when Joseph Smith announced his candidacy for the Presidency of the United States in 1846, and the announcement helped to precipitate trouble within Smith's own ranks. A schismatic group set itself up in nearby Carthage, Illinois, and began publishing an anti-Smith newspaper. Smith's men destroyed the press; the rebellious faction thereupon obtained a warrant for his arrest and that of his brother Hyrum. In jail in Carthage the brothers were murdered by a mob.

This bloody event encouraged the Mormons to move on to the relative peace and quiet of Utah. French Icarians, a group whose communal ideals were not unlike those of the Owenites of New Harmony, established a short-lived community at Nauvoo after the Mormons' departure. But the death of the God-struck Smith brothers marked the end of major efforts by utopians to establish settlements in the Heartland.

The coming of the railroads in the 1840s, following the opening of the Erie Canal in 1825 and the completion of a network of canals in the northern sections of the Heartland, reoriented the region from a north-south axis along the rivers to an east-west one. The canals and the railroads also brought a new vigor and new population to the northern area. The historian Frederick Jackson Turner noted that "the statistics of growth between 1830 and 1840, in the states of Ohio, Indiana, and Illinois, showed that the northern counties, adjacent to the Great Lakes, increased their population over eight hundred thousand, while the counties tributary to the Ohio River gained hardly more than half this

A lofty concept for utopia was embodied in an architect's design for the nucleus of New Harmony, a 19th Century model community in Indiana. Established in 1825 by Robert Owen, a Welsh manufacturer, the community attracted scientists and scholars who set up the first coeducational public school in America—but who never did build the grandiose square. In 1828 the community itself dissolved, but the unpretentious buildings that its members actually occupied are today preserved as a national historical landmark.

number. Between 1840 and 1850 southern Michigan and Wisconsin also received a tide of settlers that increased the population of these two states by nearly half a million over that at the beginning of the decade.''

Most of these new settlers pouring into the northern sections came from New York and New England; those who migrated to the southern sections were largely from the Southern states of the Union. That fact gave rise to speculation, as the Civil War approached, that the southern area was partial to the cause of the South. The abolitionist editor Elijah Lovejoy had been shot to death in downstate Alton, Illinois, in 1837. But thousands of Chicagoans attended a mammoth rally in 1856 to cheer the antislavery oratory of Jim Lane, a former lieutenant governor of Indiana who had also been one of the leaders in the abolitionist cause in Kansas. After emptying their pockets the tumultuous crowd surged through the muddy streets of Chicago singing the "Marseillaise."

When war came most of the Heartland—north and south—was solidly for the Union. Although many of its citizens were from the South, few had come from wealthy, slave-owning areas. Some, like the North Carolina Quakers who settled in Wayne County, Indiana, had left the South because of their detestation of slavery, and many of them assisted slaves bound north on the escape routes that led to Canada. Indiana was always considered the Heartland state most oriented toward the South, yet it sent 196,363 men into the Union armies, representing 74.3 per cent of its men capable of bearing arms. Most of Ohio's southern counties, whose original settlers came mostly from Kentucky and Tennessee, were never touched by the draft; they oversubscribed their quotas of volunteers in every year of the war. Midwestern regiments played the major part in sealing the doom of the Confederacy by cutting it in two along the line of the Mississippi River. And it was Heartland generals who brought the war to its successful conclusion—Phil Sheridan by defeating the Confederate cavalry of Jeb Stuart and Jubal Early, William Tecumseh Sherman by marching through Georgia to the sea, and Ulysses S. Grant by winning the series of battles of attrition around Richmond.

After the war Heartland industry and agriculture vastly expanded. Workers were so scarce that the individual states sent agents abroad to drum up emigrants. After 1880 so many emigrants swarmed in from Europe that by 1920 there were 3.5 million Heartlanders who had been born abroad, out of the region's total population of 21.5 million. This

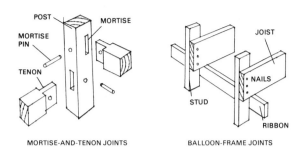

MORTISE-AND-TENON JOINTS   BALLOON-FRAME JOINTS

The revolutionary balloon frame

The need for many new houses to accommodate the influx of Heartland settlers in the 1800s, coupled with a scarcity of skilled carpenters, gave rise to an entirely new form of construction. Craftsmen of the day derisively called it the balloon frame to contrast its flimsiness—they said the first strong wind would blow it away—with the heaviness of traditional construction methods. In fact, the balloon frame not only was cheaper and quicker to put up but was stronger. In the older type, huge beams were fastened together by fitting the tenons of crossbeams into the mortise holes of uprights. The holes, however, weakened the beams and collected moisture, which promoted rot. In the newer method, thinner lumber was used, and floor supports (joists) were nailed to the uprights (studs) and reinforced by a horizontal member called a ribbon. For added strength, a skin of wooden sheathing was then applied across the studs and joists. Houses built by this method today fill the Heartland as well as most other regions of the United States.

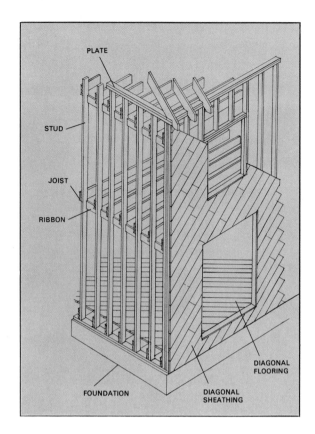

inrush of Greeks, Poles, Bohemians, Italians, Bulgars and Hungarians aroused conflicting emotions. The *Chicago Tribune* trumpeted: "Europe will open her gates like a conquered city. Her people will come forth to us subdued by admiration of our glory and envy of our perfect peace. On to the Rocky Mountains and still over to the Pacific our mighty populations will spread. . . ." But some segments of the native population feared that they would be overwhelmed. Heartland Protestants, who feared a papal conspiracy and were disturbed because so many of the newcomers were Roman Catholics, flocked to such organizations as the American Protective Association, whose members pledged to hire only their own kind. Even these xenophobic groups did not deny the American dream. The historian John Higham has observed: "The old pride in America as a home of the oppressed survived. . . . The concept of an American haven for people discontented with their own governments exerted little fascination [but] it was rarely repudiated."

The Heartland grew unsteadily—spurting ahead in booms, falling back in busts. Like the rest of the nation it also grew unevenly, with great wealth at the top and great poverty at the bottom. Charles Darwin's theory of the survival of the fittest was used to justify everything from child labor to the

12-hour day. By 1877 the Knights of Labor, a secret organization of workers whose demands included the eight-hour day, had established its first locals in Illinois. Anarchism, that ultimate expression of disgust with society, flickered through the Heartland. "Chicago," noted the historian Theodore C. Pease, "had the distinction of being the center of the radical labor movement in the United States." Clashes between strikers and police grew frequent. In May 1886 a mass meeting to protest the shooting of six strikers at the McCormick Reaper works in Chicago was called in the city's Haymarket Square at the urging of the editor of *Die Arbeiter-Zeitung*, an anarchist newspaper. Police advanced on the crowd, a bomb was tossed, eight policemen died and 65 of them were wounded.

The Haymarket Riot precipitated a spasm of fright in the Heartland. The Columbus *Journal* complained, "There are too many unhung anarchists and rebels." In the opinion of the Cleveland *Leader*, "The anarchist wolf . . . has fastened its hideous, poisonous fangs in the body corporate of the American people." Eight alleged anarchists were brought to trial for the Haymarket bombing, and although it was evident that none of them had thrown the bomb, four were hanged for the crime; the rest were imprisoned.

The cause of trade unionism was dealt a near-deadly blow by the Haymarket affair and the unions' associations with radicalism, but the tenets of anarchism lingered on. A moody young man from Michigan named Leon Czolgosz took so seriously the anarchist belief in the "propaganda of the deed" that he shot and killed President William McKinley in 1901. Disavowed by anarchist groups, Czolgosz nonetheless wrote in his confession, "I done my duty." The grammar, if not the point of view, was soon echoed by Governor Jeremiah Rusk of Wisconsin, who, on sending troops to put down a strike in Milwaukee by workers demanding the eight-hour day, said, "I seen my duty and I done it."

Despite its labor strife, the Heartland began to challenge the East for industrial primacy at the turn of the century. In 1870 John D. Rockefeller, a former Cleveland bookkeeper, and a group of associates had formed the Standard Oil Company of Ohio; by 1900 Rockefeller was the dominant figure in the American oil-refining industry. Henry Ford formed the Ford Motor Company in Detroit in 1903; in 1909 he designed his Model T, more than 15 million of which were to be sold over a 20-year period before the model was discontinued. Judge Elbert Gary, whose father had been among the founders of Wheaton, Illinois, became one of the chief organizers of U.S. Steel in 1901, and in 1905 he founded a city of his own amid the Lake Michigan sand dunes—the steel town of Gary, Indiana, which became the only city to grow from nothing to more than 150,000 people in the 20th Century.

With the U.S. entry into World War I, the Heartland, along with the rest of the nation, had one of its periodic spasms of superpatriotism. Everything German was held suspect, and sauerkraut became "liberty cabbage." The Irish were also viewed with suspicion because of their bellicose attitude toward England. But after the war, and a brief depression in 1921, the Heartland joined the rest of the country in a great surge of optimism over what seemed the boundless and endless prosperity of the 1920s, with the period's great sports heroes, flappers, and college boys in raccoon coats at the wheel of Stutz Bearcats. It was also the heady Prohibition era, when Al Capone ruled Chicago from his headquarters in what had been a modest, middle-class suburb, Cicero. The gangs provided lurid headlines, with Dion O'Bannion murdered in his Chicago florist shop across the street from the Holy Name Cathedral, and the Purple Gang running booze across the border from Canada to Detroit. The violence culminated in the St. Valentine's Day Massacre, when seven hoodlums were gunned down

ROBERT M. LA FOLLETTE

ROBERT M. LA FOLLETTE JR.

PHILIP FOX LA FOLLETTE

Wisconsin's fighting La Follettes

For much of the first half of the 20th Century, the Wisconsin political scene was dominated by one family —the La Follettes. The first of the family to enter politics was Robert M. "Fighting Bob" La Follette, who was elected Governor in 1900 and United States Senator in 1905. In 1924 La Follette ran for the Presidency on the Progressive Party ticket and polled more votes than any third-party candidate before or since. When he died in 1925, his son Robert M. "Young Bob" La Follette Jr. won Fighting Bob's Senate seat and served an additional three terms. Another son, Philip Fox La Follette, was Wisconsin's Governor for three terms. In 1931, during his first term, Wisconsin enacted the country's first unemployment relief measure. With Young Bob's defeat in 1947, the dynasty seemed to end, but in 1964 his son, Bronson Cutting La Follette, renewed the tradition by becoming Wisconsin's attorney general.

in a Chicago garage, and Chicago became a synonym for unpunished murder. In one four-year period the city had 215 unsolved gang slayings. But the Heartland had always had a penchant for violence (the first recorded U.S. train robbery took place near Seymour, Indiana, in 1866, when two brothers got away with $10,000), and since the gangsters usually killed only one another, few people were seriously concerned by the slaughter.

The speakeasy, the automobile and the new affluence caused a nationwide relaxation of morals. Girls' skirt lengths climbed above the knee, and when women began to smoke in public, preachers thundered dire warnings from their pulpits. Jazz moved upriver from New Orleans to Chicago; Bix Beiderbecke was playing his clear and lyrical cornet with the Wolverines all over the Heartland; lean, sad-visaged Hoagy Carmichael played the piano in Bloomington with a University of Indiana combo, and the Coon-Sanders Band broadcast from the Blackhawk Restaurant in Chicago.

America's "era of wonderful nonsense" ended with the 1929 crash, and the Heartland and the country plunged deep into the Great Depression. Keweenaw County, Michigan, had fully two thirds of its population on relief. Some vital Heartland spring seemed broken as people watched the collapse of public-utilities empires like Samuel Insull's in Chicago, the shuttering of banks and factories, and the lengthy bread lines and woebegone apple sellers. For two decades not a single new skyscraper was erected in Chicago. The malicious crack attributed to George Ade about his own state, "Many men come from Indiana; the better they are the quicker they come," applied to all of the Heartland. Almost the entire school of Chicago writers, including Edgar Lee Masters, Ben Hecht and Burton Rascoe, who had given the Heartland identity and a distinct voice in the 1920s, abandoned the city for Manhattan.

The Heartland did not fully revive until World War II, when it again proved how abundantly it could produce. PT boats came off the ways in Wisconsin shipyards; landing craft poured from factories swiftly raised in cornfields; two enormous munitions plants sprang up in rustic Charlestown, Indiana. Detroit switched from cars to tanks, jeeps and airplanes. But there was everywhere the nagging fear that it would all end with the end of the war, and the Heartland hedged its bets in fear of the coming of another depression.

There was indeed a pause after the war, but not a depression. The hiatus lasted until the mid-1950s and was accompanied by the flight of the middle class to the suburbs and the progressive darkening of the urban complexion. About 1955 the Heartland exploded economically, its broken spring magically repaired or replaced. Burgeoning industry discovered that it could not find the workers it needed in the mill towns. Small, sleepy cities awoke with a start as new factories moved in and began making things like transistors, which most people had never heard of. Chicago resumed its ancient love affair with architects. Designs flowed from the drawing boards of Ludwig Mies van der Rohe at the Illinois Institute of Technology and other members of a new "Chicago school," and once again shining buildings soared high against the sky. The changes went deep: tiny Winamac, Indiana, practically untouched since the Civil War, found itself suddenly invaded by branches of three manufacturing companies.

Perhaps the major instruments of change were the junior executives who accompanied the factories into the small towns and at once plunged into the lives of their new communities. It was as if a thousand windows had been flung open. A citizen of one Illinois city said, "If you had asked me fifteen years ago who ran this town, I could have named you three men. Now, with all these new executives in town, I'm damned if I know who runs it. It's a lot livelier this way."

Recognizing the importance of education in the new age, the Heartland cities began a mad scramble for colleges and technical schools. State universities put out branches in all directions, and long-moribund colleges revived with a rush. Northern Michigan University shot from 900 to more than 5,500 students in 10 years.

With more industrial muscle today than ever before, and a new glint in its eye, the Heartland is once again ready to challenge the East, or any place else, for national leadership. By 1960 the median family income in the Chicago metropolitan area had reached $7,300, some $1,700 higher than the national average. The region grants more than 25 per cent of the nation's doctoral degrees—and, to overcome the "brain drain" to California and elsewhere, is making a determined effort to keep their holders at home. "It's high time we stopped running a Point Four program for the rest of the country," said one businessman.

The Heartland's history, and its goals, can best be summed up by one of its natural features, the Kankakee River, which rises in Indiana and empties into the Illinois River. At one end of the Kankakee is an ancient Indian portage; a few miles beyond its other end is the Dresden Nuclear Power Station.

Steel wheels and floor beams are all that remain after rioters put the torch to sleeping cars during an 1894 strike against the Pullman Palace Car Company. Pullman had slashed wages but kept rents high in company-owned houses in which its employees lived.

Violence in a growing land

The vigor that men brought to the building of the Heartland has sometimes been transformed into violence: between budding industrialists, who saw an opportunity to create empires, and the workingmen who sometimes labored 60-hour weeks; between rival gang mobs in search of profit and power; between Negroes who migrated north seeking work and whites who claimed the territory—and the jobs—for themselves. Other regions have known such struggles, but in the Heartland they at times erupted with special force. Yet the violence that pitted man against man pales in comparison to the one-sided war that nature has carried on against all men. Here the weapons have been tornadoes, blizzards and rain-swollen rivers that sent human beings to their deaths with a might that made fists, tommy guns and clubs seem puny and ineffective.

The workers' search for dignity and a living wage

As elsewhere in the United States, the growth of industries and work forces in the Heartland created a widening gulf of misunderstanding—and income—between the haves and the have-nots. Although labor unions appeared early in the Heartland, and strikes were called there in the 1830s, attempts by the workers to better their lot frequently failed. During the last decades of the 19th Century and the first few of the 20th, many disputes were resolved not over a bargaining table but in the streets, where police, company thugs and strikebreakers, and workers settled differences with clubs and guns.

Wives of Chrysler auto workers march around a factory, cheered on by their striking husbands, who had in 1937 seized control of one of the company's Detroit plants. Such "sit-down" strikes were a popular labor tactic in the mid-1930s; the Chrysler workers won their strike after holding the factory for almost a month.

En route to picket, steelworkers and their families are forcibly halted by police a few blocks from Republic Steel's South Chicago works on May 30, 1937. The workers were striking for the right to unionize. The "Memorial Day Massacre" of that day left 10 workers dead and roughly 100 seriously injured—and the strike was lost.

The rise to power
of "hidden government"

For nearly two decades following the end of World War I, Chicago was the capital of the nation's underworld. Even before 1919, when the arrival of Prohibition created a huge market for bootleg liquor that provided Chicago gangsters with funds for expansion and bribery, they were prospering from gambling and prostitution. The pervasive optimism of the time, born of the mistaken notion that peace was permanent and that happy days were here to stay, helped mobsters to operate with relative impunity; in a carefree world few cared that the racketeers were the wealthiest and happiest of all. Mayor "Big Bill" Thompson, for one, was a firm believer in a wide-open town, and from city hall down to the cop on the beat—and on the take—city officials were hopelessly corrupt. By the early 1920s it was the gangsters who truly ran Chicago.

Awaiting grand-jury questioning, Al Capone *(light hat)* talks with his attorney in 1929. The king of the Chicago underworld, Capone long evaded imprisonment, but he was finally jailed in 1931. Even after his death in 1947, the Capone mob continued to flourish.

Murdered in a gangland power struggle, ex-gang leader Angelo Genna is carried in state in an $11,000 coffin. The mourners, among them state and city officials, paid their last respects as the funeral procession moved slowly through Chicago on May 30, 1925.

Bank robber, gunman and lady's man, John Dillinger *(in shirt sleeves)* awaits trial on a murder charge in January 1934. He escaped before the trial, only to be shot dead by FBI agents six months later—ironically, in that sanctuary for criminals, Chicago.

Foretaste of the future: a bloody, large-scale race riot

By 1943 labor-management violence had subsided in the Heartland. Open gang warfare had diminished, though the criminals were better organized than ever. But the region's quiet was short-lived; violence between black and white erupted in one of the northernmost cities of the region, Detroit.

The number of Negroes in Detroit had been small; in 1910 there were fewer than 6,000. But during World War I the needs of industry brought many Negroes from the South, and by 1920 their numbers had increased sevenfold. Less than 20 years later the slums were bursting with 150,000 Negroes, and World War II increased the influx. Most were employed, but their jobs were often the most menial available and slum rents were disproportionately high. On June 27, 1943, a rumor spread through one poor section that whites had murdered a Negro mother and child. The story was later proved untrue—but too late. Angry Negroes attacked whites and white-owned shops, angry whites counterattacked, and police struggled for a full day and night to put down the riot. At the end, 31 whites and Negroes were dead, a grim toll whose memory contrasts sharply with the progress in race relations that Detroit is making today.

Despite his police escort, a Negro is slapped by a white man while an angry crowd closes in. The police, although attacked by both sides, were harsher in dealing with Negroes: of the 15 rioters killed by policemen, not one was white.

Surrounded by the acrid white puffs of tear-gas bombs, Detroit policemen keep a crowd of white men at bay with the aid of a submachine gun. Outflanking the police, other whites begin to storm Negro homes across the street.

Destruction wrought
by a river run wild

Of the countless songs and poems that praise the region's beauty, perhaps the most misleading is "Beautiful Ohio." For the Ohio can be among the ugliest of rivers. Heavy winter rains or an early thaw in the more than 200,000-square-mile area the river drains can send downstream waters cascading over their banks, carrying death and destruction before the mighty tide. Since 1935 the Ohio has indulged itself in a minor flood almost every other year, and has six times gone on awesome rampages.

Riding the rails, Ohio River water pours over the Illinois Central tracks at Cairo, Illinois, in January 1937. This was only the start of the river's most terrifying spree. The flood took some 400 lives; rising to street-light level, the water scoured Cairo for a week.

Safe on high ground, dairy cows on a farm near New Albany, Indiana, are milked during the Ohio River flood of March 1964. The lessons of the Ohio's 1937 rampage had been well learned: property damage was less and only 15 persons were killed.

The taut string of the Mackinac Bridge, longest suspension bridge in the world, stretches 8,614 feet across the Straits of Mackinac at the juncture of Lakes Michigan and Huron. Completed at a cost of $99,800,000, it links the Upper and Lower Peninsulas of Michigan.

4

Vast, Interlocking Waterways

The Great Lakes are a watery staircase. From the top step of Lake Superior there is a drop of 22 feet through the St. Mary's River and the Soo Canals to Lakes Huron and Michigan, which are at the same elevation. A fall of six feet through Lake St. Clair leads to Lake Erie, from which it is a giant downward step of as much as 190 feet over the thundering Niagara Falls to Lake Ontario, which empties into the St. Lawrence River for its 1,200-mile run to the Atlantic Ocean.

If the water of the Great Lakes were spread evenly over the old 48 states, the United States would be flooded to a depth of 10 feet. The first French explorers were struck dumb with amazement at the extent of the lakes, and the Jesuit missionaries gave Lake Huron, the first they found, the felicitous name of "The Sweet Sea." The portages between the lakes were difficult. But the *voyageurs* who discovered and traversed them found the way west and south from the St. Lawrence passable for hundreds on hundreds of miles. The French were understandably convinced that in the Great Lakes they had found the long-sought Northwest Passage to the Orient. In 1634 Jean Nicolet was dispatched to make contact with China, and he dutifully donned a robe of Chinese damask when approaching a landfall in Wisconsin. Instead of being greeted by polite Chinese, Nicolet was hailed by a band of savage Winnebago. It must have been a shock to Nicolet, who returned to Quebec with a pessimistic report, but men continued to dream of—and seek—a water passage through the Heartland.

Many years were to pass before they found one. The lakes are as notable for their treachery as for their beauty. Their extent and the free sweep of prairie winds help to create sudden and dangerous seas. A single storm in 1913 sank or drove aground more than 30 ships. There are other hazards: narrow channels, shifting sand bars, reefs, sudden fogs, and freezing temperatures that make ships top-heavy with ice or create threatening, jagged floes. The pounding waves are so strong that they have pulverized great boulders into tiny grains of sand to form the splendid beaches around the lakes.

The first proper ship to sail the Great Lakes was the *Griffon*, a tidy little vessel of some 50 tons, carrying five cannon and a crew of 32. It was painstakingly built above Niagara Falls by Robert Cavelier, Sieur de La Salle. In August 1679 the *Griffon* made her maiden voyage to what is now Green Bay, Wisconsin, and took aboard a cargo of furs gathered by La Salle's agents. With sails set and the French flag unfurled, the *Griffon* fired a parting salute from her cannon and set off across the glassy water on her return voyage. Like hundreds of later lake ships, the *Griffon* vanished without a trace.

Mirages, both real and imaginary, are common on the Great Lakes. Ships on distant horizons seem to be sailing through air, sand dunes float by, and headlands appear to be cut adrift from the shore. La Salle's long-lost *Griffon* has repeatedly been sighted on Lake Superior and so have other notable wrecks, like the *Lady Elgin* and the *Bannockburn*. Isle Royale, the only island that is also a national park, occasionally appears upside down, with its base in the clouds and its pines pointing at the water. Sometimes two moons ride in the night sky. By day, sundogs, or mock suns, rival the real sun and are thought to foretell the weather.

It is no wonder that the Heartland's lakes and rivers gradually became the home of legend. The geologist Henry Schoolcraft lived for years among the Chippewa, learned the tribal language, customs and mythology, and described them in *Algic Researches*. The book fell into the hands of Henry Wadsworth Longfellow and the happy result was *The Song of Hiawatha*. Paul Bunyan, according to later legend, dug out the Great Lakes—which occupy an area the size of the United Kingdom—to assure his great Blue Ox, Babe, a supply of water.

From the beginning the Great Lakes have been carriers of actual as well as fictional wealth. As the ice loosed its grip each spring, Indians in beaded leggings and scarlet sashes loaded their canoes with furs trapped during the winter and went whooping on their way to the nearest trading post. At Michilimackinac, the present St. Ignace, at Sault Ste. Marie and at Green Bay, French clerks graded the

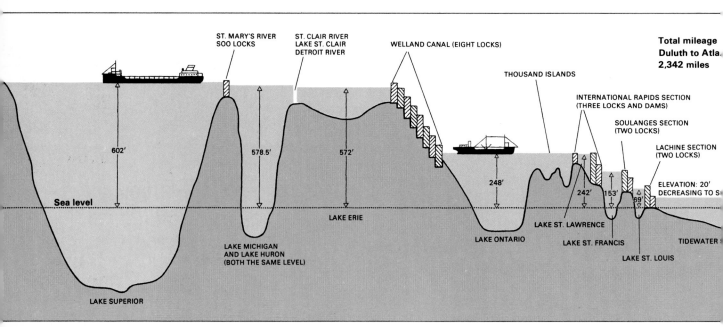

Making seaports of lake ports

This stylized cross section illustrates the complexity of the system of lakes, locks and canals that make up the vital St. Lawrence Seaway, opened to traffic in 1959. Linking the navigable waters of the St. Lawrence River with the Great Lakes, the waterway penetrates more than 2,300 miles inland from the Atlantic Ocean to the Heartland and beyond. The seaway accommodates deep-draft, oceangoing vessels as well as the smaller Great Lakes ships, lifting them in 16 locks from sea level to the surface of Lake Superior, 600 feet higher.

pelts—beaver, muskrat, marten, mink, raccoon, wolverine, lynx, wolf, elk, deer, bear and buffalo—into four categories. In return for the furs, Indians got guns, traps, blankets, knives and, inevitably, brandy. When drunk, Indians became either maudlin or murderous. At a Fort Dearborn powwow of 3,000 Ottawa, Potawatomi and Chippewa, 10 Indians were killed in drunken quarrels in one day.

One of the first Heartland boosters was Father Louis Hennepin, a huge, bearded Franciscan. Like many of the so-called Heartland "French," he was not a Frenchman at all, having been born in what is now Belgium. Hennepin, like many explorers, was prone to exaggeration—he swore that Niagara Falls was 600 feet high, three times its actual height. But Hennepin had both vision and intelligence and in 1680 declared that it would be "easy to build on the sides of these great Lakes, an infinite number of considerable towns which might have communication one with another by navigation . . . and by an inconceivable commerce which would establish itself amongst them."

This did not happen under the French. They were eager for empire, and they recognized the strategic importance of the mid-continental waterways. By 1750 they had secured both ends of America's potential water highway with fortified cities, Quebec on the St. Lawrence and New Orleans at the mouth of the Mississippi. But they were far less successful than the English in promoting immigration into the Heartland and other regions of the North American continent, and they tried to oppose the advance of English power by using the Indian tribes and bolstering them with French troops. The French administrators on the scene were growing wealthy on the fur trade and did not want settlers usurping the land and causing friction with the Indians. In addition, the Jesuits and other missionaries wanted to be let alone to reap for God a harvest of Indian souls.

Curiously, many of the European empire builders long regarded the Heartland as an inhospitable wilderness unfit for large-scale settlement. The view that it was a barren waste persisted for decades. A traveler in upper Michigan wrote that "there is not a spear of grass in the entire eternity of this country, and an ox or an ass, turned out, would starve unless he could feed on pine shadows and moss." When proposals were heard that a canal should be dug to bypass the rapids known as the Soo in the St. Mary's River and thus give access between Lake Superior and Lake Huron, Henry Clay, the "Great Compromiser" of the U.S. Senate, derided the area as "a place beyond the remotest

Simple boats for river travel

Early settlers and explorers in the Heartland built a variety of boats to carry them and their goods into the wilderness over the region's main routes of travel—the rivers. Among the earliest was the pirogue, which was little more than a platform bearing a shed, supported by two dugouts or canoes. It usually carried only a single traveler. A larger vessel was the ark, a flat-bottomed boat almost completely enclosed to protect the settler, his family and his livestock from Indian attack. The open flatboat was used when there was little danger from Indians. Dependent on the river's current for motion, such boats could travel only downstream. When the settler reached his destination, he lived in the boat until he could build a house, or he sold it for lumber.

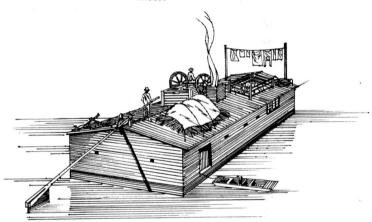

PIROGUE

ARK

OPEN FLATBOAT

Transporting a vessel to Lake Superior from Lake Huron before the Soo Canals were dug, men laboriously drag the 50-ton schooner *Algonquin* through the main street of Sault Ste. Marie, Michigan. The trip took from December 1839 to April 1840. Before the canal opened in 1855, sixteen such ships were pulled through the town to create an ore-carrying fleet on Lake Superior.

settlement of the United States, if not on the moon."

Yet the Heartland abounded in natural resources. After French power gave way to English, the British, too, began to exploit the lucrative fur trade, and after their departure, so did the Americans. In 1808 John Jacob Astor founded the American Fur Company and after the War of 1812 proceeded to lay the base for one of America's great financial dynasties by gaining a monopoly over the fur trade in Michigan's Upper Peninsula. When the supply of fur-bearing animals diminished in the 1830s, Astor moved his fur-trading operations westward; at his death in 1848 he was known as the wealthiest man in America. There were, however, other fortunes to be made in the Heartland; not long before Astor's death Douglass Houghton, the Michigan state geologist, reported the presence of copper in the Upper Peninsula. Publicity about the removal of a three-ton boulder of pure copper and rock touched off speculation that the metal could be easily mined there. Extraction and shipping costs, however, proved to be high; moreover, the labor of blasting out the ore and hauling it up the deep-sunk mine shafts was backbreaking. Many Upper Peninsula miners left for California after gold was discovered there in 1848. But eventually copper mining became big business in this area; until 1887

Michigan was the leading copper producer among the states, and it still mines an impressive amount of the metal.

One of Houghton's subordinates was a surveyor named William A. Burt. Surveying the Upper Peninsula in 1844, he had noticed that his compasses were erratic in certain areas. He had stumbled on what were subsequently described as "mountains" of iron ore. Companies were quickly organized and miners moved in. Getting the ore across the water to the smelters at Cleveland and other industrial cities on the lower lakes proved, however, to be a more formidable problem than extracting it. Cargo schooners were dragged overland at the Soo and into Lake Superior; there they were loaded with ore at the Superior port of Marquette. Back at the Soo the ore was unloaded, transported overland and reloaded aboard other schooners for shipment into Lake Huron. The job was both desperately difficult and costly; the canal through the Soo that Henry Clay had opposed was clearly a necessity. In 1852 Congress granted 750,000 acres of public lands to the state of Michigan as a subsidy for the construction of a canal; it was completed under the direction of Charles T. Harvey, a Vermont engineer who kept 1,600 men working through the bitter northern Michigan winters to finish it by the 1855 deadline set by Congress. The completion of the Soo Canal proved a boon to the Heartland and to the Union; the demand for ore greatly increased during the Civil War. By the 1890s more than eight million tons of iron ore were being shipped through the Soo and down the lakes each year.

A timber boom reached its peak in the same period. Every winter 120,000 lumberjacks swarmed through the white-pine forests of Michigan and Wisconsin. As the tall trees crashed to earth, logs cut from them were hauled by teams of horses or oxen over an iced "skid road" to the riverbank. When the ice broke up in the spring, the logs were canted into the water and sent racing downstream to the sawmill. So many logs poured down on the spring flood that water could scarcely be seen on the Fox and the Black, the Paint and the Dead, the Peshekee and the Yellow Dog, the Tittabawassee and the Shiawassee.

The logging trade has been accurately described as "dripping with blood." Few jacks came out of the woods unscathed—mangled hands and broken backs were common in Michigan and Wisconsin. The going wage was one dollar per day, usually payable in a lump sum in the spring at the end of the logging season. The wanagan, a sort of company store, followed the jacks into the pine woods,

Like apparitions from another era, the riverboats *Tom Green* (right) and *Betsy Ann* race up the Ohio River in 1930, long after most such craft had been destroyed or sold for scrap. The *Tom Green* was declared the winner, although rivermen still dispute the outcome. One of the most thrilling sights on the water, steamboat races were held as late as 1962, when the *Delta Queen* of Cincinnati raced the *Belle of Louisville*. Much of the excitement of earlier races grew out of the knowledge that riverboats were dangerous; during the 19th Century, more than 140 boats blew up from boiler explosions, usually because engineers recklessly built up steam pressure. In the famous *Moselle* disaster, in 1838, all four boilers exploded and 150 persons were killed.

selling, among other items, a noxious mixture of Jimson weed, burdock and old rope for pipe tobacco. It was called the Scandihoovian brand because "when it was smoked in Wisconsin, folks could smell it in Scandihoovia."

When payday came after the spring drive, the lumberjacks would throng into such freewheeling towns as Hurley and Saginaw. Escanaba's Ludington Street had 102 saloons selling tanglefoot whiskey strong enough to take the hair off a buffalo robe. Oshkosh, Wisconsin, which today is a sedate city, was regarded in its youth as "the wickedest town in the West." In Seney, Michigan, whose reputation became even worse, prostitutes were said to be kept in stockades guarded by ferocious dogs trained to let customers in and to keep the girls from getting out. Bruising gang fights broke out between Irish and Swedish lumberjacks—although both would combine to lambaste the Germans.

The sawmill cities were rich and careless. Alpena, Michigan, had five major fires in 10 years. In the dreadful, tinder-dry autumn of 1871 ship captains were blinded in mid-lake by the smoke from raging forest fires. Peshtigo, Wisconsin, was swept by an inferno of fire and more than 600 people burned to death or drowned in the Peshtigo River while trying to escape. Cheboygan, Michigan, and other towns cut so much lumber that sawdust mountains rose by the mills. Often the rivers were made impassable by the mass of floating sawdust, and when it was burned off, the rivers would be aflame for weeks.

Logs went down the Mississippi as well as the Great Lakes. Huge rafts covering several acres of water and guided by as many as 15 sweeps fore and aft made the dangerous passage to sawmills at Moline and Rock Island, Illinois. At night the rafts crept along like giant turtles; red and green lights winked at the bow, the sweeps creaked loudly on their tholepins, and off-duty raftsmen gathered amidships around a fiddle or accordion to sing "One-Eyed Riley" or "Buffalo Gals." Whenever a raft tied up before making a passage through rapids or around a sharp bend, villagers locked their doors and cowered behind drawn curtains. Especially feared were raftsmen from Wisconsin's Black River, above La Crosse. It was an article of faith along the upper Mississippi that "a Black River man would stab you as soon as look at you."

On the Great Lakes, shipping began with canoes and Mackinaw boats—slow, bargelike vessels with tanbark sails—and progressed to graceful skiffs, sloops and schooners. The first steamer on the upper lakes, *Walk-in-the-Water*, was launched in 1818, only 11 years after Fulton's *Clermont*. It became the forerunner of a Great Lakes fleet whose queen in the 1850s was the S.S. *Western World,* a mammoth vessel of 2,000 tons. Millions of immigrants came to their Heartland homes on lake steamers, and thousands found eternal rest as ships foundered in the sudden storms.

Summer cruises out of such lake cities as Chicago, Cleveland and Detroit became immensely popular in the 1850s. Travelers enjoyed voyages to Charlevoix, Mackinac Island and Georgian Bay, or longer runs to Duluth and the Thousand Islands of the St. Lawrence. But lake cruising, too, could be dangerous; the S.S. *Eastland,* chartered for an all-day cruise by employees of Western Electric in 1915, capsized at its Chicago dock, drowning more than 800 persons.

Wheat, coal, iron ore and lumber were originally carried on the lakes by cargo schooners, usually three-masted ships with a capacity of about 150 tons. When Great Lakes shippers switched to steam, they developed a bulk carrier that has no counterpart anywhere in the world. More than 700 feet long, the modern lake carriers can transport 25,000 tons of ore—or the yield of 32,000 acres of wheat, equal to what could be carried in 250 freight cars. Prototypes of today's freighters were built in Cleveland as early as 1882. They were 300 feet long, with engines aft and pilothouse far forward, and an uninterrupted cargo hold in between.

On the great network of Heartland rivers the canoe was again first, followed by flatboats, or broadhorns, as they were called. "Flatboat turnings" rivaled logrollings as a frontier pastime. The flatboat hulls were built upside down. The boat would then be launched and lined up across a river, and stones piled on the downriver side until their weight and the strength of the current flipped the boat over. At the end of a voyage down the river, flatboats were broken up and their timber sold. Next came slow, unwieldy keelboats, which were propelled by the current, by poles, or even by grabbing bushes on the riverbank—"bushwhacking," it was called. Keelboats were intended for longer service than flatboats; they made voyages back up the rivers as well as down.

The coming of steam brought to the rivers one of man's most beautiful creations—the paddle-wheel steamer. This graceful craft seemed the product of a genius among ship designers: a spacious, open deck for the stowage of cargo, a salon deck with staterooms, upper works filigreed like lace, and a pilothouse placed between two tall smokestacks separated by a thin spreader bar from which a proud owner might dangle a ball, a glittering star

The Lakes' worst disaster

Huddled on the hull of the capsized pleasure ship *Eastland,* survivors of one of the most extraordinary disasters on the Great Lakes await rescue a few feet from a Chicago dock on July 24, 1915. The *Eastland* had been jammed with some 2,500 Western Electric employees and their families bound for a day's outing. While a steam calliope pumped out the popular tunes of the day, the ship slowly rolled over. More than 800 persons died, many trapped below decks, others pulled underwater by panic-stricken nonswimmers. Holes were cut in the hull to reach people caught in their cabins, but few were rescued. After many lawsuits and investigations, the blame was fixed on an engineer who had failed to fill the ballast tanks, causing the ship, with its huge crowd, to become top-heavy. No one, however, was ever held guilty of criminal negligence. As a result of the accident, the federal government enacted more stringent safety regulations for Great Lakes shipping. The *Eastland* itself was refloated and served for many years under another name as a Great Lakes naval training vessel.

or some other heraldic device. The paddle boxes on side-wheel steamers were decorated with paintings.

At a distance the river steamboat moved with swanlike grace. Close to she gave an impression of power with the rat-a-tat-tat of her engines and the churning of her paddles. She was decked out with a flutter of flags and streamers, and the light skiff drawn up on davits at the stern danced in the air with the ship's movement. By night the steamboat cruised with the majesty of fire—sparks flying from the funnels, flames casting a ruddy glow from furnace doors, pine chips and resin blazing from iron baskets raised as running lights above the bow.

From the first, a premium was placed upon the "hot and fast" engineer who would pile on fuel and tie down the safety valve to get as much speed as possible. The sight of two steamboats "digging up the bottom of the river" in a race was considered the greatest spectacle of the time. The water in the boilers was kept so shallow that it barely covered the flues, and a boat "carrying dry steam" would depart from a landing in style, making sounds like pistol shots. Captains of slower boats were able to stay side by side with faster ones by employing a partial lock—a phenomenon of hydrodynamics by which the slower boat is sucked along by the faster. The technique called for seamanship of a high order, since the pilot of the slower boat had to maintain a precise distance from his rival or risk being drawn into a broadside collision. Casualties were many, and because of that fact hair-raising stories became popular along the Heartland rivers. On some vessels, it was said, passengers who had not yet paid their fares were herded to the stern as the safest part of the ship—in case the steamer blew up before their money was collected. Another story held that Irishmen were preferred to Negro slaves as firemen because their deaths caused no financial loss to the owners; slaves, of course, cost money.

Not all the stories were fictional. In the excitement of a race everything combustible was thrown into the furnace. The packet *Ocean Spray* burned and sank because the firemen were tossing dipperfuls of turpentine into the flames to get a hotter fire. The trail of drops running back to the barrel of turpentine suddenly ignited, and the raceback of fire set ablaze both barrel and ship. The effects of boiler explosions were often ghastly. When the *Moselle* blew up at Cincinnati in 1838, Second Engineer Halsey Williams dodged into a sidehouse just as a piece of boiler took off the chief engineer's head. Some 150 persons were scalded to death or drowned, but Williams got safely ashore, calmly told his story, thanked God for his deliverance and

dropped dead. While tied up at the Illinois town of Hampton, the packet *Lansing* exploded with such force that the pilot's body landed on the other side of town and the clerk was hurled across the Mississippi and into Iowa.

Every voyage was chancy. Steamboats collided, got stuck on sand bars, and ran into submerged wrecks, snags, keelboats or log rafts. If the river was low they got stranded; if it was in flood they might be carried into a forest. In the four years after the Civil War, 2,268 people perished in steamboat accidents. Dr. John Locke of Cincinnati made a study of steamboat explosions and declared that they were caused by "the present mammoth evil of our country, in the inordinate love of gain." He pointed out that each steamboat "must establish a reputation of [being] a few minutes swifter in a hundred miles than others, before she can make fortunes fast enough to satisfy the owners." Since as many as 8,000 steamboats a year landed at Cincinnati, the city fathers pigeonholed Dr. Locke's report.

The glamorous steamboats were a casualty of the railroad—sometimes literally so. The first railway bridge across the Mississippi was built by the Rock Island Railroad at a bend in the river between Rock Island, Illinois, and Davenport, Iowa. The completion of the bridge made it possible to ship

A snout-nosed whaleback boat—so called because of its peculiar shape—loads grain in Chicago in 1895. A turn-of-the-century innovation, the whaleback was an early attempt at designing a ship that had great stability, a strong yet light frame and a good cargo capacity. Although successful, it was soon replaced by larger ships with flat decks that were easier to load.

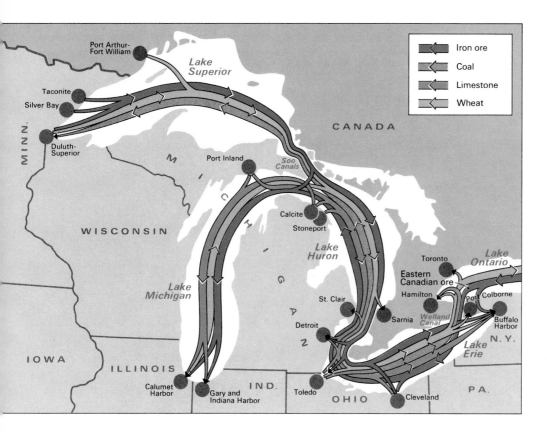

The flow of Lake shipping

The major cargoes, shipping routes and ports of the Great Lakes are shown on this map. As the arrows indicate, the bulk of the traffic flow is southward. From such northern ports as Taconite, Silver Bay and Duluth-Superior, the huge carriers transport their cargoes of iron ore to steel mills at the southern tip of Lake Michigan and along the shores of Lake Erie. With the iron-ore fields around Lake Superior gradually becoming depleted, ore has been coming in from eastern Canada, as the arrow at the right-hand edge of the map indicates. In 1965—a good year—some 88 million tons were shipped, making iron ore the largest cargo carried on the lakes. Coal, with some 55 million tons shipped, was the second largest. Limestone, also used in the manufacture of steel, was third—some 31 million tons. The fourth largest was grain: some 22 million tons were shipped.

goods by rail directly between Chicago, the eastern terminus of the Rock Island line, and areas west of the Mississippi, obviating the necessity for off-loading and transshipment across the Mississippi to the railhead on its western bank. On May 6, 1856, the packet *Effie Afton* lost power in one paddle wheel as she started under the bridge, was slammed against a pier, burst into flames and sank. The ship was owned by a firm in St. Louis, then the primary port of entry to the West and the headquarters for many of the Mississippi steamship companies. Urged on by the alarmed St. Louis Chamber of Commerce, the company brought suit against the Rock Island Railroad, charging that the bridge was a menace to navigation. A major contention of the suit was that the railroad had placed the bridge piers at an angle to the current instead of in line with it, thereby causing the current to run dangerously toward the mid-river piers.

The railroad lawyer visited the site, chartered a steamboat and made repeated runs under the bridge, noting the effect of the current at varying speeds. He also launched timbers upstream to see how the river carried them. When the trial began in Chicago it was soon evident that the railroad lawyer knew as much about Mississippi navigation as anyone present. The case resulted in a hung jury,

signaled the inevitable triumph of the railroad over the steamboat and contributed to Chicago's eventual emergence as the first city of the Heartland. The lawyer who so skillfully presented the railroad's case was soon heard from again—his name was Abraham Lincoln.

The graceful paddle-wheelers have today been replaced by muscular vessels known as towboats —despite the fact that they push, rather than pull, strings of barges up and down the Mississippi, the Ohio and the Illinois. The barges are nearly 200 feet long and, when fully loaded, draw nine feet of water—slightly less than the minimum depth of the channel in the river system. They carry everything from coal and sand to oil and machinery and come in several shapes; some are divided into watertight compartments, others look like a shoe box without its lid. Deck barges resemble a flat wooden block and are difficult to handle. If the cargo shifts, the deck barge goes over on its side. "I've seen them climb trees," says a towboat captain. "And these are trees standing on top of a six-foot canal wall."

A typical towboat is 160 feet long and 5,000 horsepower strong. It can push as much as 50,000 tons and works 24 hours a day. The day is divided into six-hour shifts, with the captain and a pilot alternating at the vessel's controls, which look like old-fashioned beer-pump handles. With its four rudders, a towboat can go in any direction, even sideways. The needs of ship and crew are met by service boats stationed in the river ports. They refuel the boats and bring out mail and food. There are also smaller towboats to add barges to the tow or remove barges for delivery in port. The Mississippi and Ohio no longer echo to the leadsman's cry of "Mark twain" (two fathoms, or 12 feet) or "Mark ta-ree" (three fathoms) as he sounds the channel; towboat captains now rely on sonar.

The glittering inland rivers and lakes gave rise to visions. Men never really found a useful Northwest Passage. But in 1959, when the St. Lawrence Seaway was officially completed, a water path was opened to deep-draft, ocean-going vessels from the mouth of the St. Lawrence River in Canada to Duluth-Superior at the western end of the Great Lakes and southward to Chicago. From there the Calumet-Sag Channel and the Chicago Sanitary and Ship Canal lead to the Illinois River and then to the Mississippi, providing a highway thousands of miles in length that splits the continent and links the North Atlantic with the Gulf of Mexico.

The idea of opening the Great Lakes to deep-draft vessels through the St. Lawrence had long been a dream held by many in the Heartland—but a dream frustrated, some believed, by adamant foes. The *Chicago Tribune* identified the opponents as "railroads and Eastern shipping interests" trying to prevent the emergence of a mid-continental rival. Life, however, is seldom that simple and the East was not the only adversary—the *Tribune* itself opposed the St. Lawrence Seaway until the late 1940s, partly on the grounds that it would bring an influx of foreigners into Chicagoland.

Actually, there had long been a seaway, but one with considerable limitations. In the 1840s Heartland grain was shipped directly to Europe through the Welland Canal, which bypasses Niagara Falls between Lake Erie and Lake Ontario, after shallow-draft canals had been constructed along the St. Lawrence. Even before then grain had reached Europe via the Great Lakes and the Erie Canal, but the route was expensive, since the grain had to be transferred to barges at Buffalo and to ships in New York City. Seaway freight was for many years carried by small cargo steamers known as "canalers," whose size was limited by the dimensions of the existing locks and the 14-foot depth of the channels.

Every U.S. President from William Howard Taft to Dwight Eisenhower recommended the improvement of the seaway. But there was little action. Committees of the U.S. Congress held hearings,

The diagram shows how the bow thruster, a device adopted on the Great Lakes in 1960, improves a ship's handling in tight places. The push or pull of the thruster propellers—mounted in a tunnel extending through the bow—swings the bow to port or starboard. With such a device, a ship can turn in less space than conventional ships and can dock without the aid of tugs.

bills died in committee or on the floor, and inconclusive conferences were held between Canada and the United States. A seaway capable of handling deep-draft vessels seemed an unattainable goal until the late 1940s, when Canada reached the conclusion that its vast, largely untouched reserves of iron ore in Labrador could be profitably exploited if the ore could be shipped by way of the St. Lawrence and the Great Lakes to American and Canadian smelters. Canada decided in 1951 that the seaway was so vitally needed that it would undertake its construction alone, if necessary.

The Canadian decision precipitated a change of heart in Washington. After all the long years of dawdling, both nations moved forward with surprising speed. But in an effort to conciliate seaway opponents while the question of building it was still under debate in Congress, Senator Arthur Vandenberg of Michigan had proposed that tolls be levied on seaway users. Despite opposition from seaway proponents who feared that tolls on the waterway would keep potential shippers from using it, and thus give an unfair advantage to rail and trucking interests, the idea of tolls became inextricably linked with the seaway. By 1954 both the Canadian and U.S. legislatures had passed bills authorizing the construction of the seaway with the proviso that tolls be collected on the 180-mile seaway section between Montreal and Lake Ontario to pay off the U.S. investment of $135 million and the Canadian share of $345 million within 50 years. (Canada's costs were greater because more of the construction work had to be done north of the border.)

Seaway advocates hotly argue to this day that the tolls (about $12,000 per iron-ore laker for each passage up and down the river) are discriminatory. They claim that this is the first time in history that the U.S. has used a waterway as a direct source of revenue, and they hark back to the Northwest Ordinance of 1787, which declared that "the navigable waters leading into the Mississippi and St. Lawrence, and the carrying places between the same, shall be common highways and forever free."

In its first year of operation, in 1959, the new seaway appeared to be a flop. Cargo amounted to a disappointing 20.6 million tons—far below the modest official estimate of 25 million. The following year was even worse, with a drop of 300,000 tons. Seaway supporters blamed the disappointing showing on everything from the weather to the tolls. Gradually, however, big bulk carriers began to use the seaway, taking advantage of the 27-foot minimum depth of the channel, which is adequate for 80 per cent of the world's cargo ships. By 1965 the seaway, carrying in excess of 43.4 million tons, had more than doubled the amount of cargo transported in its first year of operation.

The seaway is currently self-supporting. Its managers had by 1966 handed over $60 million in interest to Canada and the U.S. but had not yet paid off any of the original cost. Joseph H. McCann, Administrator of the St. Lawrence Seaway Development Corporation, the American body that built the seaway in cooperation with the Canadian St. Lawrence Seaway Authority, argues that it "can be credited with forcing transportation costs down" and with "the development of new techniques and the adoption of more efficient methods of operation by its competitors."

Success has brought renewed attack. The U.S. Congress has been urged to raise the seaway tolls to ensure that the debt is repaid within the specified 50 years. Seaway advocates cry that this would strangle traffic, and Midwestern congressmen and governors have resisted this new pressure.

The new seaway itself appeared for a time to be a threat to certain Heartland areas. The Canadian iron ore from Labrador reached the Heartland mills via the seaway just as the supply of high-grade iron ore in the Mesabi Range in Minnesota and in the smaller ranges of Gogebic and Marquette in Wisconsin and Michigan began to dwindle. At first the northern ore ports of Duluth-Superior, Marquette and Escanaba, which are dependent on the supply from those ranges, faced a bleak future, but they and the mining areas have revived with the discovery of an economical and efficient process of extracting iron ore from plentiful low-grade taconite.

Other technological developments are helping to keep the Heartland ports prosperous. The new ore boats are models of automated efficiency, and the installation of a device called a bow thruster enables the ships to maneuver with considerable ease. Through the combination of ore cars and chutes, a boat can be fully loaded in four hours, while enormous scoops attached to pivoting booms can unload it in six. When the hold is nearly empty, a tractor is lowered inside to push the remaining ore into a tidy pile for a final gulp by the scoop.

With the opening of the seaway, the Great Lakes cities have become accustomed to the flutter of foreign flags and the sight of foreign seamen. Milwaukee has shipped a paper mill to Sweden, tallow to Italy, diesel locomotives to Tunisia, earthmovers to Norway and trucks to the Far East. By dredging its harbor to seaway draft, it was able in 1965 to load 21,043 net tons of corn and soybeans aboard the S.S. *Cape Breton Miner* bound for Rotterdam— one of the largest overseas cargoes of grain in Great Lakes history. Green Bay, Wisconsin, imports pulpwood from Scandinavia and exports hides to the Netherlands and Germany. Lorain, Ohio, handled 900 ships at its five docks in the 1965 season; they brought in limestone, iron ore, gypsum, sand and gravel and carried away slag stone and coal. During the same year the port of Toledo unloaded its 100,000th Volkswagen, and Muskegon, Michigan, was the transit port for millions of Spanish olives bound for the nation's salads and martinis.

A freighter from Ghana unloaded obeche wood at Navy Pier in Chicago in the same period. The American *Maiden Creek* departed for India with 79 tractors, each weighing 40 tons. Big as it is, the port of Chicago just manages to outrank Duluth-Superior, which ships out so much iron ore and taconite that it has become the second-largest Great Lakes port. Cleveland has suddenly discovered that it is almost as close to northern Europe as is New York. Detroit auto makers have found that they can save up to $30 per car by shipping overseas through the seaway. Exporters insist that the wealth of the Heartland has so far scarcely been scratched by the seaway. Lifted on the tide of fast-growing trade, the Heartland now boasts that it is providing a fourth American seacoast.

With great crunches reverberating across the icebound silence of
Lake Huron, the *Mackinaw*, largest icebreaker on the Great Lakes,
cuts a channel to enable freighters to move during freezing weather.
Throughout much of the winter, ice completely halts shipping.

Bustling world
of an inland sea

Despite pileups of ice that close most
of their harbors and channels to shipping for
four months of each year, the Great Lakes have
long been a vital part of the huge world
of commerce on their shores. Ships of many sizes
and descriptions toil endlessly during good
weather to supply factories with the wealth of raw
material that surrounds the Great Lakes—
iron, coal, limestone, lumber and a variety of crops
from extensive farmlands. Still other ships carry
finished products to markets around the lakes
and even to ports around the globe. But not all
parts of the lakes area boast booming factories
or bustling ports. Towns, islands and long
stretches of shoreline have remained rustic, and
today as in days past the residents of the
Heartland find the lakes welcome sources
of recreation as well as routes for commerce.

Mammoth carriers
of huge cargoes

The principal cargoes on the Great Lakes consist of raw materials that can be most efficiently shipped in huge quantities. The more than 500 bulk carriers that ply the lakes transport cargoes of as much as 25,000 tons of iron ore from Lake Superior and limestone from Lake Huron to the steel mills on the lower lakes. Some carriers return from the lower lakes filled with coal for northern industries; so great are the profits in carrying ore down the lakes, however, that many return without waiting for cargoes.

Freighters on the lakes also carry vast amounts of grain. Since the St. Lawrence Seaway opened in 1959—its 27-foot minimum depth makes the lakes accessible to deep-water vessels—increasing quantities of corn, wheat and other grains have been shipped overseas direct from their Great Lakes ports.

Golden yellow grain pours down long spouts directly into the cargo
compartments of the Canadian vessel *Canadoc* for shipment
from Superior, Wisconsin. Superior, together with its sister city,
Duluth, Minnesota, is the largest shipper of grain on the lakes.

Choking dust rises as iron ore thunders down chutes into a ship's
hold at the Marquette, Michigan, ore docks on Lake Superior. The ore
is brought to Marquette by freight train from the nearby mines
of the Upper Peninsula for transshipment down the lakes.

Tons of crushed limestone lie in a massive heap on a Chicago pier
after being unloaded from a vessel docked in the Calumet River. After
being refined, the limestone is used in processes as various
as the manufacturing of glass and iron and the purification of water.

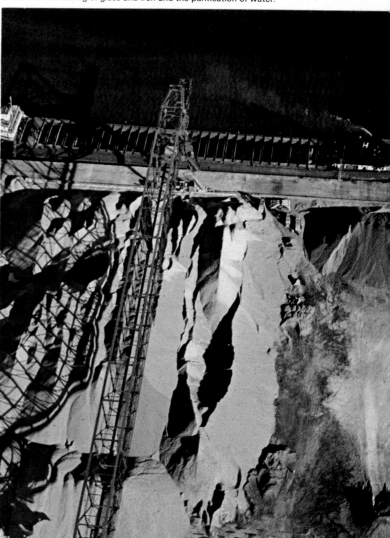

Busiest port on the nation's inland seacoast

At the southern tip of Lake Michigan is the busiest port on the Great Lakes—Chicago. Annually some 44 million tons of goods are handled at its docks, a total that ranks the city sixth among all United States ports. Chicago's widespread port facilities stretch from the municipally owned Navy Pier, on Lake Michigan near the city's center, to the docks at Lake Calumet, 15 miles to the south. Access to Lake Calumet from Lake Michigan is provided by the Calumet River (*below*). Canals connect both the Chicago River, which flows through the city from Lake Michigan, and Lake Calumet with the vast inland waterways of the Mississippi and Ohio Valleys.

Ready to move cargo, freighters tug at their moorings at a Calumet River pier. Cargoes from the Chicago port area may include raw materials or crops from the Heartland's mines and farms or such fabricated goods as the steel plates manufactured in the 574-acre South Works plant of United States Steel *(center)* on the north bank of the river. Deep-draft vessels were for many years limited in the amount of cargo they could take aboard in the Calumet; they had to be loaded short of capacity to clear the river's 21-foot bottom. Since the opening of the St. Lawrence Seaway, the Calumet has been dredged to the seaway depth of 27 feet.

A quiet oasis
amid active seas

Beaver Island, the largest of a series of small dots of land in northern Lake Michigan, is an outpost of quietude in the busy Great Lakes. In 1846 Mormons led by James Jesse Strang arrived on Beaver Island and proceeded to deport the local population. Strang ruled as king until he was assassinated in 1856. His Mormon subjects were in turn driven out by neighboring fishermen. Irishmen then settled on Beaver, and fishing became the main industry until an invasion of sea lampreys, an eel-like predator, decimated the lake fish. Today some 180 residents live on the island, compared with 900 in 1922. But summer vacationers swell the number, and residents are attempting to use the island's rustic charm to make tourism a steady industry.

Checking supplies, the proprietor of one of the island's two general stores, Vernon LaFreniere, inspects his stock, which includes hardware, groceries, clothing and coffins (the island has no funeral parlor).

Mementos of the Mormon era are displayed in the only Mormon building still standing. In it Strang printed a newspaper in which he published church documents, township ordinances and divine revelations.

LaFreniere's general store was built in 1898. Supplies are brought by boat during summer, but extensive winter stores are stocked in the fall, since only fresh goods are flown in after the lake freezes.

Island fishermen prepare to raise their nets in nearby waters. In the 1920s Beaver Island fishermen shipped out as much as a million pounds of fish a year; the annual catch now totals only about 1,400 pounds.

Hardy visitors climb Sleeping Bear Dunes, a sand mountain that rises almost 500 feet above the shore of Lake Michigan. Seven miles long and more than two miles wide, the dunes move eastward about two feet a year, burying trees and grass in their path.

An extensive playground for millions

Although industrial pollution has transformed parts of the Great Lakes into a great wasteland, unspoiled sections remain. Among them are wide, sandy beaches along upper Lake Michigan, majestic, rocky cliffs on Lake Superior, and rugged Isle Royale in northern Superior. To ensure access to such areas while retaining their character, conservationist forces are pressing to have more and more parts of the lakes' shorelines set aside in preserves.

Bathers dot the sands at Rainbow Beach, where 76th Street meets Lake Michigan on Chicago's South Side. Nearly 18 miles of the 22-mile distance from the Indiana state line to the northern city limits of Chicago are set aside for recreation.

5

The Coming of Industrial Greatness

A century and a half ago the southerly bend of Lake Michigan was a quiet and peaceful place. Sand dunes made a wind-rippled wall along the shore of the lake and were home to sandpipers and gulls. Three hundred miles to the east, in the valleys of the Cuyahoga and Mahoning Rivers, lay the quiet towns of Cleveland and Youngstown, hard by hills veined with bituminous coal. These pastoral areas were to make the Heartland industrially great—the greatest producing region of a producing nation. But their time was long in coming, and together the Heartland and the country were to witness long years of strife before that time arrived.

Until the Civil War the region was largely a producer of food and raw materials like minerals and lumber. Many of its copper mines were opened up by Eastern interests and worked by Cornish miners brought in to Wisconsin and upper Michigan. Industry native to the region sprang mostly from the needs of agriculture and the railroads—iron rails, John Deere's plows, Cyrus McCormick's reapers

and binders. Secretary of War Edwin Stanton credited the McCormick reaper with being a prime cause of Union victory because it freed so many men to bear arms. "The reaper is to the North," said Stanton, "what slavery is to the South."

The Deeres and McCormicks were the spiritual ancestors of whole generations of gifted Heartland tinkerers. Henry Ford built his first car in 1896, and he was only one of a number of men in the region experimenting with automobiles in the 1890s. In 1894 Elwood Haynes built an 820-pound horseless carriage powered by a marine engine from Grand Rapids, and drove it through Kokomo, Indiana, at a speed of seven miles per hour. Another Hoosier, Clem Studebaker, saw in his lifetime the change from the frontier to the machine age. Studebaker's wagons hauled supplies for the Union Army in the Civil War and he was one of the crowd that cheered the arrival of the first train in Indianapolis, yet he and his brothers lived to build an experimental auto in 1898. Thomas Alva Edison experimented with telegraphic communications in Cincinnati; the Wright brothers in nearby Dayton grappled with the problems of powered flight. Many of these men became major industrialists. The huge A. O. Smith manufacturing complex grew out of a Milwaukee bicycle shop. In Detroit Ford perfected

A soft haze settles over a group of Cleveland steel mills, as if to mute the clangor of blast furnaces within. The city's extensive mills, in an industrial section known as the Cuyahoga River "Flats," make the Cleveland area one of the nation's largest steel producers.

the technique of producing automobiles on mass-production assembly lines to make himself one of the wealthiest men in the world. Some of these captains of industry displayed a dazzling versatility: self-educated Carl Fisher helped develop the Prest-O-Lite storage battery, was the founder of a bicycle-manufacturing business, helped build the Indianapolis Speedway, piloted the balloon *Indiana* in Aero Club meets and went on to create Miami Beach out of a desolate Florida swamp.

The early Heartland industrialists were convinced that both God and nature approved of their elite position. David Parry, who became president of the National Association of Manufacturers in 1902, once declared: "It is the business of every man to honestly get all he can." Others, less scrupulous, corrected Parry's split infinitive by dropping "honestly." Business lived by the rule of dog eat dog. In 1887 Edward L. "Crazy" Harper tried to corner all the wheat in the West, fell short by only a million dollars, and went to prison. Benjamin P. "Old Hutch" Hutchinson succeeded in 1888 where Harper had failed.

Building his oil empire in Cleveland, John D. Rockefeller tied Darwinism and Christianity into a single package and explained that business was "merely the . . . working out of a law of Nature and God." The doctrine that the race was open to all and that only the fit survived had little appeal to small operators trying to compete with such giants as Standard Oil and U.S. Steel. As one Populist put it: "You might have the 'opportunity' of engaging in a clawin' match with a bear, but who the hell would want to?"

George M. Pullman epitomized the hard-bitten industrialist of the period. Born in western New York, he made an early success of moving houses threatened with destruction because of the widening of the Erie Canal. He was a man capable of capitalizing on opportunities others had overlooked; after Pullman moved to Chicago in 1855, he conceived the idea of building comfortable railroad sleeping cars. The territory was virgin; previously the railroads had provided for overnight passengers merely by installing three uncomfortable tiers of wooden bunks on each side of a passenger car. Pullman was a man of gigantic stubbornness; he not only built his sleeping cars with great care and at great expense but, after they had gained public acceptance, insisted on retaining ownership of the cars; the railroads could use them only under contract. The roads even agreed to allow Pullman to staff the cars with his own specially trained men. The first of the palatial cars he built—"Pioneer"—

was coincidentally completed just in time to be attached to the funeral train carrying the body of Abraham Lincoln home to Springfield, Illinois.

Pullman prospered greatly and came to employ thousands of men in his shops, but by 20th Century standards he was hardly an ideal employer. In 1880 he created the first planned factory town in the United States. Named for him and situated just south of Chicago on the shores of Lake Calumet, the town provided large brick homes for Pullman shop managers and foremen, various-sized row houses for skilled workers and large blockhouses for other employees. Pullman's aversion to selling the things he built extended to his company town; all the homes were rented, and for several years all rents were deducted from company paychecks. The city of Pullman had its own firehouse, school, brickyard, bandstand and athletic field.

There was, however, no self-government and no voice for the worker-tenants in the running of the town. The atmosphere was stultifying, but the residents, as employees of Pullman, were afraid to leave. The library contained only such books as Pullman thought proper, and the theater presented only those plays of which he approved. To get a drink of beer, a worker had to leave the town. One contemporary marveled that "here is now a town of 12,000 in which there is not one house of ill repute." After visiting Pullman a journalist wrote: "The corporation is everything and everywhere. The corporation trims your lawn and attends to your trees; the corporation sweeps your street and sends a man around to pick up every cigar stump . . . the corporation does practically everything but sweep your room and make your bed, and the corporation expects you to enjoy it and hold your tongue."

Like many employers of the period, Pullman used the piecework system: a worker received no hourly wage but was paid so much for each piece of work that he turned out in a specified period. During the panic and depression of 1893, Pullman cut the contract price for each piece of work and reduced the amount of time an employee had to complete the work on it; at the same time, he refused to lower rents in the town. He did not, however, cut pay for Pullman foremen and executives. A year later the company made additional slashes in workers' pay because of "hard times," but declared the regular 8 per cent dividend for stockholders. Some employees, after rent and other deductions, were taking home as little as seven cents a week. There were protests by workers' committees, but they meant little to Pullman; rents clearly had nothing to do with wages. "There is," the workers were told, "nothing to arbitrate." Even some fellow capitalists were appalled. The Republican political leader Mark Hanna, no mean entrepreneur himself, snapped: "A man who won't meet his men halfway is just a God-damn fool." The Pullman workers struck on May 11, 1894.

The strike was bloody and bitter. Pullman's workers found an ally in Eugene Victor Debs of Terre Haute, Indiana, who had created the American Railway Union, a nationwide organization of railroad workers. A visionary man of great charm, Debs later expressed his personal credo as:

> *While there is a lower class I am in it;*
> *While there is a criminal element I am of it;*
> *While there's a soul in prison I am not free.*

Debs's union declared a boycott of Pullman cars —trains could go through, but only after the sleeping cars were detached. Despite their earlier differences with Pullman, the railway owners closed ranks around their own organization, the General Managers' Association, and cannily attached U.S. mail cars to the ends of their trains. Railway workers who attempted to cut out Pullman cars, or who refused to move trains with Pullman cars, were automatically discharged; the workers were also guilty

of obstructing the United States mails. That, as the General Managers' Association had intended, brought the federal government into the matter. Thousands of miles of rail lines were affected; as far away as California, workers refused to move trains and troops were called out. The Pullman strike was no longer a Chicago issue; for the first time in American history there was a nationwide confrontation of labor and management, with the federal government involved.

Over the objections of Governor John Peter Altgeld of Illinois, President Grover Cleveland ordered General Nelson Miles into Chicago with 2,000 regulars. As Altgeld had feared, the situation soon got out of hand. Federal troops clashed with workers, both employed and unemployed, who were sympathetic to the Pullman strikers; state militiamen and railroad deputies engaged in bloody battles with working-class mobs. Judge William Howard Taft of Cincinnati, who would later become the 27th President of the United States, wrote his wife: "It will be necessary for the military to kill some of the mob before the trouble can be stayed. They have only killed six . . . as yet. This is hardly enough to make an impression." Ultimately, 20 rioters died and 60 were wounded, but the strike was not broken until the federal courts issued a

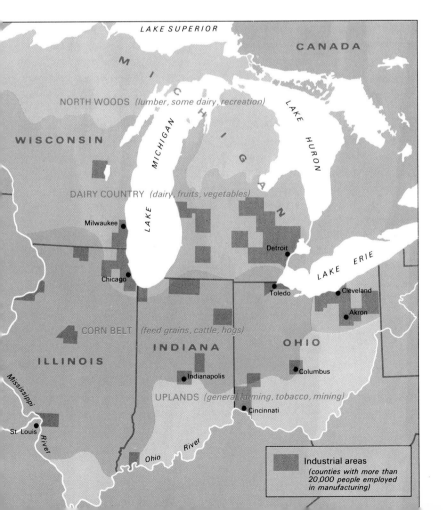

Belts of economic activity

Varying combinations of soil, topography and climate separate the Heartland into remarkably distinct areas that stretch across the region in bands. The northernmost belt is a land of poor soils and short growing seasons, where lumbering and recreation are the principal activities. South of this area is dairy country. Next is the Corn Belt, one of the world's greatest grain-producing regions, with deep soils rich in organic material. These two agricultural belts also contain most of the region's industry. Heavy manufacturing and the larger cities are located mainly in the dairy country, near the main transportation routes. In the Corn Belt many industries are related to agriculture—farm-machinery manufacturing, meat packing and corn processing. The poorest of the belts is the Uplands, whose rough topography makes large-scale farming difficult.

91

Father of the mass-produced car

Mustached and gloved, Henry Ford sits in his first automobile shortly after building it in Detroit in 1896. The "quadricycle"—forerunner of all Ford cars—had bicycle-type balloon tires, a two-cylinder motor, and two speeds: 10 and 20 miles an hour. Ford, raised on the family farm near Dearborn, Michigan, had shown a mechanical bent from an early age. At 16 he was an apprentice machinist. At 30 he built his first gasoline engine. In 1903, at the age of 40, he incorporated the Ford Motor Company, with liquid assets of $14,500. Within 24 days that sum fell to $223.65, but less than 20 years later annual profits were exceeding $93 million. He had long since been acknowledged as the automotive industry's most influential innovator.

Sails begins on the drawing board

Throughout his life he scrawled in notebooks and on odd paper scraps badly spelled maxims, serious thoughts and laconic comments like the one above, which probably meant "Sales begin on the drawing board." The jottings were found only after his death in 1947; Henry Ford never threw anything away.

series of injunctions that included the forbidding of "malicious" conspiracies that might damage an employer's business, and Debs and other labor leaders were clapped in jail for contempt of court.

The Pullman conflict had a profound effect on men's minds. To Debs it was a battle in the war between "the producing classes and the money power of the country," and he came to believe that capitalism was so strong that it could never be reformed and that it must therefore be destroyed. But other labor theorists despaired of the future of unionism on the ground that nothing could stand up to the alliance of business and government. One of them, the socialist writer J. A. Wayland, later committed suicide, leaving a note that read: "The struggle under the capitalistic system isn't worth the effort. Let it pass." The country stood in fear of anarchism and revolt. The economist Henry George warned of the "open-mouthed relentless hell which yawns beneath civilized society" because of the threatened war by the "House of Want upon the House of Have." Theodore Roosevelt, who was to come to the Presidency in 1901 on the assassination of William McKinley by an avowed anarchist, declared: "The sentiments now animating a large proportion of our people can only be suppressed as the [Paris] Commune was suppressed, by taking

ten or a dozen of their leaders out, standing them against a wall and shooting them dead. I believe it will come to that."

Fortunately, both George and Roosevelt were wrong. The Heartland was to witness a succession of bitter confrontations between management and labor, and the struggle continues to this day. But the general bloodbath that was feared did not come. Even back at the turn of the century more than one businessman, disturbed by the growing class war and the intransigence of both sides, tried hard to redress the balance. William Hapgood, owner of a canning plant in Indianapolis, went so far as to turn his business over to his employees. Tom L. Johnson, a wealthy Ohio industrialist, read Henry George's *Social Problems* and then set out to defeat monopolism. Johnson was elected mayor of Cleveland in 1901; he did not succeed in his plans to have the city assume ownership of all public utilities, but he made Cleveland for a time the best-run municipality in the nation.

The Heartland came of age industrially in this period—a development made possible by the perfection in the middle of the 19th Century of the Bessemer-converter and the open-hearth processes of making steel. Before these technological advances, steelmaking had been a slow and difficult art. With the new methods—Cleveland plants were producing steel by the Bessemer process as early as 1868—great quantities of quality steel could be made. All of the necessities were abundantly present. The mountain ranges bordering Lake Superior were rich in iron ore, and the man who signed the bill of lading for the first shipment of ore from Marquette, Michigan, in 1852—it consisted of six barrels—lived to see 42 million tons shipped from Lake Superior in the season of 1907. Vast amounts of coal were discovered in southern Illinois, Indiana and Ohio, and an excellent grade of limestone was at hand in Michigan. As for another vital element, water, the Great Lakes were full of it—and they and the Heartland rivers and railroads provided a superlative means of transport for bringing all the ingredients together and for transporting finished products to mass markets. To this day, in fact, this neat admixture of raw materials, technical skills, efficient factories, mechanized farms and food-processing plants, coupled with a superb transportation system, gives the Heartland one of the most viable and integrated economies in the world.

In the last decade of the 19th Century the rush of steel wealth arrived almost simultaneously in Ohio's Mahoning Valley, where rows of mill chimneys were raised in and around Youngstown, and in the area around the southerly bend of Lake Michigan, near Chicago. On the tripod of the Cleveland area and these two other strongholds of steel has grown the industrial might of the Heartland: they provide the underpinning for the manufacture of everything from autos and farm machinery to jet engines and missile pumps.

One of the first companies on the Chicago scene was the Inland Steel Corporation. Inland was organized in 1893, the year of panic and depression in which Pullman cut the contract prices for his workers and precipitated the country's first national labor-management crisis. There is a certain significance in the coincidence of dates. The Pullman company of the 1890s was a one-man show; George Pullman pulled its strings and was responsible to no man, whether worker or railroad president. Inland Steel of the mid-1960s is a publicly owned corporation that is deeply concerned with its corporate image; it strives not only to be efficient but to maintain positive relations with its workers. The story of Inland is in many ways the story of the growth of big industry in the Heartland, and it exemplifies the manner in which such industry operates in the region today.

Inland's beginnings were simple. On a visit to Chicago to attend the Columbian Exposition, a Cincinnati scrap-steel merchant named Joseph Block discovered that a local realtor was offering land to anyone who would reactivate an idle plant in Chicago Heights that had belonged to the bankrupt Chicago Steel Works. To take advantage of this opportunity, Block formed a syndicate with seven other men, including a professor of astronomy, a farm-tool maker and the foreman of the defunct plant. Together, they bought the property of Chicago Steel. Adopting the name Inland Steel, the new group began production with a total capital investment of $65,000 in borrowed money. The firm started by rerolling used steel rails into bars and other shapes. In the first six months of 1894 Inland produced 2,000 tons of finished steel—a little less than it makes in four hours today.

By 1901 the company was ready to expand, and another realtor was ready with an offer of 50 acres in East Chicago, Indiana, to anyone who would spend one million dollars on an open-hearth furnace. The move to the Indiana lakefront made it possible to have coal, iron ore and limestone delivered cheaply by water.

Block was soon joined in the management of the company by his two sons, Philip and Leopold; in later years Inland acquired a group of gifted executives—Edward L. Ryerson, who served as chairman of the board from 1940 to 1953; Wilfred Sykes, president from 1940 to 1949; and Clarence B. Randall, who served first as president and then as chairman from 1949 to 1956. Joseph L. Block, a grandson of the founder, became president in 1953 and chairman of the board in 1959, but there is little evidence of nepotism since the combined stockholdings of the Block and Ryerson families total less than 8 per cent of the voting stock.

As Inland grew, so did its subsidiaries: today Joseph T. Ryerson & Son, Inc., is the world's largest steel distributor; Inland Steel Container Division is a major maker of drums and pails; and Inland Steel Products Company is one of the largest fabricators of steel building products.

Inland is a "fully integrated" steel company: it is its own supplier of iron ore from Inland reserves in Michigan, Minnesota, Ontario and Labrador, has its own sources of coal in West Virginia and Illinois, and operates a limestone quarry in Gulliver, Michigan. Inland's Indiana Harbor Works is a fully integrated steel complex in the sense that it smelts ore into iron, refines steel from molten pig iron, and rolls and ships finished steel products. Yet so specialized is the business today that the handsome Inland Steel headquarters building in Chicago was in part built with steel alloys supplied by a competitor, Allegheny-Ludlum; Inland itself makes few alloys.

The Indiana Harbor Works is one of the largest steel complexes in the United States, occupying 1,500 acres on a man-made peninsula jutting two miles into Lake Michigan. Among its principal features are big, cylindrical blast furnaces, lined with heat-resistant brick and seemingly almost strangled by encircling pipes. The furnaces are packed with iron ore, limestone and coke, and this mixture is injected with a furious blast of air preheated to 1,250° Fahrenheit. As the coke burns at temperatures as high as 3,000 degrees, oxygen is removed from the ore by a chemical reaction with the carbon that produces carbon monoxide, which helps to dispose of other impurities; the limestone, fused into a liquid, also absorbs impurities; the heavy iron that remains sinks to the bottom of the furnace and is drawn off four or five times a day. The molten iron runs down a trough into a ladle car and is trundled to the open-hearth and basic-oxygen furnaces to be turned into steel.

At Inland's open-hearth plant seven huge furnaces breathe tongues of fire and spit coruscating sparks into the gloom. Inside the long, cavernous shed the goggled workers in hard hats who tend the furnaces seem to be servitors in some menacing pagan rite. The furnaces stand in a row on a center line. On the floor a mobile charging machine rams boxes of steel scrap, crushed limestone and iron ore into the furnace bottoms. When the scrap has partly melted, molten iron is dumped into the furnaces from round-bellied ladles suspended in the air alongside them by the giant hooks of an overhead traveling crane. At a middle level the three men servicing each furnace move back and forth between the raging fire and a battery of dials that record the progress of the batch. Now and again one of the workers inspects the process by taking out a sample of the boiling steel, using a long rod with a metal cup attached to its end.

When the furnace is tapped it seems like Fourth of July in hell: the dazzle of molten metal spouting from the furnace is so blinding that eyes must be averted or shielded with purple safety glasses. The steel is then poured into molds in which ingots weighing as much as 20 tons are cast. Through all the flame and smoke and tumult, there sounds from time to time the eerie moaning of warning sirens. To allow heat and gases to escape, the sides and roof of a steel mill are pierced with openings; despite the bedlam, pigeons occasionally flutter in the rafters.

If the furnaces suggest inferno, the rolling and strip mills have the aspect of the forge of Vulcan. Into one end of the mill comes a steady succession of glaring, white-hot ingots, traveling toward the big-muscled machines that will pummel and roll them into various shapes—flat sheets or strips, from which such objects as auto bodies and refrigerators are made, or heavy plates, bars and beams for construction uses.

Making some 6.5 million tons of steel a year, Inland has annual sales of more than $950 million. The company is far from being the largest of the nation's major steelmakers—in the 1960s it was the seventh-largest producer in the United States—but it was one of the most efficient. During that period, it was second in earnings per ton of ingots. The company had 50 per cent more employees in the mid-1960s than it had at the end of World War II, but they were producing more than twice as much steel. Because of the voracious Heartland appetite for this output, 90 per cent of Inland's product is sold within 400 miles of the Indiana Harbor Works.

In Inland's Chicago headquarters all the top executives are housed on a single floor where doors are never closed. Informality is a company tradition and it helps Inland to keep sales high. "At Inland," remarks one major buyer of sheet steel, "you deal with individuals, not with a branch office of a faraway outfit. When we have a problem, we can go down and talk with the boss." In addition, instant availability and the absence of barriers of rank within the company help Inland to reach decisions quickly, and to maintain a reputation for corporate independence. One of the more important demonstrations of this company trait came during the 1962 steel-price dispute between President John F. Kennedy and Roger Blough of U.S. Steel. Blough had announced a rise in prices and Kennedy had objected vociferously; the major question was whether other steel companies would follow U.S. Steel's lead. After talking the problem over in Chicago, Inland's top management phoned Joseph L. Block, who was vacationing in Japan. Block recalls: "My people made the decision. After hearing their arguments, I agreed with them." Inland then announced that it would not raise its prices. When Kaiser and Bethlehem fell into line with Inland, U.S. Steel capitulated and rescinded its increase. Four years later Inland was again the bellwether, but this time by raising prices in defiance of President Lyndon B. Johnson's efforts to keep prices from moving upward too swiftly.

The contrast between the worker-and-public-be-damned attitude of so many of the early Heartland industrialists and the operational philosophy of modern companies like Inland is diametric. Inland takes pride in a publicly released platform of goals whose value, like motherhood, is beyond criticism. "Merit and experience alone should govern," reads a typical plank, "and all should have equal opportunity irrespective of race, color or creed." The company's platform does not overlook the essential purpose of a profit-making organization—it avers that Inland will "serve our customers so well that we will merit a volume of business from them relatively as great or greater than that enjoyed by any of our competitors"—but it also urges Inland employees of all levels to be ceaselessly active in the affairs of their communities.

Although Inland's platform might appear to be the product of an alert public-relations staff, the fact is that the code was drawn up by Joseph Block, and, to a great degree, Inland practices what its chairman preaches. Inland people are found on all sorts of civic committees that seem far afield from steelmaking, and its executives tend to take more controversial stands on public issues than do those of other U.S. corporations. Vice President William Caples, for example, says flatly that the only intelligent solution to the Negro problem in the North is "open occupancy." Wiry John Sargent, president of Local 1010 of the United Steelworkers of America, regards Inland as a "forward-looking organization which, by and large, deals fairly with its people and the community," though he adds that this is "partly due to union and community pressure." Sargent also thinks that Inland has given more thoughtful attention to the effects of automation on its work force than most of the nation's other steel companies. Inland and the union have agreed on several steps to ease the transition: an advance in the effective date in new pension arrangements, for example, to encourage earlier retirement.

Business in the Heartland, as elsewhere, has discovered a need that has long been recognized by the professions: it must continually re-educate its personnel. This is true all down the line, in the crafts as well as among executives. Companies like Inland have retraining courses that workers can take free of charge on their own time. Says Vice President Caples: "Hell, Inland will give a man a college education if he shows that that's what he wants and if he is capable of handling the work." Under an agreement with Purdue University, Inland offers its employees courses in steelmaking, electricity and mechanics. Classes are held at Purdue's Calumet Center, located in Hammond, Indiana, five miles from the Indiana Harbor Works.

Inland is in a way representative of the long road

Railroad center to the nation

Chicago is the largest railroad center not only in the U.S. but in the world in volume of tonnage and extent of facilities; it handles about 7 per cent of the entire nation's freight-car loadings and 6 per cent of the unloadings. The symbols above belong to the 18 major trunk lines (the Chesapeake and Ohio and the Baltimore and Ohio affiliated in 1963) operating in the Chicago Terminal District, the name given to the area covered by the city's railroad facilities. In addition to these giant trunk lines, six industrial railroads, six switching lines and one of the nation's few remaining all-electric railways operate within the CTD. The district itself forms a huge crescent around Chicago's downtown Loop. Larger than the state of Rhode Island, it covers some 1,750 square miles and contains 7,708 miles of track, divided roughly into three bands. The band closest to the Loop includes six passenger terminals and a number of freight stations. The middle band has classification yards, sidings and freight stations. The third band, known as the Outer Belt, contains the tracks that carry trains around the city as well as to and from the inner belts.

that Heartland industry has traveled since the days of George Pullman. Not all companies, within or without the Heartland, follow the Inland style, as many a worker—and many an executive—would be willing to attest. But Inland is not alone in its progressive policies—nor are such policies restricted to heavy industry.

For example, certain parallels can be drawn between Inland's corporate manner and that of the Jones Dairy Farm of Fort Atkinson, Wisconsin, one of the Heartland's many small, personalized businesses. The Jones Dairy advertising is folksy in character, but despite that and its name, it is a highly efficient packing operation that sells a variety of pork products and that has been owned and run by the same family for five generations.

The first Milo Jones arrived in Fort Atkinson from Vermont in 1840 and built a handsome white farmhouse that still stands on the banks of the Rock River. His son, also named Milo, ran the family farm until he became bedridden with arthritis. Casting about for a means of supporting his family, Milo recalled his mother's recipe for making succulent sausage and hit upon the idea of packaging sausage for customers in one- and two-pound packages. Most butchers of the time made their own sausage and were not interested in carrying a competing brand. Jones began advertising locally and aimed his advertisements at the carriage trade, pricing his product up to 25 per cent higher than the average. In time, he was able to build up a sizable mail-order business, and in 1904 Jones began advertising on a national scale. This eventually provided the lever needed for regional distribution: a specific retailer in a metropolitan area would get a franchise for Jones products, together with a list of local Jones customers.

The mainstay of the business is Jones's "little pork sausages," which are made from the more expensive ham and shoulder cuts. Alan P. Jones, chairman of the board and a grandson of Milo, the founder, says: "We actually run a disassembly line, like taking an auto apart and reducing it to its component parts. We kill hogs on the day we buy them, using what are called humane methods—that is, the hog is unconscious when killed. The carcass is then cleaned, broken up, and made into sausage." Like other packers, the company has its own secret formula of ingredients. Unlike other packers who cater to regional tastes (for example, putting more red pepper in sausage intended for the South), the Jones company sells the same sausage throughout the country.

The Jones plant consists of five modern buildings that house offices, butchering and cutting plants, a sausage kitchen and a processing plant. Practically all the hogs used come from neighboring farmers, and in 1965 Jones slaughtered only some 150,000 hogs—which makes it, in packers' terms, a "watch-charm operation." Just how successful the company is remains a secret. "Ours is a small, mechanized operation," says Executive Vice President Edward Jones, another of the founder's grandsons. "We give out absolutely no information about profits or anything else." As a closed corporation Jones makes its annual report available only to its 12 stockholders —all members of the family—and to the company's bankers.

The firm is currently being run by Joneses of the fourth and fifth generations, and there are already five Jones boys of the sixth generation who will presumably be ready to take over in their turn. Although members of the Jones family have nothing to say publicly about profits or losses, they can be voluble on related subjects. Like other packers, the company was hurt by the unexpected scarcity of hogs in 1965. But it nonetheless managed to increase sales during that year and placed a confident bet on the future by putting in new sausage kitchens and broadening its line of products.

Jones has long enjoyed good labor relations. Some of its workers have spent as much as 50 years with the company. One Fort Atkinson man went to work for Jones in 1909; since then 14 members of his family have held long-term jobs with the company. In a widely unionized industry, Jones remained an exception until 1966, when its 200 employees voted in a National Labor Relations Board election to be represented by the United Packinghouse Workers.

Whether large or small, looking hopefully forward or nostalgically backward, Heartland industry is subject to the same stresses as business elsewhere. Just as fewer farmers are producing more and more food, so fewer workers are producing more and more goods, and there is general agreement that the trend will grow more pronounced. In the region as a whole an estimated 8 per cent of the labor force is engaged in agriculture, and 40 per cent in manufacturing and construction. Some experts believe that in the near future fully 80 per cent of the work force will be in service functions of some kind, and thus will not be making or growing anything at all. Yet for the foreseeable future, it is indisputable that the businesses of the Heartland—growing, modernizing, adjusting to the ever-changing demands of an ever-changing society—will remain at the forefront of all American production, the industrial center of the entire nation.

One of the thousands of people who help build each car, a worker at Chrysler's Lynch Road Assembly Plant in Detroit installs interior trim on a Coronet. On the windshield are cards and other work forms that tell him which of many alternative items he should attach.

A region-sized assembly line

The mass production of automobiles, long recognized as one of America's industrial achievements, can best be seen in the Heartland. The area around Detroit controls the building of cars all across the U.S. and also contains many of the final assembly lines. More importantly, the Heartland is laced with factories and subassembly points that provide products essential to auto construction. These plants are vital components of one mammoth assembly line directed by—and focused on—Detroit. The system, which constitutes a major bond in the region's economic unity, produces a remarkable variety of cars. Not only does each company have many models, but each model has countless possible variations. The cumulative steps that give birth to one such car, a Dodge Coronet 500 hardtop, are shown here and on the following pages.

A far-flung network controlled by computer

The key to the entire complex auto-building process is organization and control, and to a large extent the operation is today regulated by computers. When customers order cars from dealers around the country, the specifications for each car are sent to regional sales offices for punching onto data-processing cards and transmittal to a final assembly plant. Chrysler maintains seven of these plants, three of which it uses to assemble the Dodge Coronet. At the final assembly plant the cards are fed to computers that tell how many cars are ordered, what parts—some 15,000 for a Coronet—will be needed, and where each car should eventually be sent. The computerized information determines which car will be assembled at what time. Computers are also used to ensure that parts will be at the right place on the assembly line at the right time.

A technician at the Dodge assembly plant in Hamtramck, Michigan, checks orders just transmitted to his computer from another in a regional sales office. The data-processing cards he holds contain the individual specifications for each car that has been ordered.

MICHIGAN

WISCONSIN

SPARTA
Vehicle identification card

NECEDAH
Back-seat window grommets

MILWAUKEE
Throttle cables, air-conditioner control valves, front-suspension upper control arms

BARABOO
Radiator-core shields

SOUTH BELOIT
Air-conditioner compressors

DELAVAN
Clocks

STOCKTON
Front-seat adjusters

WOODSTOCK
Rear-deck trim

CHICAGO
Rear-cushion seat springs, front-cushion back springs, bumper-guard shock absorbers

GARY
Windshield wi

SPRING VALLEY
Interior lights, automatic gearshift dial lights

GALESBURG
Air-conditioner hoses

WARSAW
Batteries

ILLINOIS

QUINCY
Radios

DECATUR
Door-lock strikers

MOUNT ZION
Side-window glass

GRAYSVILLE
Steering wheels

FLORA
Horns

HERRIN
Door panels

MINNESOTA
Glove-compartment lights, "Dodge" lettering for rear deck

IOWA
Dashboard crash pads

NEBRASKA
Rear-cushion back springs

MISSOURI
Carburetors, rear-cushion pads

Suppliers of some of the key parts for the Coronet are located on the map. Black dots indicate where parts shown in this picture essay are made; gray dots represent other suppliers. Locations of suppliers outside the Heartland are listed on the edges of the map.

ONTARIO
Rear bumpers, wheels

NEW HAMPSHIRE
Armrest pads

NEW YORK
Rear-view mirrors,
antennas

MASSACHUSETTS
"Pentastar" medallions

CONNECTICUT
Cigarette lighters

NEW JERSEY
Headlights

PENNSYLVANIA
Seat belts

PETOSKEY
Fender ornaments

BOYNE CITY
Backup-light switches

MICHIGAN

GON
rings

ND RAPIDS
rgency-brake
ing lights,
window handles,
e door handles,
deck trim

TROY
Back-seat armrest
bases

MOUNT CLEMENS
Front-seat armrest bases

HIGHLAND PARK
Pistons, power
brakes

HAMTRAMCK
Interior roof
covering

JACKSON
Tires, jacks

DETROIT
Windshield and
rear-window glass,
stop and rear signal
lights, steering wheels,
rear axles, gas tanks,
engine frames, vinyl
outer roof coverings

ANN ARBOR
Instrument panels

ADRIAN
Front-cushion seat
springs

KA
covering
ers

TOLEDO
Spark plugs, horn
rings

CLEVELAND
Bumper guards, paint

TWINSBURG
Body stampings

ANA

UNION CITY
Outside rear-view
mirrors, outside
door handles

UPPER SANDUSKY
Weather stripping

AKRON
Front-cushion seat pads

ons

OHIO

GREENVILLE
Oil filters

LONDON
Radiators

CASTLE
k absorbers

POLIS

LOGAN
Dashboard crash pads

GREENFIELD
Front-cushion back
pads

YMOUR
l pipes

PORTSMOUTH
Water pumps

MARYLAND
Automatic gearshift
dials

TENNESSEE
Headlights, outside
rear-view mirrors

GEORGIA
Radiator grilles

NORTH CAROLINA
Carpeting, fan belts

MISSISSIPPI
Wheel disks

A sales analyst in Hamtramck totals orders to detect buying trends.
Once a month, using these trends, he makes or revises a
five-month forecast of supplies needed at the assembly plants,
ranging from different paints to kinds of glass to types of engines.

Product engineers at Hamtramck discuss a modification of the
Coronet's rear-window molding with a production control supervisor
(left foreground). The supervisor informs the appropriate suppliers
and sees that parts engineered to the modification reach the plant.

A system of assembly plants to make body and engine parts

GRAND RAPIDS
Emergency-brake
warning lights,
vent-window handles,
inside door handles,
rear-deck trim

JACKSON
Tires, jacks

MISHAWAKA
Vinyl seat covering,
front bumpers

TWINSBURG
Body stampings

LONDON
Radiators

The suppliers of equipment for the Detroit assembly lines manufacture their products in factories that are themselves assembly plants. For instance, the Coronet's radiator and tires are made on assembly lines, but their components often come from the production lines of other factories. Before being shipped to Detroit for the final assembly line, a completed part is in some cases sent to a subassembly point, where it becomes one of the items on still another line. The black dots on the map on this and the following pages locate plants shown on those pages.

Finished tires are swiftly checked for balance on an electronic machine before going to further tests under simulated road conditions at the Jackson, Michigan, Goodyear plant. The machine, called a Micro-Poise, can perform tests on 350 tires an hour.

Crashing down with 2,000 tons of pressure per square inch, a press stamps out the Coronet's trunk floor in a Chrysler-owned plant in Twinsburg, Ohio. Some 2,000 stamping operations go into the making of a Coronet; this plant alone contains 520 stamping machines. All the steel used in this plant is made within 200 miles.

Spreading folds of Naugahyde, a vinyl plastic used for seat covers in the Coronet, an inspector at the U.S. Rubber plant in Mishawaka, Indiana, gives the material a final check. The Naugahyde has already been embossed with leatherlike folds and wrinkles.

Housed in temporary frames, radiator cores are hooked to the moving production line by a worker in the McCord Corporation plant in London, Ohio. In later steps the cores will be placed in permanent frames and shipped to Detroit.

Chrome-plated trim pieces for the Coronet's trunk lid —previously shaped in Woodstock, Illinois—emerge from the final stage of a 38-bath process and are prepared for drying at Preston Products, Grand Rapids, Michigan.

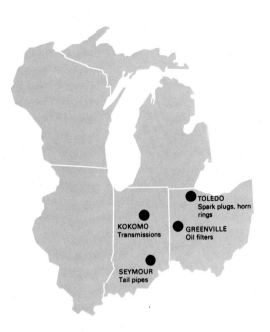

TOLEDO
Spark plugs, horn rings

KOKOMO
Transmissions

GREENVILLE
Oil filters

SEYMOUR
Tail pipes

Producers
of the power train

The Coronet's power train—the engine and other parts that move the car—is, like every other component of the auto, not only a product of a number of assembly lines but of the workers who actually man the lines. In their workers, the Heartland's manufacturers are fortunate. Assembly-line jobs are both demanding and, frequently, repetitive. To their jobs, however, workers like those shown here, who assemble sections of the power train, bring a high degree of proficiency and a considerable amount of pride.

Three women workers assemble oil filters on a continuously moving belt at the Fram Corporation in Greenville, Ohio. In the 10 years they have worked together they have become good friends and work effortlessly as they talk of home and family.

102

A die caster strips scrap metal from an aluminum transmission case before loading it on an overhead conveyor at the Chrysler Casting Plant in Kokomo, Indiana. This operator turns out 45 cases an hour, making adjustments to the die-cast machine to maintain quality.

A press operator prepares to cut a Coronet tail pipe to the proper length at Arvin Industries in Seymour, Indiana. One employee says of this type of work: "Some of the jobs you've got to think about. Others the machine does the thinking."

An assembly-line worker removes spark plugs from a gap-setting machine at Champion Spark Plugs in Toledo. An inspector at the plant says: "I wouldn't think of putting a spark plug in the 'passed' tray without looking closely at it. It's a matter of conscience."

Precise work and tough tests for safety and glamor

Each year cars grow more glamorous and more complicated, creating increasing quality-control problems for automotive engineers. Some of their complex instruments, like the speedometer, have long been essential to auto safety. Other somewhat less essential items placed in modern automobiles—like radios and clocks and stereophonic tape systems—are nonetheless also intricate pieces of machinery and require the same kind of rigorous testing and careful precision work on the assembly lines.

DELAVAN
Clocks

ANN ARBOR
Instrument panels

QUINCY
Radios

Radios quickly take form under the skilled hands of workers at the Motorola plant in Quincy, Illinois. When finished, each set is hit with a rubber mallet to test it under stress.

Speedometers are raced at high speeds for 24 hours in a durability test at the King-Seeley Thermos factory in Ann Arbor, Michigan. Picked at random, they are junked after testing.

An electric-clock motor is checked by the watchful eye of an inspector at the Borg Corporation in Delavan, Wisconsin. Every finished clock is test-run for a total of six days.

The pay-off: final assembly line in Detroit

As parts pour in from the scattered suppliers, workers at the final Coronet assembly line in Detroit piece the car together almost as if it were a toy model. They attach the preassembled power train to the painted body, mount the tires, and fill the body with carpeting, seats and other equipment. While the car moves by, each worker has a specified length of time to do his job, whether it is tightening bolts or installing the steering wheel. All along the line, inspectors check the cars to ensure that each job has been done correctly. Then, at the end of the line, the finished Coronet rolls off, to be shipped to the dealer and to the waiting customer who had started the process less than three weeks before.

A worker on the engine line swings a transmission, suspended by a power hoist, into position on the Coronet's engine so that another man can bolt it on. The engine was subassembled in Trenton, Michigan, the transmission in Kokomo, Indiana.

An inspector checks the Coronet against its "hardware build sheet," which carries specifications for each car—whether, for example, it should have dual or single exhausts. Each inspector examines only a certain section of the car.

Inserting the rear seat, a worker swings it into the car by hand. The seats reach this "station" on an overhead belt. The worker has one minute in which to insert the seat; assembly of a complete car on the final line requires two days.

At the end of the line, inspectors give the Coronet a final check. If they find a fault, the car is driven to a repair area. If it passes this check, it is driven through a wax-spray booth and then to an outdoor marshaling yard.

With other new cars in the right foreground, the finished Coronet *(the gold car on the left, second from rear)* awaits shipment at Chrysler's Lynch Road Assembly Plant, not far from downtown Detroit *(background)*. Behind the cars, another is coming out of the plant and Chrysler trucks are unloading equipment for the assembly line. In a 16-hour shift, more than 800 cars a day are built in this plant—all of them spectacular examples of a kind of industrial ingenuity that is largely taken for granted by Americans.

6

Thriving
Urban Centers

The cities of the Heartland possess a number of traditions in common. Many were born combative and sought to grow at the expense of neighboring towns. Many have progressed from rule by tyrannical bosses to democratic reform. Some, like Chicago, boldly and brashly set forth to establish themselves as leaders and builders; some few others, like Cincinnati, came to reject brashness and have with conscious civic pride quietly attempted to build splendid metropolises.

Many of the cities began in myth and had—or purported to have—a newspaper, hotel and sawmill long before they had actual inhabitants. The myths were usually created by land speculators, and out of their verbal improvisations grew the boosterish belief that if something were only said loud and long enough it would ultimately come true. In the 1830s a pictorial map was circulated in the Eastern U.S. depicting the splendors of White Rock City, on the shores of Lake Huron. It showed a river crowded with shipping, a public square ringed by churches, a courthouse and a bank, and busy

factories on the outskirts beyond the residential neighborhoods. Curious about this thriving city in the wilderness, two Michigan men went looking for it. The bustling river proved to be a shallow creek barely navigable by their canoe, and in place of docks, homes and mills, there was only the leafy forest. Three large beech trees stood in the clearing that was the site of the public square. Carving their names on the smooth bark of one tree, the two men congratulated each other on being the first guests to register at the White Rock City Hotel.

Even when towns were really settled by real people they often came to untimely ends. The railroad was a killer as well as a creator. The lumbering town of Newport, Wisconsin, died when the railroad bypassed it; Grand Detour, on the great bend of the Rock River, hoped to outdo Chicago, but is today only a hamlet surrounded by cornfields. When the rail line was laid elsewhere, the people of Stacey Corners, Illinois, put their homes on rollers and moved to Wheaton, the nearest town with a railway station. Astute settlers often made under-the-counter deals to make sure the right of way would go through their land. Daniel Harmon Brush bought up the site of what is now Carbondale, Illinois, and then gave a number of acres to Illinois Central officials. In return Brush got not only a railroad station but a freight yard and a warehouse. With everyone clamoring for a site on the railway, Bourbonnais, Illinois, astonished Heartland entrepreneurs by objecting to the laying of track through the village. The railroad obligingly shifted the line of survey through nearby Kankakee, which today has a population of 30,000 to Bourbonnais' 3,000.

To survive and prosper, towns bid frantically against one another to gain the cash advantages of harboring state institutions. Of four rivals for the University of Illinois, Champaign-Urbana got the prize; its lobbyist in Springfield had paid lavish bribes to the state legislators. Springfield, originally only the county seat of Sangamon County, became the state capital because Abraham Lincoln and a group of other legislators from Sangamon County —all tall men like Lincoln, they were collectively known as the "Long Nine"—traded their votes on matters of interest to other lawmakers in return for votes on the seat-of-government question.

When there was talk after the Civil War of moving the national capital from Washington to somewhere in the Heartland, Chicago hurriedly put in its bid. Amused by Chicago's presumption, the Cincinnati *Gazette* speculated that the city on Lake Michigan might soon pass out of existence. Chicago's lack of permanence was evident, said the *Gazette*, in "the temporary character of [its] buildings, the transient feeling of [its] citizens, the general recklessness as to business reputation, the gambling character of their trade and the general looseness of their morals." On the other hand, the *Gazette* went on in all seriousness: "Cincinnati offers all the beauties of site, climate and civilization, but Cincinnati does not need the capital. If the country desires to put it here . . . we shall acquiesce as a patriotic duty." The self-assurance of those closing lines was the sort of thing that made a Louisville, Kentucky, paper refer to Cincinnati as "our clever but rather vain sister up the river."

The experts were frequently wrong in their estimates of which city would gain the ascendancy in the Heartland. A writer for the New York *Merchants Magazine* provided a classic example. In 1843 he gave the palm not to Detroit, Chicago or Cleveland, but to the budding seaport of Maumee, which is now a suburb of Toledo. When citizens of young Chicago decided to develop the muddy bog that was their town, they applied for a loan from the bank at Shawneetown, then one of the state's leading cities. The bank's investigators took one look at Chicago and decided that it was uninhabitable. The loan was refused.

The bank's disdain was understandable. Chicago now sits firmly on pilings and caissons driven into the bedrock below its initially swampy streets, but it appeared for a time to be a place that nature did not intend men to settle in any numbers. The land had so little elevation that it was annually flooded by Lake Michigan and the Chicago River. Moreover, it was not a restful spot. One of the first settlers was Jean Baptiste Point du Sable, who prospered to the extent of owning a house, two barns, a mill, bakehouse, workshop, dairy and smokehouse, all of which he sold to Jean La Lime in 1800 before moving on to Peoria. La Lime was later stabbed to death by another settler, a prominent trader named John Kinzie, after an argument between them of unknown origin. In 1812 the Potawatomi Indians massacred the garrison at Chicago's fort—although Kinzie, his family and his home were spared.

Chicago never got the message that its site was unsuitable for a city, even though early residents complained that the Chicago River was too shallow for boats and the streets too bottomless for wagons. North and west of the town—known to the rest of the country as the "Mud Hole of the Prairie"— stretched an area sometimes referred to as "Dismal Swamp." Eventually deciding that they had to take action, Chicagoans in 1855 began the herculean task of raising the city above the lake level. Some sections were lifted as much as 12 feet. Engineers dredged the malodorous Chicago River to get the fill needed for the elevation, and in the process deepened the river channel. The streets were frequently raised first; it thus became possible for pedestrians to saunter along and peer into second-floor bedrooms. George M. Pullman, who later built the first modern railroad sleeping cars, made his early reputation by assembling 5,000 jack-screws and 1,200 men in the basement of the Tremont House and raising the hotel eight feet "without disturbing a guest or cracking a cup."

Chicago was growing at a fantastic rate during this period. Settlers poured into the area from the East through the Erie Canal and across the Great Lakes and on the railroads that were completed during the 1850s. Within the next three decades the city's population surged past that of much older St. Louis, reaching a total of some 500,000. The new residents of Chicago acted, as had the old, in the bold manner that seemed to be becoming a part of the city's character. Chicago's primary source of drinking water was Lake Michigan; in 1871 the city began work on reversing the course of the Chicago River, which then emptied into the lake, to make the river carry the city's sewage away from the lake through a series of canals for eventual dumping into the Illinois and the Mississippi Rivers.

The move partially succeeded, but the river soon returned to its old course; in the 1890s the city dug the deep Sanitary and Ship Canal to make the change permanent. There were immediate outcries. Downstate Illinois cities were indignant at the prospect of being deluged by Chicago sewage; St. Louis, Chicago's old antagonist, went to court to prevent the opening of the canal. But while St. Louis was appealing to the law, Chicagoans stole out by night and dynamited the last barrier, and since that time the Chicago River has flowed out of Lake Michigan instead of into it.

Disaster kept pace with the city's growth. An ice jam in 1849 carried away all the bridges and destroyed many of the ships in the harbor. In 1871, shortly after the initial reversal of the river, Chicago's Great Fire began in back of the house of one Patrick O'Leary (giving rise to the legend that Mrs. O'Leary's cow had started the blaze by kicking over a lantern) and roared through the city for two nights and a day. One eyewitness reported that the flames made diagonal arches as they leaped high into the air to cross streets and the river, and the atmosphere was so thick with cinders that the scene looked "like a snowstorm lit by colored fire."

As flames swept the downtown district, businessmen gathered in the exclusive Chicago Club to toast one another's ruin in champagne, and when the club itself caught fire they adjourned to the lakefront to finish the wine. Escaping from his burning Tremont House (the establishment that had been so painstakingly lifted by Pullman), John B. Drake walked into the Michigan Avenue Hotel and offered to buy it, $1,000 down, the balance in two weeks. Expecting the building to follow the Tremont into oblivion, the owners quickly took the offer, but the hotel survived and Drake renamed it the Tremont House. So extensive was the damage to Chicago that 100,000 people were left homeless, and in the East the poet John Greenleaf Whittier lamented: "The City of the West is dead!"

Like most Eastern opinions about Chicago, Whittier's was wrong. The realtor W. D. Kerfoot erected a sign reading: "All gone but wife, children and energy!" Joseph Medill of the *Chicago Tribune* wrote: "Chicago still exists. She was not a mere collection of stone, and bricks and lumber." Potter Palmer, a successful merchant and hotel man, was shaken by the holocaust and thought of moving away, but his beautiful wife admonished him: "Mr. Palmer, it's the duty of every Chicagoan

A capacity crowd rides on an interurban electric trolley line to Elkhart Lake, Wisconsin, in the early 1900s. Introduced in the 1890s, the "interurbans" offered cheap, clean and rapid transportation to Americans otherwise isolated in small towns and on farms. They were an immediate success, particularly in the Heartland. By 1917 nearly 10,000 cars were in use in the U.S. on more than 18,000 miles of track, 40 per cent of it in Indiana and Ohio. However, in the 1920s the interurbans fell victim to the convenience of the automobile.

Classical columns of a bank building rise above the rubble left after the Great Chicago Fire swept through three and a half square miles of the city in 1871. In two days the flames destroyed $200 million worth of property, took at least 250 lives and left almost 100,000 homeless. Ironically, Mrs. O'Leary's barn, where legend says the fire started, escaped virtually unscathed.

to stay here and help rebuild this stricken city."

One of the first undertakings after the fire was the opening of a public library in an empty water tank, with volumes donated by such luminaries as Queen Victoria, Charles Darwin, Thomas Carlyle and Benjamin Disraeli. As the city responded to its motto, "I Will!," new buildings seemed to rise almost overnight. Within six years of the fire, Chicago could boast of 16 new hotels with as many as 800 rooms each, and 150 smaller ones. Understandably, the city took pride in its achievement. In later years the University of Chicago adopted the phoenix rising from the ashes as its seal. The crenelated Gothic water tower on North Michigan Avenue that survived the fire became so greatly venerated that Chicagoans in 1928 adamantly refused to allow it to be torn down for a street-widening project.

The city's vitality in the rebuilding years was intellectual as well as structural. The English poet Robert Browning wrote with some surprise: "Of all the places in the world, the one which from its literary societies sends me the most intelligent and thoughtful criticism upon my poetry is Chicago."

Architects swarmed to Chicago, understandably excited by the opportunity to rebuild a major city practically from scratch. Daniel H. Burnham and John W. Root combined their talents to perfect a

steel-and-concrete raft that "floated" on the city's marshy ground while supporting one of the world's first skyscrapers. Louis Sullivan and Dankmar Adler devised the method of sinking caissons down into bedrock to give buildings solid footing. Old Chicago had followed the various European styles popular in the East, and commercial buildings usually had been no more than five stories high. Now, taking advantage of the power-driven elevator perfected a few years before the Great Fire, and of the technique developed by William LeBaron Jenney of supporting structures by an internal iron framework rather than by heavy external walls, the buildings of the 1890s soared up to 20 stories and more, and were given light and air by the bay windows that became a distinctive trademark of "the Chicago school." Carl Condit of Northwestern University has observed: "Today recognition of the school is world-wide, and its . . . principles now constitute the basis of architecture as it is practiced on every continent."

Chicago is a sprawling city, stretching as far as 12 miles inland from its more than 20 miles of waterfront along Lake Michigan. At the heart of the city, near the lake, lies the downtown district known as the Chicago Loop, so called because it is roughly encircled by an elevated railway. The coastline is a continuous string of sandy beaches, green parks, yacht basins, marinas, lagoons, fountains, statues, museums, stadiums and playgrounds. Threaded along almost its entire length is a wide express boulevard, Lake Shore Drive—informally known as the Outer Drive. On its northern section, lane dividers can be raised or lowered depending upon which direction—uptown or downtown—the bulk of traffic is flowing.

The British architectural critic Reyner Banham writes: "From the steps of the Art Institute [which lies close to the lakefront] you have a kind of offshore view of the Chicago Loop. It's almost like looking back at Venice from the island of San Giorgio—almost; you have to make gondolas of the cars on Michigan Avenue, but beyond them, and beyond the irregular cliff of masonry and brick, steel and glass and aluminum that confronts you, is one of the richest lodes of architectural treasure in the world. And, as in Venice, it is packed into a small enough space to be looked at (and looked into) within the space of an afternoon's reasonable walking."

Chicago's shining lakefront is so handsome that it can lead a casual visitor to believe that the entire metropolitan area is beautiful. Unfortunately he is likely to be in for disappointments in addition to

Chicagoans stroll in 1918 on fashionable Michigan Avenue. Thoroughly rebuilt after the Great Fire (opposite page), it became the showcase boulevard of the city. It was resplendent with towering office buildings, grand hotels, smart shops, elaborate street lights and the bronze lions that still guard the entrance to the city's Art Institute. Before the fire the avenue had been a quiet, tree-lined street of elegant homes and residential hotels. In the wake of the fire 40,000 people had deserted the city, but many more soon arrived. With donations from around the world, the people started putting Chicago together again, replacing the former wood structures with fireproof stone and brick. As early as 1890 the city had become second only to New York in size in the U.S.

rewards. In the south, Chicago runs into the ugly industrial cities of the Calumet River area, where factory chimneys, steel mills and refineries stain the sky. Northward, the city ends at Calvary Cemetery, beyond which lies prim and leafy Evanston, home to Methodism, Temperance, Rotary International and Northwestern University. To go any distance west from Chicago's shoreline is to plunge into an anonymous urban sprawl of brick factories, warehouses, printing plants, two-family houses, low apartment buildings with courtyards, and old corner saloons. Wandering through this maze is the Chicago River, spanned by innumerable bridges that range upward on their trunnions for the passage of freighters. The landscape architect Jens Jensen once created or rehabilitated a string of West Side parks filled with regional trees and plants, but a number of them are now dreary from neglect. Even so, Chicago is a park city, with 6,662 acres set aside for horseback riding, golf, tennis, boating, fishing and swimming.

Beyond the western city limits lies a pleasant area, the green chain of the Forest Preserves, where generations of Chicagoans have picnicked and played in the summertime. Some distance past the Forest Preserves is the Outer Belt, a ring of rail lines on which run the thousands of freight and passenger cars that daily travel into, around and out of Chicago. Along the Outer Belt lie the satellite industrial cities, adding their smoke and flame to the atmosphere around the mother city. Without its famous wind, which scatters the smoke across the Midwest and the Great Lakes, Chicago would choke of air pollution. Sufficient grime and cinders descend to grit the city's face, but the sky is usually clear.

Between the Outer Belt and the city are cluster on cluster of suburbs dotted with shopping centers and modern factories—windowless, antiseptic, functionally trim—each with its landscaping and its plaintive "Help Wanted" signs. Along the North Shore, beyond Evanston, lies a succession of more affluent suburbs like Wilmette, Winnetka, Glencoe, Highland Park and Lake Forest.

This vast metropolis that grew so fast, 700 miles inland from the Atlantic Coast, was long a victim of municipal chaos. Its mayors have ranged from occasional earnest reformers, who were usually ineffective, to party hacks and occasional cosmopolites like Carter Harrison and his son Carter Harrison II, who were elected to five mayoralty terms each between 1879 and 1915. Chicago was long noted for a sort of genial corruption that was accepted by its citizens with an almost world-weary

Boisterous Prohibition-era Chicago was briefly the jazz capital of the U.S. and one of its greatest bands was "King" Oliver's, seen in this 1923 photograph. Oliver *(third from right)*, himself a jazz pioneer, brought north from New Orleans the young man standing next to him, cornet in hand—Louis Armstrong, who, more than any other musician, would shape the course of jazz history.

apathy. Members of the city council were nicknamed the "Gray Wolves" for their eagerness in selling out the city to private corporations. Charles T. Yerkes, who around the turn of the century built Chicago's first urban transit system, was so skillful in buying up politicians that he obtained his franchises at a fraction of their value. In the same period a company obtained the right to bore holes beneath the city streets to carry telephone wires, but by the time the work was finished the enterprising owners of the company were discovered to have actually completed 60 miles of potentially profitable subway tunnels 14 feet high and 12 feet wide connecting the city's major freight terminals and business houses. When someone belatedly examined the company's permit it was discovered that the license had been altered after its issuance by the city council. As has so often happened in Chicago, nothing was done about the matter, and the tunnels remained in use until 1959.

The only mayor of Chicago to achieve nationwide notoriety was William Hale Thompson, who presided over the city during World War I and the Prohibition era. "Big Bill" answered his numerous critics by suggesting that they "throw away your hammer and get a horn." He sought to divert attention from his association with the Capone mob by combatively offering to take on the British Empire singlehanded, and more than once threatened to punch King George V "in the snoot" if the King ever happened to drop by Chicago.

As the nation's premier convention city, Chicago was—and still is—indulgent toward fleshpots, although it is not so relaxed today as it once was. Mayor Carter Harrison and his son both believed that gambling and prostitution could be controlled but not eradicated, and although the younger Harrison closed the Everleigh Club, one of the world's most elegant houses of ill repute, the "Levee" district remained a vast brothel. Municipal corruption reached a peak during the Prohibition era, when Capone and his boys were busily engaged in wiping out such rivals in the rackets as Dion O'Bannion and Earl "Hymie" Weiss. Chicago's police force was better known for bribetaking than for law enforcement, and for years Chicago motorists, as a matter of course, attached $5 or $10 bills to their drivers' licenses.

Mayor Richard Daley seemed completely in the Chicago tradition when he took office in 1955—rotund, of Irish descent and, as an orator, addicted to platitudes. But Daley proved to be a better man than anticipated. During his administration an outraged West Side burglar revealed that he could scarcely make ends meet because he had to cut so many policemen in on his jobs. There was a public outcry; Daley responded by naming Orlando W. Wilson, a California professor of criminology, as his chief of police and backed Wilson in a thoroughgoing reorganization of the city force. He also refused to allow the existing scandal to be hushed up, as might have been done under previous administrations, and the case ended with the conviction of eight patrolmen for burglary.

Daley in addition moved to refurbish and develop the city physically and economically, and he saw to it that the time-honored corrupt methods of conducting municipal business were done away with. When the Inland Steel Company proposed erecting the first new building in the Loop in a quarter of a century, Daley gave assurances that the company need pay no kickbacks to city officials. An Inland executive recalls that on three occasions work was held up because city permits were mysteriously delayed. In each case a word to Daley's office proved sufficient to get things moving again.

Chicago is unmistakably masculine and perennially young. The city is at its best when given some seemingly insuperable task like raising the city streets, reversing the course of the Chicago River, rebuilding itself after the Great Fire or engaging

A pioneering settlement house

Hull-House, one of the most famous settlement houses in the nation, was established in Chicago in 1889 by a crusader for social justice, Jane Addams, shown at left reading to neighborhood children in the 1930s. Miss Addams opened the institution with the revolutionary credo that social workers should live in the slums they serve and that the poor themselves should suggest the programs of aid. The concept was so successful that other cities started similar ventures and Hull-House itself grew from its single original structure on a South Halsted Street corner *(above)* on Chicago's West Side to 13 buildings. Today Hull Mansion is a museum, but the Hull House Association maintains centers in other areas of Chicago to aid the city's poor.

in some great crusade—as when the merchant-entrepreneur Montgomery Ward fought other businessmen, local politicians and public apathy to prevent the burned-out lakefront near the Loop from being used for commercial purposes and thus preserved it for the people of Chicago.

The city is, on the other hand, historically unsure of itself. The local magazine *Chicago* once asked a number of people familiar with the city to try to define its essence. Claudia Cassidy, then a *Chicago Tribune* critic, reported acidly that "Chicago is the place I seldom recognize when I read about it." The advertising executive Leo Burnett protested that the national image of Chicago as the "Windy City" and the hub of organized crime was wildly distorted. "We can't," Burnett wrote, "go around explaining to every person we talk to that, according to U.S. weather department figures, we are only the 19th windiest city, and that New York City is the windiest of all. Nor . . . can we hope to explain that the last F.B.I. annual report says that in 'murder and negligent manslaughter' 51 metropolitan areas ranked ahead of Chicago." Burnett might well have added that still another image of Chicago —that of "hog butcher to the world," inadvertently propounded by a generation of U.S. schoolteachers assigning their charges the reading of Carl

Sandburg's poem "Chicago"—is also outdated. The slaughterhouses in the old stockyards stand dark and silent; the packers moved west years ago to be nearer to the pigs and cattle.

The Irish poet Sean O'Faolain was struck by the fact that "Chicagoans burst into wild praise of Chicago if you decry it; but you can make them go into ferocious reverse the next moment by praising their city." The author Richard Stern thinks that "Chicago is what happens to you here. It is hard to separate what it is from what you are." Edna Ferber, fresh from Wisconsin, found Chicago "one of the most vital, unformed, fascinating, horrible, brutal, civilized and beautiful cities in the world." John Reich, director of the Goodman Theater, comments: "There is a terrible inferiority complex here . . . After I had been here three years, one well-known public personality . . . said to me: 'John, how come you are still in Chicago? I thought you were talented?' I think that sums it all up."

Not entirely. The sum total of Chicago is more than that—and it adds up differently every day. "That's how it is here," said Frank Lloyd Wright, "nothing stays, everything changes." A big and disquieting city, forever pulsing with energy, Chicago seems to put an indelible mark on its children. Whether they go or stay, whether they rejoice in

Chicago or abominate it, few seem able to rid themselves of an intimate love-hate relationship with this most archetypal of American cities. After living in Manhattan for 20 years, the novelist Saul Bellow came back to his native city because he found that he was wasting his time in New York searching for the equivalents of the friends and relatives "I had grown up with here and knew well." Another writer, Studs Terkel, who had stayed in Chicago, laments: "Our incapacity to accept criticism, a criticism built on a love for what *can be*, appears to be hardening rather than softening. It is our own cold war against the world: You're either with us or against us."

In total contrast to hastening, busy Chicago is Cincinnati, a metropolis at the other end of the Heartland urban spectrum. Reclining on its lovely hills along a bend of the Ohio River, Cincinnati once held Chicago's position as the largest Heartland metropolis. Today it is not even the largest city in Ohio, ranking third behind Cleveland and Columbus—but Cincinnati could scarcely care less. Long before President Lyndon Baines Johnson announced his dream of the Great Society in the mid-1960s, Cincinnatians were convinced that they had achieved such a society. A great society is, they

know, a delicate blend of the material and the cultural, and it must be constantly maintained. The story may be apocryphal but Cincinnatians firmly believe that Henry Ford came, hat in hand, to propose building automobiles in Cincinnati but was turned away by the city fathers who decided that they wanted the metropolis to remain as it was.

Cincinnati is almost European in its reverence for the past, in the leisurely pace of its existence, and in its citizens' docility and obedience to the law. Yet the city is not stodgy. When of a mind, it can move as fast and as purposefully as Chicago. After the Civil War Cincinnati sought to regain its status as the principal supplier of the South but found that Louisville, Kentucky, using improved rail lines extending into the South from that city, had taken over Cincinnati's prewar role. Cincinnati citizens voted a $10 million bond issue, and the city built and operated a new rail line to Chattanooga, which it later leased to the Southern Railroad. Among the city's other achievements are the first shipment of airmail, carried by balloon in 1835; the first chartered municipal university; the first Jewish theological seminary; the first salaried fire department; and the first salaried baseball team, the Cincinnati Red Stockings, now the Reds.

The river steamboat made Cincinnati the Queen

Chicago's city-sized market

Beside the Chicago River stands the world's largest commercial building, the two-block-square, 24-floor Merchandise Mart. The Mart has 97 acres of floor space, most of it rented to manufacturers and wholesalers who display more than two million

items of clothing and interior furnishings to the more than 50,000 interior designers and buyers for stores who visit it each year. To handle the flow of goods and people, the building has its own pier, railway station and truck-loading facilities. It has a 20-man police force, 35 elevators and its own post office.

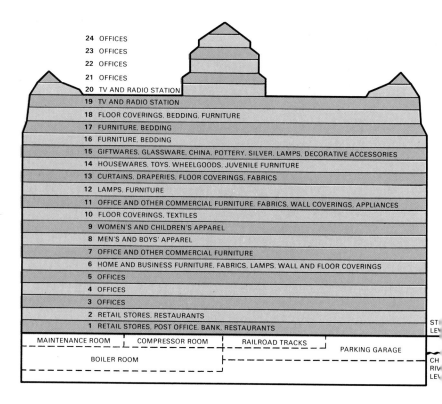

Floor	Use
24	OFFICES
23	OFFICES
22	OFFICES
21	OFFICES
20	TV AND RADIO STATION
19	TV AND RADIO STATION
18	FLOOR COVERINGS, BEDDING, FURNITURE
17	FURNITURE, BEDDING
16	FURNITURE, BEDDING
15	GIFTWARES, GLASSWARE, CHINA, POTTERY, SILVER, LAMPS, DECORATIVE ACCESSORIES
14	HOUSEWARES, TOYS, WHEELGOODS, JUVENILE FURNITURE
13	CURTAINS, DRAPERIES, FLOOR COVERINGS, FABRICS
12	LAMPS, FURNITURE
11	OFFICE AND OTHER COMMERCIAL FURNITURE, FABRICS, WALL COVERINGS, APPLIANCES
10	FLOOR COVERINGS, TEXTILES
9	WOMEN'S AND CHILDREN'S APPAREL
8	MEN'S AND BOYS' APPAREL
7	OFFICE AND OTHER COMMERCIAL FURNITURE
6	HOME AND BUSINESS FURNITURE, FABRICS, LAMPS, WALL AND FLOOR COVERINGS
5	OFFICES
4	OFFICES
3	OFFICES
2	RETAIL STORES, RESTAURANTS
1	RETAIL STORES, POST OFFICE, BANK, RESTAURANTS

MAINTENANCE ROOM   COMPRESSOR ROOM   RAILROAD TRACKS   PARKING GARAGE

BOILER ROOM

ST LEV

CH RIV LEV

City of the west. The first industrial city of the Heartland, it shipped its products west and south. Farmers all over the United States worked their fields with Cincinnati plows and lived in homes protected by Cincinnati lightning rods; congregations trooped to church on Sunday mornings to the tolling of Cincinnati bells; the lacy ironwork on plantation houses of the Old South is usually said to have come from France but much of it was actually made in Cincinnati. The city turned wheat and corn into flour and whiskey. So many droves of pigs crowded the streets that Cincinnati was known as "Porkopolis," and its ham became so justly renowned that it was specifically ordered by Queen Victoria.

A line ("Vas you efer in Zinzinnati?") from a turn-of-the-century operetta, *The Prince of Pilsen*, convinced many Americans that the city was filled to the brim with German burghers, and there was some truth in the belief. Although Cincinnati has for many years had more native-born than foreign-born citizens, many Cincinnatians are of German origin. In the early 1900s the Germans were concentrated in an area north of Mill Creek that was known as Over-the-Rhine. German as well as English was taught in the public schools until World War I. Although the language is seldom heard in public today, a Teutonic imprint survives in the city's speech: when a Cincinnatian does not catch a remark, he is likely to say, "Please?"—a reflection of the German "*Bitte?*"

Cincinnati originally bore the name Losantiville, a complex French-Greek-Latin acronym. According to the word's creator, a scholarly surveyor named John Filson, Losantiville read backward meant the "city opposite the mouth of the Licking River" (*ville* meaning "city," *anti* meaning "opposite," *os* meaning "mouth," "L" standing for the Licking River). A story goes that when General Arthur St. Clair, first Governor of the Northwest Territory, landed at Losantiville, he boomed, "What an awful name! God damn it, call it Cincinnati!"—thereby honoring the Cincinnati, a society of Revolutionary War officers to which he belonged.

The city first clustered around its Public Landing on the Ohio, then spread backward to the plateau known as the Basin before it began climbing the surrounding hills. It grew quickly and was both lively and dangerous to live in. Gangs fought one another in Gas Alley and Rat Row, young rowdies prowled the dock area on the lookout for drunks they could roll, and the favorite weapon of footpads was a blackjack. But the city also had cultural proclivities. One of the city's first physicians, Dr. William Goforth, collected fossils, flowers and Indian artifacts. His successor, Dr. Daniel Drake, founded —or helped to found—a library, museum, debating club, college, medical school, eye clinic, medical journal and drug store—among other things.

Perhaps the city's most outstanding characteristic today is its tolerance in intellectual matters. Partly because of the influx of freethinkers who arrived in the German immigration that reached a peak around 1848, agnostics and atheists have not found the kind of hostility in Cincinnati that they have encountered in other American cities. One prominent freethinker was permitted to mount a sphinx indicating his doubts about a future life atop his family tomb in one of the city's leading cemeteries. In 1868 Alcander Longley published a journal called *The Communist* in Cincinnati.

In the hectic decades after the Civil War Cincinnati was as badly governed as any other Heartland city. Chief of Police Tom Snelbaker spent as much time supervising the risqué shows at his Vine Street Opera House as he did chasing criminals. George B. Cox, a saloonkeeper, rose to run the city as a Republican boss and genially gave interviews to the journalist Lincoln Steffens for his muckraking articles on city government.

Boss Cox was eventually succeeded by Boss Rud Hynicka, who often exercised control from New

A precedent-making design

A prototype of many modern skyscrapers *(below left)* was submitted by a Finnish architect, Eliel Saarinen, in a 1922 contest for a building to house the Chicago Tribune Company. Another design *(right)*, by John Mead Howells and Raymond Hood, won (Saarinen took second place) and became a Chicago landmark, but Saarinen's design had wide influence on architects of the day.

York City, headquarters of his burlesque interests. Municipal offices were filled with ward heelers and other incompetents, a few of them illiterate. As was generally the case throughout the Heartland, politics were thought "too dirty" for the better element. A number of businessmen made mutually profitable deals with the Hynicka machine, and most citizens, as elsewhere, concluded that there was no sense in fighting city hall. An occasional reform mayor was elected, but the reformers seldom had the time or talent to clean out the Augean stables of municipal government.

Yet reform was in the air. The city's rebirth began with the Cincinnatus Association, organized by a few public-minded citizens after World War I to discuss and act on city problems. They had what other reform groups had lacked, a tenacity of purpose that enabled them to harass the Hynicka machine year after year. When a machine-backed bond issue was defeated at the polls in 1923, the bosses retaliated by turning off street lights and otherwise cutting back on municipal services in the name of economy. The reformers then produced a new charter for Cincinnati, which established a city-manager system and provided for a city council, and the city's voters accepted the charter in 1925 by a 2-to-1 majority.

Cincinnati has been well governed ever since. During the Depression a New York reporter marveled: "What a town! Money in the bank. A balanced budget. A steadily decreasing bonded debt. Lowest tax delinquency in America. No defaults. . . . No deficits." The Charter Party—made up mostly of independents and dissident Republicans —contests control of the city council with the Democrats and the orthodox Republicans, normally the dominant party in Cincinnati. Although majority control has shifted from the Charterites to the Republicans, municipal policies remain largely unchanged. Cincinnatians seem agreed that they are best served by the city-manager form of government. They are not surprised that few other major U.S. cities have followed their lead. Since Cincinnati is unique, it naturally should be unusually governed.

The Heartland paradoxes are carried to the extreme in the Queen City. Its radicals are conservative, and its conservatives radical. An early merchant prince, Reese Evans Price, renounced his U.S. citizenship because he disapproved of the war with Mexico in 1846. Charles P. Taft II, a prominent Republican in a prominent Cincinnati Republican family that has given the nation a good President, William Howard Taft, and an outstanding Senator, Robert A. Taft, once submitted a report to the World Council of Churches that described both Communism and capitalism as inconsistent with the Christian way of life.

Cincinnati's industry is so diversified—it is the leading world producer of machine tools, playing cards and soap products—and so cannily run that the city seems almost depression-proof. Slumps affect Cincinnati much more slowly than the rest of the country. It is one of the few U.S. industrial cities that cherishes its past and its traditions. Plans for urban reconstruction continually collide with Cincinnati's stubborn refusal to change just for the sake of change. In the mid-1960s the heart of Cincinnati was almost totally demolished to provide for renewal, and the Queen City plans further development. But the downtown scheme provided for the retention of the city's beloved Fountain Square, with its ornamental bronze-and-porphyry monument that was brought from Germany in 1871 by Henry Probasco as a memorial to his brother-in-law, Tyler Davidson. Much of what has always been handsome and civilized in the old Cincinnati will remain, as well as the tolerant attitude that finds Protestants and Jews joining Roman Catholic pilgrims in the annual Good Friday ascent to the monastery atop lovely Mount Adams.

Chicago and Cincinnati represent the poles of Heartland cities. Between the poles lie the dozens of others that survived the threats of Indians, wars, droughts, and disasters both financial and natural. The noontime carillon of the Old Stone Church sounds over the statuary and flower beds of Public Square in Cleveland while, 65 feet below in the grimy trough of the Cuyahoga, long, low ore freighters twist and turn along the tortuous river. Detroit, with its two business districts set down with apparent absent-mindedness a few miles from each other, is a city of many homes and even more automobiles and one that probably contains more public-spirited men and women per square mile than any other. Indianapolis sits flat on the prairie, with the brisk wind whipping along Pennsylvania Avenue and flags snapping on poles beside the grandiose plinth of the War Memorial. Milwaukee is serenely busy on its bluff overlooking the sun-dancing water of Lake Michigan and the smoky haze of the industrial valley of the Kinnickinnic. Between them, the thriving cities of the Heartland have brought to reality the prediction made three centuries ago by Father Louis Hennepin, who foresaw that the region would produce "an infinite number of considerable towns" that would establish "an inconceivable commerce."

His city's undisputed leader for more than a decade, hard-driving
Richard J. Daley has been called "the best mayor Chicago ever had."
Behind him is one of the monuments to his bold campaign for civic
betterment, the University of Illinois' new Chicago Circle campus.

The leaders
who build cities

Cities—unlike other political subdivisions,
which are for the most part merely designations
of territory—owe their existence primarily to
man's presence. Men choose the site and begin
building, and each generation must continue to
build—and rebuild. Men decide the direction
cities take, and for more than a century
exceptional Heartlanders have stepped forward
to lead their cities. Some of these leaders have
been exceptionally bad—scoundrels who put
personal ambition first—but most have been
selfless and dedicated. Today almost all the
region's cities are undergoing a transformation.
Led by elected officials and men of the church,
by industrialists and labor organizers, they are
reaching for new heights—literally, in the form of
soaring buildings; and figuratively, in tangible
efforts to improve the lot of their inhabitants.

119

1   Enormously wealthy Mrs. Potter Palmer (1849-
    1918) reigned over Chicago's social set for 40 years.

2   Julius Rosenwald (1862-1932), of Sears, Roebuck,
    seen with his wife, was a noted philanthropist.

3   Marshall Field III (1893-1956) founded *The
    Chicago Sun* in 1941 to combat the *Tribune*.

4   William Hale Thompson (1869-1944), known as
    "Big Bill," was a colorful mayor for three terms.

5   Colonel Robert R. McCormick (1880-1955)
    published the *Tribune* from 1914 until his death.

6   Aaron Montgomery Ward (1843-1913), mail-order
    innovator, fought for civic improvements.

7   Philip D. Armour (1832-1901) made his millions
    by selling pork at a 100 per cent markup.

David Kennedy, standing in the plaza of Chicago's striking new Civic Center, has two important roles: he is a key financial adviser to Mayor Daley, and he is board chairman of the Continental Bank, which underwrote the bond issue for the center.

Chicago: the aggressive "I Will" city

If any city deserves the motto "I Will," it is Chicago. With its overlay of broad freeways, its border of parklands and beaches, and its imaginatively designed skyscrapers, Chicago seems to deny the difficulties of its birth and the problems that accompanied its growth. Chicagoans built their city on swampland; raised it to avoid a muddy death; reconstructed it after a holocaust that left a third of the population homeless; and bequeathed it an unmatched combination of port, railroad and airline facilities. Some of those whose names are indissolubly linked with Chicago's eventful history are pictured opposite. Today, having survived an era of underworld rule and governmental corruption, the city still looks to the future and says, "I Will."

One of the ablest railroad executives in the nation, Ben W. Heineman,
president of the Chicago and North Western Railway, gained
his reputation by making commuter service efficient and profitable
—a feat that has immeasurably aided Chicago's business community.

In the world's most modern police communications center,
Superintendent Orlando W. Wilson visits the men on duty.
Wilson's system has cut to 15 seconds the time needed to dispatch
a police car; in 1965 Chicago was able to boast a reduction in crime.

magination and talent
or a bold new renaissance

Chicago's climb to importance has been based on more than its size or its unusual location, and it is urrently undergoing a revival that has been compared to the renaissance that followed the Great ire of 1871. To many people, the undisputed leader of this revival has been Richard Daley (*see page 19*), who began serving as mayor in 1955. Urbanrenewal projects are steadily erasing some of the ity's worst slums, and the new Civic Center, housing courtrooms and government agencies, provides a handsome municipal focus. In a broad plaza fronting the Civic Center, an airy 50-foot sculpture by Pablo Picasso is a significant sign of the city's realization that it must take a more active role in promoting and sustaining the arts. Similarly, the $150 million new University of Illinois campus marks the increased interest in advancing higher education. There have been many other improvements, including an efficient commuter service (*above*) and a major overhaul of the formerly corruption-ridden police force (*far left*). In each case, Chicago has been able to call in the help of its citizens, who number some of the liveliest brains in the country.

arol Fox, the woman who brought opera back to Chicago, confers ith an assistant at the Lyric Opera. Distressed because the city ad been without a grand-opera company for several years, Miss ox founded her group in 1952, and it now ranks with the best.

"The man who built Detroit," Albert Kahn (1869-1942) designed factories for every major auto company.

Walter Chrysler (1875-1940) moved his small company past established giants to join the "Big Three."

A charter member of the Baseball Hall of Fame, Ty Cobb (1886-1961), of the Detroit Tigers, set 90 records.

An expert in auto assembly, William Knudsen (1879-1948) helped make Chevrolet the biggest car producer.

Detroit: a new image for the auto's town

The center of the automobile industry, Detroit was until recently one of the least prepossessing cities in the Heartland. Its setting—much of it faithfully reflecting Detroit's grim factory-town past—helped explain the city's record of poor relations between races. But Detroit is rapidly changing, largely because of the efforts of labor and industry leaders and of the man who became mayor in 1962, Jerome P. Cavanagh. Welding together the efforts of many groups, Cavanagh helped the city to move purposefully in securing equal opportunity for Negroes and in promoting cultural affairs. Today, a new and forward-looking Detroit is rapidly coming into being.

A leading developer of Michigan's first atomic-power plant, Walker L. Cisler, of Detroit Edison, sits in the plant's control room. The plant's reactor, the largest of its kind in the world, uses uranium not only to generate electricity but to create plutonium as a by-product.

An enlightened art patron, Mrs. Edsel Ford attends the opening of a new wing of the Detroit Institute of Arts. Mrs. Ford, shown here with Mayor Jerome P. Cavanagh, has consistently supported the institute, and contributed one fourth of the wing's $3.8 million cost.

One of America's most influential labor leaders, Walter P. Reuther *(right, front)*, head of the United Auto Workers, marches in a Labor Day parade. The founder of Detroit's Citizens Committee for Equal Opportunity, he has been especially active in race relations.

Indianapolis: challenge to an old conservatism

Indianapolis is Indiana's state capital and its largest city. Yet its atmosphere is that of a small town, and its people like it that way. With no natural barriers to restrict it, Indianapolis has chosen to sprawl over as large an area as it needs; there are few high buildings. Its small-town character has given the city an outlook that is basically conservative, and municipal leaders have reflected this conservatism. Following World War I the Ku Klux Klan demonstrated openly and dictated the election of politicians up to U.S. senator. Another organization that has contributed to the city's conservative viewpoint is the American Legion, whose national headquarters is here. But today Indianapolis is changing. The privately financed James Whitcomb Riley Center, an urban-renewal project, has added several tall apartment buildings to the skyline. And the repeal in 1965 of an old law that forbade the acceptance of federal aid has opened the door to further rehabilitation efforts. Finally, the representatives of minority groups are being heard—and sometimes heeded.

A leader of the young, active, more liberal group in Indianapolis, Mrs. David Cook wor with a children's interracial group. She serves on many municipal committees concerned with social welfare and educatic

The "poet laureate of Indiana," James Whitcomb Riley (1849-1916), who wrote "The Old Swimmin' Hole," among other verses, chats in 1916 with a group of children outside his home in Indianapolis.

Known for his nostalgic *Penrod* trilogy, Booth Tarkington (1869-1946) won Pulitzer Prizes for two serious novels, *The Magnificent Ambersons* and *Alice Adams*.

Indianapolis' No. 1 citizen, Frank E. McKinney stands before the city's ornate war memorial. In the left background is the headquarters of McKinney's America Fletcher National Bank, through which he wields stron and progressive influence over civic affairs.

The Reverend James Armstrong *(center)* became concerned with urban renewal because of its effect on members of his congregation. Here he discusses relocation with two dispossessed residents and with James Beatty, a Democratic leader *(second from right)*.

Mark A. Hanna (1837-1904), of Cleveland, made money from coal, iron, shipping and banking. Politically powerful, he engineered McKinley's election as President.

The Van Sweringen brothers, M. J. (1881-1935) *(top)* and O. P. (1879-1936), railroad magnates, were prime movers in renovating downtown Cleveland in the 1920s.

Tom L. Johnson (1854-1911), a steel tycoon who served as reform mayor of Cleveland, fought for lower streetcar fares, better sanitation, and penal reform.

Former Secretary of the Treasury George M. Humphrey *(right)* is one of Cleveland's most respected citizens. Here he tours ore docks operated by a subsidiary of the M. A. Hanna Company, of which he is honorary chairman.

Louis Seltzer, who retired in 1966 after 38 years as editor of *The Cleveland Press*, reads his paper next to the fountains and park that flank the city's Erieview renewal project. The *Press* crusaded for the project and has backed a number of others like it.

Cleveland: an industrial city's cultural heritage

Founded in 1796, Cleveland was only a small town until the Civil War, when it became a key industrial center. Men like Mark Hanna and Samuel L. Mather reaped their fortunes from the burgeoning iron industry, and John D. Rockefeller founded the Standard Oil Company there. In time, such wealth was transformed by gifts into a public asset in the form of museums, theaters and concert halls, and today Cleveland can take pride in its cultural legacy.

Industrialist Cyrus Eaton, reputed to be worth more than $100 million, stands in Kirtland Hall of the Natural Science Museum, which he helped found. Continually active in civic affairs, Eaton has aided education on every level and has worked to create new parks.

129

Jacob Laubenheimer (1874-1936) was chief of Milwaukee's honest, efficient police for 15 years.

Victor Berger (1860-1929) led Milwaukee's Socialists in a reform of the city government.

Lucius Nieman (1857-1935), owner of the *Journal* for 53 years, crusaded against corruption.

Captain Fred Pabst (1836-190 wealthy beer baron, campaigne for the city's park system.

The only Negro in the Wisconsin legislature, Lloyd Barbee pickets with a Catholic priest on behalf of MUSIC—Milwaukee United School Integration Committee—of which he is chairman. Barbee has led school boycotts in attempts to end de facto segregation.

Milwaukee: the city that beer made famous

In the Heartland the mere mention of the word "beer" rarely fails to elicit the response "Milwaukee"—and vice versa. It was in 1840 that the city's first brewery began bubbling, and more than two dozen major firms, most of them owned and operated by German-Americans, subsequently located there. The industry is still an important one, but today Milwaukee, like other Heartland cities, boasts great economic diversity. And as in the other cities, a combination of businessmen—led by the brewers —and other civic-minded people have taken an active role in promoting the welfare of the community.

130

President of *The Milwaukee Journal*, Irwin Maier *(right)* looks over the front page in the paper's city room. The *Journal*, 80 per cent employee-owned, pursues a policy of civic involvement, and Maier often acts as a behind-the-scenes mediator in community disputes.

A community-minded brewery president, Robert Uihlein Jr., head of Schlitz, appears with an array of circus wagons that are used in the annual four-day Old Milwaukee Days celebration sponsored by the brewery. In addition, Schlitz sponsors free outdoor concerts.

7

Challenges Imposed by Success

Containing some 38 million people—a greater number than any other region of the United States, turning out more goods than any other region, ranking as one of the largest producers of food in the world, possessing an abundance of thriving cities, the Heartland is superlatively blessed. It is also, in consequence of these blessings, beset with all of the difficulties that today accompany progress. With urban deterioration and suburban sprawl, with despoliation and deterioration of natural resources, and with increases in population year after year, the Heartland faces virtually every problem plaguing every other region of the United States. In the main, like the nation at large, the Heartland is attempting to deal with those problems. In some areas its successes have been great; in others the region is only now becoming aware of the challenges progress has imposed on it.

For a long period the Heartland lived by the psychology of the American frontier; the past never happened and the inevitable reckoning of the future would never come. Anything old was certain

Carrying many kinds of waste, covered with a gummy oil slick and alive with bacteria, the Cuyahoga River pours pollutants into Lake Erie at Cleveland in a shocking manifestation of a problem the Heartland shares with the entire nation.

to be torn down; anything new was built for a quick return; whatever took long-range planning was left undone. From the beginning the Heartland has demonstrated the pioneer's ability to triumph over trouble. Chicago survived fire and typhoid fever. Cincinnati withstood cholera, insect plagues and floods. Detroit, once described by proud local citizens as "the most beautiful city in America," paid little attention to urban esthetics while putting the nation on wheels. Originally laid out on the plan of Washington, D.C., with broad, handsome avenues radiating out from circular plazas, Detroit, along the way to industrialization, impatiently superimposed a gridiron plan, to become one of the most confusing and esthetically unsatisfying cities in the nation. In the mid-1960s, however, the city began work on a long-range program that promised to restore to it a measure of beauty.

One reason for the long decline of the cities in the Heartland, as elsewhere, has been the fact that for many years a large number of their most energetic and able citizens have not lived in them. Most businessmen retreat to the suburbs when day is done. Only one of the top executives at Milwaukee's Marine National Exchange Bank, for example, lives in town, and a similar situation prevails in other Milwaukee business firms. Top Cincinnatians flee

argument and protest—a very large assumption indeed—it is by no means certain that Negroes want to be dispersed among white neighborhoods to the point where they become "absorbed." Even with open-occupancy laws, experts doubt that any widespread dispersal of Negroes will occur, if only because such a dispersal would cause Negroes to lose whatever political power they now possess—or may in the future acquire. It is axiomatic that the Negro wants what the white man wants—not only possessions but opportunity and options for his children as well as himself. If he can obtain them without all the heartache of attempting to move into a hostile white community, he may elect to establish communities of his own in which such amenities are available—as have other ethnic groups. James Downs, board chairman of the Real Estate Research Corporation of Chicago, points out that the Negro middle class is expanding as fast as is the middle class of any other ethnic group, and he believes that both Negro and white middle-class families share a similar objective: "To see to it that their children are segregated to their greater personal advantage.

"This is not," Downs explains, "from the point of view of race, but from the point of view of selecting their children's companions—separating them from bums, hoods, slum people and addicts. The major drive of families is not only to segregate their children from improper companions, but also from improper surroundings or environment." Downs was involved in the development of Lake Meadows, a high-rise apartment community intended for middle-class Negroes in the Negro section of Chicago's South Side. At first the Lake Meadows apartments that were intended for families with children went unrented, largely because the only grammar school in the neighborhood was attended solely by the children of underprivileged Negroes. When the city built a new school specifically for Lake Meadows residents, the vacant apartments were quickly filled.

Communities like Lake Meadows represent one approach to the problem of housing the urban Negro, but that approach by no means offers a universal solution. For some Negroes the problem is simply compounded. In the mid-1950s, for example, the trustees of the University of Chicago, whose South Side campus in the Hyde Park-Kenwood neighborhood was being surrounded by the expanding Negro ghetto, seriously discussed moving the entire institution to another Chicago location or even to another city because of the area's deterioration. But the university finally decided to stay where it was and to put its power and prestige behind efforts to halt the spreading blight in the neighborhood. The result was the almost total rehabilitation of the Hyde Park-Kenwood neighborhood. With federal funds, acres of ancient buildings were leveled, and town houses, 10-story apartment buildings and new shopping centers were constructed by private developers on the cleared land. Hyde Park-Kenwood is now about half Negro and half white, a middle-class and upper-middle-class neighborhood of great variety. However, the rehabilitation of the area was achieved at the cost of pushing lower-income Negro families out of it and farther into the city's dismal ghetto neighborhoods.

The ghetto problem is greater in Chicago than in any other Heartland city. In a 1964 study of 207 major municipalities, the sociologist Karl Taeuber concluded that Chicago is residentially the most segregated Northern city in the nation. He gave it a segregation index of 92.6, compared with an average of 86. The index means that to achieve residential integration in Chicago 93 out of every 100 Negroes then living in ghetto neighborhoods would have to move to predominantly white areas.

Within the Chicago ghetto neighborhoods 41 per cent of all housing units are dilapidated, deteriorating or lacking in plumbing facilities (the comparable figure for white neighborhoods is 18 per cent). Where plumbing facilities exist—to give one indication of the frustrations of life in the Negro slum—it is virtually impossible to have repairs made when breakdowns occur. Plumbers from nearby white neighborhoods invariably plead that they are occupied when called to a Negro home, and there are few Negro plumbers; neither in the Heartland nor elsewhere have Negroes managed to break through the color barriers of the craft unions. In the Negro neighborhoods rats abound; where there are no rats there are cockroaches.

Rats, cockroaches and leaky bathroom fixtures do not, however, constitute the real horror of the Negro ghetto. Horrors they are, but as the Reverend Martin Luther King, the militant leader of the nonviolent Southern Christian Leadership Conference, has observed, "the problem of the urban Negro is not slums but slumism." He defines slumism as an attitude of mind, a cult of despair and impotence imposed on the Negro community from without, which pervades body and spirit throughout every ghetto area in the nation.

In 1966 Dr. King and a group of his supporters launched an all-out attack on residential segregation in Chicago. There were marches and demonstrations; more important, King persuaded slum

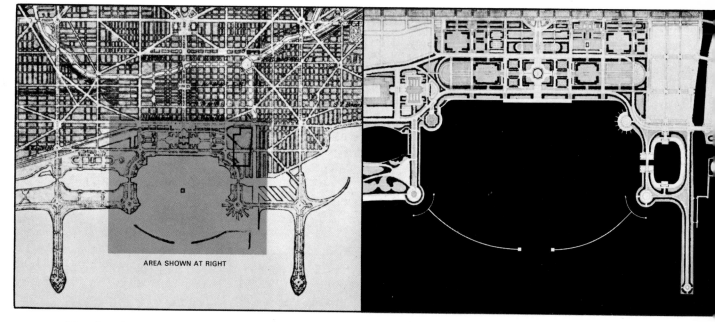

The plan that shaped Chicago

An outstanding example of farsighted planning in the Heartland was the 1909 Burnham Plan for Chicago, which set forth a coordinated scheme for the development of the city and surrounding land within a 60-mile radius. Proposed by the architect Daniel Burnham, the plan took as its focus Grant Park on the lakefront *(above left)*. It still shapes Chicago's growth: the city's 1966 plan for further development of Grant Park *(above right)* is almost identical to the original. Beyond the lakefront much of the old plan has also been kept.

dwellers to withhold the money they would normally have paid as rent to their landlords. With the funds, repairs to slum buildings were made and accumulated garbage and dirt were cleared out. King himself described the action as "supralegal," but the withholding of rents, coupled with the demonstrations, worked; after months of pressure, city officials and private realtors capitulated. All municipal and private bodies concerned with housing and real estate in Chicago signed a compact with King and his associates in which they pledged themselves to work for open occupancy throughout the city.

Under the compact the city's Housing Authority agreed that it would scatter its new housing projects throughout the city instead of concentrating them in Negro neighborhoods; the Chicago Real Estate Board, an association of real-estate agencies and brokers, withdrew its opposition to open occupancy and agreed to advise its members that they had a duty to comply with the city's fair-housing ordinance. "It's a historic day," said Mayor Richard J. Daley of the agreement. Initially, there were doubts that action would be taken to follow through on the compact, but a committee called the Leadership Council for Metropolitan Open Communities was presently formed to implement the agreement's provisions, and James W. Cook, president of the Illinois

Bell Telephone Company, was appointed the council's president.

Out of such developments arises a belief in the Heartland that it will come to terms with the Negro's efforts to win a place in the sun sooner than any other U.S. region. Stanford Williamson, a gifted designer of books for the Follette Publishing Company of Chicago, agrees. Owner of a house on East 48th Place, which he describes as "right on the buckle of the Black Belt," Williamson is a successful Negro who could easily leave the ghetto if he wished. "People here," he says, "are good at working things out. They're open-minded enough to know that the Negro only wants the same sort of thing they already have, that he doesn't want to take it away from them but just to enjoy the same thing."

That judgment about the Negro problem (or the white problem), which will remain the Heartland's and the nation's most pressing piece of domestic business for decades to come, may be excessively hopeful. But there is ample precedent for the belief that the region is "good at working things out." And the determination with which Heartlanders are attacking the problems of their long-deteriorating cities makes their optimism about the future understandable. In Chicago, for instance, ever since 1909 there has existed a master plan for the development of the city, created by D. H. Burnham, architect of the Chicago Planning Commission. From time to time over the years Chicago has taken certain steps to implement the plan, but progress has been slow. In recent years, however, the city has been moving rapidly within the general outline of the plan. One major step envisioned in the plan is the removal of the downtown elevated railway that delineates the Loop area. With the railway gone, the area would be more open to sky and air, and the new tall buildings that have recently been erected in the Loop would alternate with tree-lined plazas and be surrounded by a large residential area. Some new Loop structures, like the $95 million Hancock Center, combine offices with apartments, so that residents can commute to their work by elevator.

The Heartland city of the future may contain a number of small communities, each with its own identity—a curious throwback to the old ethnic neighborhoods that are now seen to have had something of value in their cohesive spirit, cultural unity, and distinctive customs and cuisines. What the ethnic neighborhoods offered naturally, new communities, lacking the bond of ethnic traditions, will have to create artificially. The planners intend to provide a variety of housing sufficient to meet all the changing needs of the life cycle of community dwellers. This would mean modest-sized apartments for newlyweds and small families, houses for growing families, and efficiency apartments for single persons and the elderly.

Bertrand Goldberg, architect of the 60-story Marina City on the Chicago River, believes that Chicago will become even more of "a city of communities" than it is today and that "there will certainly be a community in the downtown area."

Private citizens also see advantages in re-establishing cohesive communities in the Heartland cities. Handsome old frame houses in Cincinnati's Mount Adams section are being modernized internally and brightened externally with paint and flowers; German Village, a section on the South Side of Columbus, Ohio, was once a solidly German neighborhood, but now its unity comes from the care and dedication with which new homeowners are reclaiming the comfortable old brick houses. Householders in the old company-owned town of Pullman, now within Chicago's city limits, are restoring the community's turn-of-the-century architectural distinctiveness.

All of these actions are part of a general recognition that urban life will deteriorate unless there is forthright action. Edwin C. Berry of Chicago's Urban League says bluntly, "We can allow the city to commit suicide by doing nothing—or we can breathe new vigor into it." Charles A. Blessing, Detroit's official city planner, is in accord. He predicts that by the year 2000 Detroit will have grown northwest toward Lansing and Flint and west toward Ann Arbor, and that the population of the metropolis will number more than 11 million. Blessing shares the widely held belief that in so extensive an urban sprawl, human beings will tend to feel lost if all they see is a vast, dull, gray area that extends for miles without relief or variation.

With the enthusiastic backing of Mayor Jerome Cavanagh, Blessing in the mid-1960s spent more than $150,000 of the city's money to survey future needs and to build scale models of what the Detroit of the year 2000 could be. To enable its citizens to preserve a sense of identification with their city, he proposed organizing the future metropolis into three separate but interconnected areas, or subcities, that would flow out of and away from the present central business district on the Detroit River. One of these subcities would be the Woodward Corridor, which will stretch northwest from the present business district. The Woodward Corridor, which already houses the city's Public Library, Historical Museum and Institute of Arts, would be expanded as the cultural nucleus of all of Detroit, containing shops and small parks as well as a college, theaters, concert halls and additional museums. Flanking the corridor would be the two other subcities, Forest Park and University Park, each with its own public- and private-housing units to serve the needs of different economic and family groups. Both Forest Park and University Park would have community colleges to serve as cultural centers. The Woodward Corridor would serve as Detroit's overall focal point, linking the two other subcities with the downtown business district.

To build the Detroit of the 21st Century will cost something like one billion dollars, Blessing and his staff believe. They are well aware that neither the city nor the state, nor even both together, can pay for so mammoth a project. But, with assistance from the federal government, Detroit officials believe that rebuilding can go forward.

The citizens of the rural Heartland face problems as difficult as those found within the cities and their satellite towns. One area of concern, surprisingly, is agriculture. Today mechanization, scientific crossbreeding and feeding, and technological advances are making it possible for fewer and fewer farmers to produce increasing amounts of food. Only a quarter of a century ago all the Heartland states had more farmers than they have today; Michigan, for example, saw the number of its farms drop from 187,000 in 1940 to fewer than 110,000 in the mid-1960s. Those farmers who have survived are on the whole prosperous; what is happening is that smaller farmers are being squeezed out, for modern farmers not only need large amounts of capital to purchase the mechanized equipment necessary to compete in today's farm market, but they must also own farms that are large enough to make use of the equipment efficiently.

Even established dairymen are chronically in debt to pay for new equipment, from milk-cooling tanks and storage silos to tractors and forage harvesters— a form of reaper used today to gather feed for delivery to livestock that live indoors and never emerge to graze for themselves. It is estimated that a dairy farmer starting out from scratch would need close to $200,000 in capital. Lyman McKee, an agricultural expert and former president of the American Grange, has a 1,100-acre dairy farm outside Madison, Wisconsin, on which he also raises corn and hogs. He asks: "If a man has that kind of money, why would he want to be a farmer?"

McKee and others like him wonder where the next generation of farmers is coming from. McKee's farm, or at least its nucleus, has been in his family for three generations. It is worked by McKee and his brother William; another brother, Albert, got off the farm early and became a successful businessman in Chicago. There seems little likelihood that a fourth generation of McKees will be on the land. Lyman's son and nephews are not attracted to dairying, and he can see why: "Unless you love livestock, and love working all day long all week long, it's an impossible business." As nearby Madison continues to grow (the city's population climbed from 96,000 in 1950 to 160,000 in the mid-1960s), the McKee acres, instead of producing corn and cows, will probably sprout ranch houses.

Paradoxically, some of the earlier alterations of the landscape, made to create additional farmland, have resulted in the irretrievable loss of natural wonders. The great Kankakee Swamp originally covered 600,000 acres south of Lake Michigan in Indiana and Illinois. Several miles wide and some 60 miles long, it was bordered by a tangle of rushes and alders and dotted with small, tree-covered islands. In 1906 the draining of the vast swamp was begun. Gradually, and at great cost, the wild-rice fields, oxbow lakes and bayous were dried up. Over much of its course the Kankakee River today flows through a concrete-lined ditch, and the oaks, sugar maples, poplars and white pines that stood in the swamp are gone. What was gained was a flat valley

A bloodsucking sea lamprey dangles from a Great Lakes trout while its small, sharp teeth rasp a hole in the fish's side. The eel-like predators first entered the lakes in the 1920s, decimating the lake fish. Then in 1955 a compound was developed that killed lamprey larvae. This gave promise of eventual victory over the invader, but treatment of the lakes may take years.

floor with a rich, loamy soil that is today largely planted in corn and soybeans. Although parts of the old swamp are now preserved for wildlife, gone is a vast bird sanctuary, a superb fishing ground, and a valuable stretch of natural wilderness that once resounded to the croak of bullfrogs and the honk of wild geese.

The constant infringement of man on the land creates ever more pressing problems. Most of the rivers that run through industrial or urban areas are little more than open sewers. At Cleveland the Cuyahoga is so solid with refuse and debris that it can almost be walked on. The Great Lakes are close to becoming a disaster area. Only Lake Superior, deep and relatively remote from urban and industrial wastes, remains largely uncontaminated.

Lake Erie is being turned into a dead sea by what man is dumping into the rivers that supply it. The Maumee, for example, flows from Fort Wayne, Indiana, through Defiance, Ohio, and empties into the lake at Toledo. Along the way steel mills and glass-fiber companies dump carbolic acid into the stream, plating plants disgorge cyanide, and foundries deposit cinders and ashes on its surface. When its storm sewers overflow, Defiance gives the Maumee a dosage of raw sewage; at Toledo the river receives a final injection of city sewage as well as oil, metallic deposits and toxic materials from local industries. Ammonia compounds pour into the river via its tributary, the Auglaize, which is even more grossly polluted than the Maumee. A report issued by the U.S. Public Health Service states that "taste and odor problems are prevalent throughout most of the year in the water supplies at Defiance and Napoleon."

The unfortunate Cuyahoga, heavily loaded with disease-producing coliform and salmonella bacteria, also empties into Lake Erie. The Cuyahoga carries so much oil slick that it sometimes catches fire, and Cleveland has been forced to build firebreaks out into the water to deflect the flames from riverside industries.

In a 2,600-square-mile central section of Lake Erie, fish have disappeared and have been replaced by bloodworms, sow bugs, leeches and sludgeworms. The lake bottom is alive with weeds and algae. Senator Gaylord Nelson of Wisconsin observed in 1965 that the algae were "blooming in a tank of liquid fertilizer." The Senator claims that the algae are "sealing the lake's doom," and he may be right. Ecologists believe that when a body of fresh water has become infested with algae to the point that Lake Erie has, the life of the lake may be beyond saving. Some scientists actually think that the point of no return has already been reached in Lake Erie. Dense meadows of algae are also present at the southerly bend of Lake Michigan, from which Chicago takes its drinking water, and have become so thick that on occasion they have clogged the city's water-intake pipes. The pollution level is rising in Lake Huron as well.

The federal government, industry and the states are at last making efforts to attack the causes of contamination. Secretary of the Interior Stewart Udall urged support for a six-billion-dollar pollution-control program at a 1966 Cleveland conference. "My feeling is that Lake Erie is the big challenge," said Udall. "It is the best test case we have. If we can lick water pollution here in the next few years then we can lick it in the country at large."

Meanwhile a number of industries have acted on their own. U.S. Steel estimates that close to $200 million of its five-billion-dollar spending for capital improvements in the past 15 years has gone into air- and water-pollution control measures. A notion of the magnitude of these cleansing operations can be obtained in Gary, Indiana, where the water-treatment plants being built by U.S. Steel will be three times the size of the mill they will serve. Some air-cleaning towers will soar as high as 10 stories. Efforts like this have been spurred by the realization on the part of some businessmen that there can be profit in pollution control. A grain-elevator company in Maumee, Ohio, has installed highly efficient filtering devices to collect grain dust that was previously lost in the air. The recovered dust can be mixed into cattle feed for profitable sale. A partner in the firm said he expected the company to earn back the $750,000 cost of the equipment within a few years.

The Heartland, as usual, is sanguine about the prospects of licking large-scale pollution, and with some reason: it has met a similar problem before and helped find a solution. At the end of World War II the Ohio River was so badly polluted that fish could not live, nor people swim, in it. In 1948 eight states drained by the Ohio and its tributaries—Illinois, Indiana, Kentucky, Ohio, Pennsylvania, New York, West Virginia and Virginia—established an interstate authority entitled the Ohio River Valley Water Sanitation Commission, known generally as ORSANCO, with headquarters in Cincinnati. ORSANCO was empowered to issue antipollution orders on its own and to go to court to enforce compliance. Generally, however, it has acted through the member states and has obtained results by persuasion rather than by compulsion.

When ORSANCO began operations, fully 100 per cent of the sewage being discharged into the Ohio along its 981-mile course was raw and untreated. Today only 1 per cent is untreated. Fifteen years and close to one billion dollars were required to clean up the Ohio, but the river is now clean enough so that a city can make river water safe for drinking at reasonable cost and without adding so many chemicals that the taste changes. The Cincinnati Waterworks could not do that in 1944, but it could by 1964.

Progress has been almost as impressive in the disposal of industrial wastes. By 1966 fully 94 per cent of all the plants discharging wastes into the Ohio and its tributaries had installed facilities for processing them. What is perhaps most heartening about ORSANCO is that it represents cooperative action on a vital matter by the eight states concerned: the agency has had to go to Washington only to get federal approval of the interstate compact.

With the example of success on the Ohio, the Heartland is confident that as much can be done with the Great Lakes and such rivers as the Maumee and the Cuyahoga. This is a tall order, but the region has seldom been daunted by crises in the past. Indeed, the challenge of cleaning up the lakes and rivers is precisely the sort of difficult task to which the Heartland has always responded with vigor.

A young passenger disembarks at Greencastle's Monon Railroad Station, which was built in 1897. This line was once the town's principal link with Chicago; today most of its passengers are students. The railroad runs through four university towns.

A small town in a time of change

While the cities of the Heartland are in a state of flux, the small towns still seem to pursue a way of life long considered traditionally American. The land around the towns remains largely farm country; the county fair is still one of the year's main events. The many small colleges in the region are flourishing. Seeing buildings unchanged from the 1890s, observing the relaxed pace, a visitor to the town squares and railroad stations might imagine himself in the last century. Behind this placid exterior the towns are changing. Farming is no longer the dominant way of life. Industries are locating near the towns. The people are seeking new creative outlets. And like the cities, the towns are faced with problems of growth. Such a town is Greencastle, Indiana, located in Putnam County, southwest of Indianapolis, in the middle of the Heartland.

The Putnam County Court House *(left)*, the third on this site, dominates Greencastle's square. Some of the stores around the square have changed their façades very little since the 1800s, when most of them, and many of the town's houses, were built.

Interdependent parts that form a town's harmony

Greencastle is composed of many elements, out of which emerges the harmonious life of the town. One element is its business section, which, as in many Heartland towns, spreads around the town square. Another element is DePauw University. Its students make up a fourth of the town's present population of 10,000, which is almost twice what it was in 1950. Workers in factories, such as the Greencastle branch of International Business Machines, and farmers form other groups. Working to retain the harmony in the face of the recent growth are the town's leaders, some of whom are shown on pages 144-145.

udents, housewives and businessmen stroll
Washington Street, one of the four streets that make
the square, on a spring day. The telephoto lens
akes the street seem more congested than it actually is.

DePauw students take a break at The Fluttering Duck,
a café not far from the square, where DePauw
professors sometimes hold informal classes and student
entertainers frequently play jazz or read poetry.

143

DePauw University marshals Howard Youse *(left)* and Harry Hawkins lead a commencement procession. Like many colleges in the Heartland, the university was founded by a local church and has over the years educated many leading citizens of its town.

The president of the First Citizens Bank and Trust Company, Simpson Stoner discusses loans with an assistant. Stoner was born on a farm near Greencastle and was graduated from DePauw. He is the chairman of the local Industrial Development Committee.

The president of Greencastle Federal Savings and Loan, Ernest Collins inspects a house built with money from his institution. A city councilman, Collins is also active in the Greencastle Development Corporation, formed to maintain the downtown area.

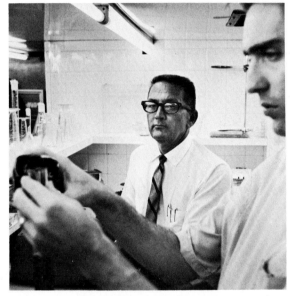

A druggist, Chester Coan (left) watches a pharmacist mix prescriptions in one of his two stores, which together employ 26 people. To help create new recreational facilities for the town, Coan was instrumental in getting a country club built in 1958.

A Greencastle real-estate and insurance broker, Charles Shuee (center) is also the county Democratic chairman. Like most Heartland towns, Greencastle holds Republican sentiments, but it is willing to switch. It voted for Lyndon Johnson in 1964.

Men who lead
their community

The chairman of the board of the Central National Bank of Greencastle, Fred O'Hair presides over a small committee meeting in the bank that his father helped found in 1883. O'Hair was a charter member of the Greencastle Development Corporation.

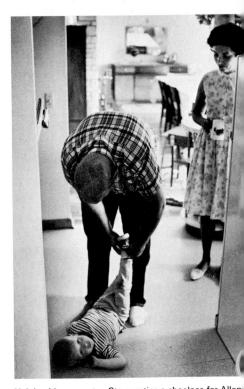

Helping his youngster, Stevens ties a shoelace for Allen Lee in the family kitchen. Stevens has just returned home from his job at IBM, and his wife, Martha Ellen, has supper waiting so that he can get into the fields.

To be with his son, Allen Lee, Stevens takes him along while tilling his fields, but the tractor's chugging lulls the boy to sleep. During the April-May cultivating season, Stevens usually spends seven hours a day on the tractor and works all night on weekends.

Resting a moment from their arduous round, the Stevenses sit on the porch of the three-bedroom house he and his father-in-law built in 1959. Like other farmers in the area combining farming with an industrial job, Stevens plans eventually to farm full time.

A young farmer struggling to maintain his land

Farmers throughout the Heartland are in a time of transition. Since World War II, soaring land prices and rising farm expenses have forced many farmers to leave the soil. Others whose love of the land is strong enough have attempted the difficult task of commuting daily to industrial jobs in nearby towns and cities and running their farms as well. Walter Stevens reflects this trend. He works from 7 a.m. to 3:30 p.m. at the International Business Machines' branch in Greencastle. Then he toils evenings and frequently all night on his 132-acre farm outside the town. He grows corn on 85 acres and raises Herefords on most of the rest, but the work involved is well worth the rewards, he feels. "I grew up on a farm," says Stevens. "Farming is born in you."

After running data-processing cards off a press, his usual job at the IBM plant, Stevens stacks them in cartons for shipment. He started work at IBM in 1956, the year he graduated from high school, and made his down payment on the farm in 1963.

Hearty Herefords are paraded for judging at the Putnam fair by members of the local 4-H Club. An organization strong throughout the Heartland, 4-H encourages youths to learn modern agricultural techniques and to assume civic responsibilities.

An annual display of farm products and spirit

In midsummer the people of Greencastle and the surrounding farmlands flock to the Putnam County Fair. Like such events throughout the Heartland, the fair is a combination of circus and school, with animal shows and educational displays intended to teach better ways of farming. Attendance is heavy during fair week, and understandably so. The county's residents in general welcome industry, but the working of the land remains their major interest.

Flower-show entries are displayed after the fair's judges have broken
the hearts of the losing growers. Prizes at fair events range
from 50 cents to $10. But there is no lack of entries for such titles
as loveliest girl or most-freckled child of Putnam County.

Crowds gather at the fair's popular horse and pony show.
Although county fairs in other Heartland towns hold horse races on
which bets may be laid, the Putnam fair has no facilities for
horse racing. Betting is prohibited by Indiana law.

149

Amateur actors from the Putnam County Playhouse put on a production of the *Wizard of Oz*. Organized in 1960, the playhouse plans four plays each summer, part of a trend in the Heartland to create cultural entertainment by local groups.

Members of the Moose Lodge dance to the music of a small band. Other dances are given periodically throughout the year at the country club and by various other social groups. Teenagers dance on Saturday nights at a local spot called the Blue Wolf.

A round of traditional social activities

Like people everywhere in the United States, Greencastle residents have such nationwide amusements as movies and television available to them. But they also pursue a round of social activities traditional in Heartland towns. Greencastle has no fewer than 20 churches, which hold "socials" and suppers, and more than 40 fraternal, social and service groups like the Optimists and the Elks, which offer lunches and other entertainments. In addition, the university presents a free symphony or other program each Wednesday evening, as well as plays throughout the year, to which the townspeople are invited.

Pies and cakes made by members of the First Christian Church grace the table at an annual barbecue *(right)*. More than 600 people belong to First Christian. It and Gobin Memorial Methodist, affiliated with DePauw, are Greencastle's leading churches.

8

A Many-faceted Character

A Midwestern Rip van Winkle, returning to the Heartland after an absence of several decades, would be startled by the changes. Only the great natural landmarks remain the same: the austere ranges of the north, the blue hump of the Baraboo hills in southern Wisconsin, the high bluffs of Mackinac Island, the Pictured Rocks along Lake Superior's shore, the Sleeping Bear Dunes bordering Lake Michigan, Tahquamenon Falls in Michigan's Upper Peninsula. Though crisscrossed now by superhighways, the wide prairie remains largely unaltered.

Everything else seems different—from the rebuilt and rebuilding cities to their ever-expanding suburbs to the steel mills and assembly plants sprawled across the cornfields. At night the once-dark countryside glows with the blue flowers of mercury-vapor lamps that go on at dusk in farmsteads at the command of an electric eye and go off at daybreak. Curiously, the Indian, who departed so long ago, has returned. The 1940 census found only about 400 Indians in Chicago, but today they number

more than 10,000 and have their own American Indian Center in the city, complete with a salaried, non-Indian director.

The pace of the place has stepped up. The people of the Heartland have always been mobile, but never so much as in recent years. A Wilmette, Illinois, housewife found that in one three-year period she had five different next-door neighbors. Of six newly arrived families in another suburb, one had just returned from Tokyo, another was fresh from Peru, a third was back in the Heartland after several years in New Jersey, and the remaining three had come from Michigan, Indiana and Florida.

Yet, in noting the more rapid tempo, our returning Rip van Winkle might recognize that some things have not altered in the slightest. Basically unchanged in the region is its tradition of helpful neighborliness. Newcomers arrive, but they are not ignored; there is scarcely a small city or a suburb without a local club whose sole purpose is to welcome, introduce and incorporate new families into the community. Neighborliness often goes to astonishing lengths—as in Mascoutah, Illinois, where a 38-year-old housewife was stricken with an incurable kidney disease. Her friends and neighbors raised $15,000 to buy an artificial-kidney machine; local carpenters, electricians and plumbers gave

Three cheerful waifs, children of Chicago's West Side slums, beam at the camera in Jane Addams' Hull-House in the 1920s. The settlement house became world-famous for its welfare work among thousands of the city's Irish, Russian, Italian and Polish immigrants.

Late in the 19th Century, three generations of a Central European family gather for a group portrait. In 1850, when the first federal statistics on immigration were compiled, 15 per cent of the region's residents were foreign-born, a proportion that was maintained through 1920 before it started to drop. Most newcomers were drawn by the industries and mills in the cities.

their time to build a basement room and install the device; a physician's wife baked salt-free bread for the invalid; and dozens of townspeople regularly drove to nearby St. Louis to give blood for the patient's weekly transfusions.

"Friendliness," in fact, is the word most often used in defining the Heartland character. The trait of neighborliness can be traced back to the days of the early settlers, when the difference between success and failure—and even between life and death—was community cooperation. In those days, when settlers were beset by dangers on every side, neighbors were both highly valued and eagerly sought. It was out of the cooperation and clash between people of different traditions that the character of the Heartland—which encompasses much more than simple folksiness—emerged. The earliest settlers were largely Yankees from New England and Scotch-Irish from the Upland South—probably two of the most disparate types in the U.S. The historian R. Carlyle Buley, in discussing the Northwest Territory, writes that "the American had the dual heritage of Puritanism with its desire to regulate the other fellow's conduct and of Scotch-Irish frontier individualism . . ." Cultural confusion was compounded by the fact that French *habitants* had already established themselves in the region and had

created a society that blended primitive simplicity and Continental sophistication. The French scandalized both the Yankees and the Scotch-Irish by the dances, card games and horse races with which they lightheartedly observed Sunday. In addition to giving the Heartland a needed gaiety, these River French—so called because they had settled primarily along the rivers—supplied considerable leadership: Pierre Menard became the first lieutenant governor of Illinois; Father Gabriel Richard of Michigan became the first, and only, Roman Catholic priest elected to Congress.

What the settlers did not bring to the Heartland was as important as what they did. The Yankees left behind them their New England class consciousness and their insistence on property qualifications for voting. The Scotch-Irish, though they were from the South, espoused neither slavery nor the Southerner's aristocratic code; in fact, many of them had migrated north to escape these institutions. One of the very few Heartland duels, for example, occurred at Belleville, Illinois, in 1820, when one William Bennett shot and killed a certain Alphonso Stewart. Bennett was arrested in Arkansas two years later, brought back to Illinois, tried, found guilty of murder and hanged—something that would not have happened in the South. His fate, observed a contemporary, "made duelling discreditable and unpopular" in Illinois.

From the various elements of Puritanism, Scotch-Irish individualism and French sophistication developed a society with a strongly egalitarian bent. Heartland society has never jelled sufficiently to produce rigidly fixed classes—a man or a family could rise with astonishing speed and fall with equal celerity. Thomas Ford, the third Governor of Illinois, is a case in point. His father disappeared when he was three and he was raised in grinding poverty in Illinois, yet he managed to attend Kentucky's Transylvania University. Ford served in Illinois judicial offices before being elected governor in 1842. Yet his two sons, Seuel and Thomas, who had every advantage their father had lacked, were hanged as horse thieves in Kansas.

As the years went on, additional groups of settlers reached the region from Europe. The first large wave was chiefly English, Scottish, Irish, German and Scandinavian, and it was followed by an even greater inundation of Italians, Greeks and Eastern Europeans. This surge of newcomers caused surprisingly few modifications in the Heartland character; the immigrants were virtually recast in the Heartland mold, becoming egalitarian-minded and convinced that they were as good as the next man.

EDWARD EGGLESTON

One of the nation's pioneers in both realistic fiction and social history was a Heartlander, Edward Eggleston, whose first book, *The Hoosier School-Master,* was based on his youthful experiences in southern Indiana. The woodcut above, captioned "First acquaintance with Flat Creek," is an illustration from the book, which, published in 1871, described a naïve teacher's adventures in a crude backwoods community. Eggleston, who was born in 1837 in the southern Indiana town of Vevay, went on to write other novels, and spent the last years before his death in 1902 on a social history of the U.S. With his emphasis on the common people, he influenced other writers and historians, but he is best remembered for his first book, which has never gone out of print.

The English observer Lord Bryce thought this 19th Century process of amalgamation to be "the most distinctively American part of America." Since the amalgamation took place on so widespread a scale in western America, Lord Bryce believed that the West, of which the Heartland was of course then considered a part, contained the national essence, that it was the area "where those features which distinguish America from Europe come out in the strongest relief."

Paradoxically coexisting with the neighborliness and the egalitarianism, however, was an element of suspicion and distrust. There was a time when the racial antagonisms of Europe reappeared in the Heartland. The Irish were antagonistic to the English; the Dutch cold-shouldered the Belgians; the Poles and the Ukrainians did not particularly like each other but both detested the Russians; the Germans retained a low-grade animosity toward the English, French and Poles. A Roman Catholic bishop of Cincinnati, who was of German descent, refused to solemnize a marriage between Clara Longworth, an Episcopalian and a member of one of Cincinnati's most prominent families, and the Roman Catholic French Count Aldebert de Chambrun on the grounds that he was opposed to all "mixed marriages"—and, besides,

Frenchmen were "rotten and immoral." Miss Longworth and the count were eventually married by an archbishop from out of town.

In only one area did the immigrants add weight to a native conviction—in their tendency toward isolationism. Many of the people who had originally come to the region were descendants of Europeans who had left the Old World to build a better life in the New; some had fought to free America from European control in the Revolutionary War. These settlers, situated about 700 miles from the Atlantic, were naturally apathetic toward foreign affairs and were especially wary of European entanglements. The immigrants who came to the Heartland in later years were also in flight from the troubles of Europe, yet they held sentimental feelings about their former homelands, and they carried old prejudices to the New World with them. Particularly in the early years of World War I, the millions of Heartlanders of German descent were understandably reluctant to see the U.S. become involved in a war against Germany. They had the support of other millions of Irish descent, who had little enthusiasm for a war they saw as only an effort to bail England out of trouble. Some historians feel, incidentally, that the celebrated isolationism of the Heartland was based as much on lingering ethnic

Fairgoers promenade around the Court of Honor in Chicago's epochal World's Columbian Exposition of 1893. Intended to commemorate the 400th anniversary of Christopher Columbus' 1492 voyage, the fair was so complex that its construction took a year longer than scheduled. The Midway featured gambling halls, restaurants and entertainments from around the world, as well as the world's first Ferris wheel. In the exposition center were displays from every state in the Union and from many nations. The most enduring influence of the fair, however, was its architecture. The exposition's buildings, in classical Greek style, set the tone of American civic architecture—post offices, railroad stations and other public structures—for 50 years.

animosities as on the area's geographic remoteness.

Today, most of these old tensions have faded. Intermarriage is so common that many Heartlanders can trace a dozen racial strains in their ancestry—including Indian. The poet Kenneth Rexroth, born in South Bend, Indiana, says he is part German, part River French, part Irish, part Huron Indian and, perhaps, part Negro on the Indian side.

The continual Heartland mix is evident in wedding announcements and obituary notices. When Andrew Pavlacka of Chicago died, in 1966, he left, in addition to his widow and five sons, four daughters whose married names were Knutson, Jurkiewicz, Bassett and Tocik. Leo A. Ruswick, also of Chicago, was survived by his widow, Rose; three daughters whose married names were Tomiello, Stolz and Fattori; four sons; and two sisters, Mrs. Pearl Wilmington and Mrs. Celia Szymanski.

Most third- and fourth-generation Midwesterners have little interest in their ancestral country except as a place of fond remembrance or as a source of ethnic jokes. This is not to say, however, that origins have been forgotten. There is some lamentation for "the good old days" of ghetto existence. A Chicagoan of Greek descent fondly recalls the old Greektown section, southwest of the Loop, which has been bulldozed out of existence to make way for the Chicago campus of the University of Illinois. He regrets the disappearance of the old coffeehouses, which excluded women, and of the street vendors who sold such Hellenic delicacies as calves' heads seasoned with garlic and freshly ground oregano. The children and grandchildren of Greektown have scattered to the suburbs and are now somewhat saddened that their own children have never seen a slum or residential streets that are crowded, or known the heady joys and terrors of fights with gangs of Irish and Italian kids.

Ethnic islands evoking the European origins of such peoples have survived outside the large cities. Monroe, in southern Wisconsin, is so self-consciously Swiss in ancestry that the coats of arms of the Swiss cantons adorn the courthouse square. Tiny Washington Island, Wisconsin, lying on Lake Michigan's Green Bay, is still primarily Scandinavian; the towns of Hancock and Houghton, both in Michigan, are predominantly Finnish. Ethnic islands are so common in the Midwest that its people are unaware that such communities are unusual elsewhere in the United States, perhaps because the men and women of these towns and villages are so markedly Midwestern American—but with certain unusual characteristics. Swiss Monroe, for example, won the 1965 Wisconsin high-school basketball championship, and was cheered to its victory by coeds in Swiss costumes chanting in pure Midwestern accents.

People of all classes and groups, in fact, seem united in the intensity of their devotion to basketball, which seems almost a part of the regional character. The game is a Midwestern madness and each town is deeply involved in the fortunes of its team. When Michigan City's Red Devils reached the final round of the 1966 Indiana tourney, the mayor dyed his beard red, and the sympathetic magic seems to have worked, for Michigan City won. A high-school field house sometimes seats more than a town's population—and needs to, because the sport draws enormous and sharply partisan crowds. The intensity of feeling has its unpleasant side: following a poor season, a basketball coach at the Manitowoc, Wisconsin, high school was hounded from his job by a barrage of menacing letters and phone calls.

Other sports receive similar zealous attention, and some observers believe that the violent aspect of the Heartland character is reflected in the style of play of its professional football and hockey teams. In these two strenuous sports, the Chicago clubs—the Bears and the Black Hawks—have a reputation as the kings of mayhem. The Bears were long

dubbed the "Monsters of the Midway" (referring vaguely to an avenue in Chicago near which other football teams used to play) and are owned and coached by George Halas, a strong-willed individualist who was a rough-tough end in his own playing days and has always by choice hired players in his own pugnacious image. A mighty Chicago Bear fullback of the 1930s, Bronko Nagurski, is reputed to have been the toughest man ever to play the game.

The Heartland teams are pre-eminently exponents of size and power. The Green Bay Packers have dominated the National Football League's Western Conference in recent years and carry with them the hopes of the entire state of Wisconsin, especially in encounters with their traditional rivals, the Chicago Bears. The tactics of the Detroit Lions and the Cleveland Browns are also based on a bruising ground game. One curious sports anomaly, however, is Indiana, which is the only Heartland state that does not field a major professional team in any sport.

A further characteristic of Heartlanders past and present is their strange sense of being under siege, with an accompanying urge to lash out in retaliation. Despite the region's contemporary political and economic power, it frequently seems to feel it

Two years after the 1893 Chicago exposition had glorified classic architecture, a vehemently antitraditionalist architect named Frank Lloyd Wright opened his first office, in Oak Park, Illinois. Many of Wright's highly original ideas were formed under the tutelage of the architect Louis Sullivan. Among Wright's most noted contributions was the "prairie house," exemplified by the Robie House *(below)*, built in Chicago in 1908. The then-radical style—low silhouette, great overhanging eaves, open interiors—was designed to harmonize with the Midwest's flat topography while providing protection against the weather. Wright, who died in 1959, lived to see his concepts embodied in much of modern U.S. architecture.

FRANK LLOYD WRIGHT

THE ROBIE HOUSE

must scare the rest of the nation half to death. From the Democratic Presidential candidate William Jennings Bryan to the Right-Wing Republican Senator Joseph R. McCarthy, a long succession of characters has emerged from the Heartland to spread panic throughout the land, especially in the East. An Ohio reformer, Jacob Coxey, led a ragtag army of unemployed men on Washington in the 1890s, giving the country both a fright and a phrase —"Coxey's Army" came to mean an undisciplined crew haphazardly setting out to demand its own reforms in the body politic.

Although historians agree that the voice of the Midwest has been "a voice of protest," there is little agreement as to what, precisely, the region has protested against. The Heartland speaks loudly, with many voices—and sometimes the same voices say different things. Before World War II the Republican Senator Arthur Vandenberg of Michigan called for nonentanglement in European affairs; after the war Vandenberg was one of the Senate's most active advocates of American aid to Europe. Senator Robert Taft of Ohio, also a Republican and a prewar isolationist, backed U.S. participation in the United Nations. Long regarded as the country's leading conservative, Taft also fought in the late 1940s for expanded social security measures and for federal aid to education.

True to its individualistic tradition, the Heartland refuses to be politically predictable. Most of the big cities tend to be Democratic, while the small towns and suburbs are Republican; the states can go either way in national elections. Voters like those in Wheaton, Illinois, will elect a Right-Wing mayor and later saddle him with liberal councilmen.

Nonconformism seems endemic to the region. Paul Percy Harris, who founded Rotary in 1905, was far from being the quintessence of conventional middle-class behavior that his organization has come to symbolize. On graduating from college at 23 he gave himself five years in which "to study life in as many cities as possible," and successively worked as a reporter in San Francisco, an actor in Denver, a cowboy on the plains, a hotel clerk in Florida and a marble salesman in the South. He then extended his study of life to Europe by working his way across the Atlantic on a cattle boat. Harris' wanderlust was not unusual in the Heartland, whose people have often wanted to see beyond the next ridge. Warren Wheaton, one of the founders of Wheaton, Illinois, in the 1830s, roamed the land each fall when the summer's work was done. Setting out from his cabin, which was so remote that from his doorway he could see only two

plumes of smoke rising from neighbors' chimneys, he made his way on foot or by stage to such distant points as St. Louis, Missouri, or Dubuque, Iowa, and to most of the towns in Illinois.

The struggle to get to the top and to stay there has been fought with a savage zest by the Heartland's individualists. In writing of Frank A. Cowperwood, his archetypal Heartland businessman, Theodore Dreiser gave him the motto, "I satisfy myself." Once arrived at the top, men did not hesitate to take advantage of their position. The region was virtually a fiefdom for the 19th Century railroad barons in their great days. The owners of a Wisconsin railway admitted that in a single year in the 1870s they paid $50,000 to the governor, $10,000 each to the state comptroller and a first secretary, and a total of $125,000 to 13 legislators.

Despite their individualism, the people of the Midwest have historically looked to the federal government for help. As with other regions, their land was sold cheaply to them by the government, the U.S. Army protected them as they settled in, the railroads were built by government subsidy, and Washington governed the region until its states were ready to join the Union. But in perhaps no other part of the country is the federal government viewed with such suspicion as in the Heartland;

The Chicago writers

Starting about 1910, a number of famous and soon-to-be-famous writers, some of them shown at right, came to Chicago and fostered what historians later termed the city's literary renaissance. The writers frequented the same restaurants, clubs and bookstores, and were sometimes referred to as "the 57th Street colony," for a South Side quarter where they occasionally gathered. Many published in Chicago magazines, such as Harriet Monroe's *Poetry*, which began appearing in 1912, and Margaret Anderson's *Little Review*, which was founded in Chicago in 1914 but moved to New York in 1917. Much of what they wrote was concerned with Chicago and the Heartland, which they glorified and vilified by turn, but with an eye for sociological detail. However, about a decade after the movement started, many of the writers left the area. Despite its short life, this group left such classics as Masters' *Spoon River Anthology*; Anderson's *Winesburg, Ohio*; and Sandburg's *Chicago Poems* as well as Hecht's short stories; poems by Lindsay, such as "Abraham Lincoln Walks at Midnight"; and essays by Dreiser showing the promise that would later result in the novel *An American Tragedy*.

CARL SANDBURG

for years the anti-Washington fulminations of the late Colonel Robert R. McCormick filled the pages of the *Chicago Tribune*.

On the state level, political power becomes increasingly diffused in the region. Roger Branigin, the brisk and intelligent Governor of Indiana during the mid-1960s, noted that power is seldom centered in a single person. Branigin numbered as many as 25 separate power blocs functioning in his own state, ranging from the teachers' associations to the mental-health bloc, and from the Farm Bureau—"though it doesn't speak for all the farmers"—to the American Legion—"though it's weaker than before."

The Governor's attitude toward his electorate —a sort of affectionate irritation—is very common among Heartland politicians. Indianans, he has said, "have an ability to see sin at a distance but never at their very feet. Indianapolis is shocked by vice in East Chicago; Bloomington is horrified by what goes on in Terre Haute or South Bend, and so on."

The Heartland has a lively sense of self-derision. Stillman's Run, in northern Illinois, is not a creek but the site of an encounter in 1832 between a handful of Black Hawk's Indian braves and a party of Illinois militia whose commander, Major Isaiah Stillman, led their panicky flight from the field. Battle Creek, Michigan, commemorates a ferocious combat between two Indians and a couple of American surveyors in which no one was badly injured. A folk saying describes a hick town as "anything smaller than the town you live in." The Society of Midland Authors, an organization headquartered in Chicago, is sometimes called the "Society of Middling Authors" by its members.

Such a wisecrack is unfair to the writers of the region, although many of them take a wry delight in it. Literary accomplishment has been substantial. William McGuffey began a trend toward popularizing the classics with his *Eclectic Readers*. Bestsellers dripped from the pen of General Lew Wallace, author of such romanticizations of history as *Ben-Hur*. Edgar Rice Burroughs, perennially popular, brought a fund of misinformation about Africa and anthropology to fascinating life in the pages of the Tarzan series. But the highly successful Booth Tarkington did seem to say something meaningful about what boys were made of in *Penrod* and *Seventeen*. The Heartland has supplied deeper and more probing writing in the stories, sketches, novels and commentaries of Hamlin Garland, Theodore Dreiser, Thorstein Veblen and John

EDGAR LEE MASTERS

BEN HECHT

VACHEL LINDSAY

SHERWOOD ANDERSON

THEODORE DREISER

Dos Passos. The litany of Heartland writers includes such giants as Sherwood Anderson, a some-time paint-plant manager; Edgar Lee Masters, a lawyer turned poet; and Carl Sandburg, who experimented with a number of occupations before becoming the unofficial poet laureate of the prairie.

In the 1920s H. L. Mencken noted that all of America's top contemporary authors sprang "from the Middle Empire that has Chicago for its capital." Many of them, like Ring Lardner and Ernest Hemingway, chose not to remain in their native region. However, at one Manhattan cocktail party some years ago, a New Yorker grew restive as a group of expatriate Ohioans recited praises for their state. He asked, "Look here, if Ohio's such a great state, why the hell didn't all of you stay there?" The late James Thurber replied, "Well, you see, out there the competition is too tough."

The Heartland's Negro authors are as articulate at its white ones. From Paul Laurence Dunbar of Dayton to Gwendolyn Brooks of Chicago, the names of Negro poets and writers have bulked large in the Midwest. Of Chicago's Willard Motley, the novelist Nelson Algren writes: "He was a Negro and a writer but he was not a Negro writer." In the 1940s, after the success of Motley's *Knock on Any Door*, "Motley afforded Bohemia a brief revival in his big house on Wells Street," Algren has noted. "Though its decor was literary, its climate was languid and its tone one of acquiescence to everything."

For both white and black writers, the old Chicago Bohemia has surrendered, like so much else, to the new affluence. Such Negro authors as Lerone Bennett Jr. appear in the glossy pages of *Ebony*. There seem to be very few Heartland writers, white or Negro, scribbling in garrets today. New authors like Harry Mark Petrakis and Charles Newman are more likely to be working by day in universities or business organizations and writing by night.

While it is true that many of the Heartland's poets and authors have felt compelled to leave for more congenial surroundings, the region has been generally kind to working journalists. The early newspapers were both vituperative and popular. Travelers repeatedly noted that the typical Heartland posture was that of a man tilted back on the hind legs of a chair, his nose in a newspaper. An Indiana editor, laying down the aims of his new journal in the 19th Century, stated: "Politically, we shall be independent; on all other matters we shall endeavor to tell the truth." Chicago's *Inter-Ocean* was blunter in its slogan: "Republican in everything; independent in nothing."

In the early decades of this century, Chicago

Two men and a university

The University of Chicago, a top-ranked school almost from the moment it opened, was established by two unusual men, multimillionaire John D. Rockefeller *(above center)* and educator William Rainey Harper *(right)*. The partnership began in 1888 when Rockefeller suggested that Harper, then a professor at Yale, start a Baptist college. Harper delayed until Rockefeller would agree to underwrite a full university. When the institution opened in 1892, it had 742 students from 33 states and 15 foreign countries, a graduate school and a highly trained faculty. Rockefeller and Harper not only created an excellent school but introduced many innovations; among them were courses for women, as in the wood-carving class at right, when most colleges were for men only. The university also pioneered in adult education and had one of the first graduate schools for social work.

produced the stereotype of the American newspaperman—cynical, wisecracking, incapable of surprise, yet sentimental and endowed with a heart of gold. Those who should know insist that every character and every event in the hard-boiled 1928 play by Charles MacArthur and Ben Hecht about Chicago newsmen, *The Front Page*, was totally true to life. The best journalists spoke out frankly on the folly and foolishness of their time. Finley Peter Dunne's Mr. Hennessy observed: "We're a gr-reat people," to which Mr. Dooley replied, "We ar-re . . . An' th' best iv it is, we know we ar-re." Ambrose Bierce put into words another Heartland cynicism when he described a Conservative as "a statesman who is enamored of existing evils, as distinguished from the Liberal, who wishes to replace them with others." Herman Fetzer of Ohio, who wrote as Jake Falstaff, has been unjustly forgotten and reads with much the same wit and immediacy today as he did in the 1930s. "There's only one thing for Chicago to do," he once observed, "and that's to move to a better neighborhood."

The consistent cutting edge of Heartland journalism is as evident today in the work of Chicago's Mike Royko and Len O'Connor as it was before in that of Jack Malloy and Lionel Moise. One of Royko's finer conceits in his *Chicago Daily News*

column was his proposal for the celebration in 1966 of a Chicago "Hit Festival" on the occasion of the city's 1,000th gangland slaying. Noting that Chicago was only nine short of the 1,000 mark, Royko urged that preparations be made for the festival—including, perhaps, a fireworks display at Soldier Field, complete with exploding cars.

There is a popular view that the Heartland is anti-intellectual and far more interested in facts than in abstractions. Moreover, as the historian Daniel Boorstin has noted, the practical organizer has certainly been triumphant in Heartland society. Midwestern authors like Theodore Dreiser have buttressed this theory with scathing accounts of Heartland life. But the region has by no means been intellectually barren, and it has consistently produced men and women of genius and vision who have helped redirect the national culture. For this the region's schools and universities can take much credit. Admittedly, many of these institutions in the early days were less culturally oriented and tied more closely to the needs of the people than were those of the East: Purdue University, for instance, taught farmers to raise peppermint, onions and potatoes in the black mucklands of northern Indiana that had been thought worthless; now Purdue is working closely with such steel cities

as East Chicago in an effort to help solve their monumental civic problems.

But today the colleges and universities are also throwing a wider net and serve not only their own areas with intellectual distinction but also the nation and the world. The University of Chicago, once noted as a Big Ten football power, years ago began concentrating more and more on scholastic matters to enhance its standing as one of the most prestigious centers of higher education in the country, and in 1939 dropped intercollegiate football altogether. Lake Forest College, attractively situated on a wooded bluff above Lake Michigan, was for decades a small Presbyterian institution drawing its students almost exclusively from northern Illinois villages and towns. Today it pays high salaries to attract an excellent faculty, and of the 1,290 students at Lake Forest in 1966 only a third were from the five states of the Heartland. The rest were drawn from 37 other states and from 27 foreign countries.

Historically, women have been the custodians of culture in the Heartland. For nearly a century most men simply did not have the time—they were too busy building, tearing down and rebuilding. Philip Armour spoke for a generation of self-made millionaires when he said that his culture was "in my wife's name." The men are more involved now, but women still contribute the greater share of volunteer cultural effort for they seem to have a limitless passion for self-improvement in the arts, or for anything else that lifts them above the level of being "just housewives." It is a rare woman of the Heartland middle class who does not belong to a worthy study group of some kind.

Women have often been the Heartland's conscience as well. Mary McDowell, who became director of the University of Chicago Settlement House in the 1890s, frequently mediated the conflicts between the packing-house owners and their workers, and became known as the "Angel of the Stockyards." Jane Addams in 1889 founded Hull-House on Chicago's slum-ridden West Side. A reformer who mixed humanity with help, she has been called "the only saint America has produced."

Like every place else, of course, the Heartland has produced more sinners than saints. The lawlessness of the gaudy Prohibition era in Chicago is matched by the indiscriminate warfare that cursed Williamson County in southern Illinois for close to a century. Beginning with the tangled blood feuds of the Bulliners, Hendersons, Sisneys and Crains in the 1860s, the area experienced troubles that lasted into the 1930s, with gang wars, Ku Klux Klan atrocities and labor strife. Some sort of gory record was set in June of 1922, when strikebreakers working a strip mine belonging to the Southern Illinois Coal Company were besieged by strikers carrying rifles and revolvers. The strikebreakers fought back and killed three of their attackers but finally surrendered. The strikers assured their prisoners safe-conduct out of the county, but then, on a march while leading them toward the town of Herrin, the union men began shooting down the strikebreakers one by one. Nineteen of the fleeing strikebreakers were shot or beaten to death.

Violence still seems ingrained in Heartland life today, but no one has yet provided a satisfactory answer to the question of whether the trait sprang from the bloody manner in which the land was originally won, from the fact that the region was so long a frontier, or from the rowdy competitiveness that long characterized both the politics and the business of the area. One is left with the feeling that the people of the Heartland often seem to use force as a purgative before settling down peaceably —as they almost always have—to get a difficult task accomplished.

They also have a deep love for their homeland. The architect Frank Lloyd Wright thought his native southwestern Wisconsin "more like Tuscany, perhaps, than any other land, but the Florentines that roamed those hills never saw such wild flowers as we see any spring, if the snow has been plentiful." And he rhapsodized over the Wisconsin red barn: "A farmstead here is somehow warmed and given life by the red of the barns as they stand about me over the green hills and among the yellow fields with the sun on them." The novelist Saul Bellow writes with a backhanded affection for his native city: "Clumsy, stinking, tender Chicago, dumped on its ancient lake bottom; and this murky orange west, and the hoarseness of factories and trains, spilling gases and soot on the newborn summer." The writer and former diplomat John Bartlow Martin remarked as late as 1947 on the timelessness of Indiana towns, with their "loafers on the curb around the shaded courthouse lawn, cars parked slantwise on the broad brick street, parking meters, the red front of Montgomery Ward's . . . old stone or painted brick business 'block' . . . drugstores and hardware stores with cluttered windows, narrow staircases going up to law offices, a tavern or two."

But above all other features, the Heartlanders love their endless prairie. Most visitors feel dwarfed and depressed by its monotonous reach from horizon to horizon. But to the people of the region, the prairie has a peculiar charm and the timeless fascination of an ocean. Some of them have tried hard to put the feeling in words. Wilhelm Miller wrote: "The contemplation of a vast prairie stirs every soul with the suggestion of the Infinite." Carl Sandburg wrote:

I was born on the prairie and the milk of its wheat, the red of its clover, the eyes of its women, gave me a song and a slogan.

Here the water went down, the icebergs slid with gravel, the gaps and the valleys hissed, and the black loam came, and the yellow sandy loam.

Here between the sheds of the Rocky Mountains and the Appalachians, here now a morning star fixes a fire sign over the timber claims and cow pastures, the corn belt, the cotton belt, the cattle ranches.

Here the gray geese go five hundred miles and back with a wind under their wings honking the cry for a new home.

Here I know I will hanker after nothing so much as one more sunrise or a sky moon of fire doubled to a river moon of water.

The prairie sings to me in the forenoon and I know in the night I rest easy in the prairie arms, on the prairie heart.

Leaping just for the fun of it—and for the thrill of jumping back again—Ashley Bennett hurtles a five-and-a-half-foot gap. The picture was taken in 1888 at Stand Rock, in Wisconsin, by Ashley's father, the pioneer photographer Henry Hamilton Bennett.

The exuberance of a robust people

Recreation is almost a passion in the Heartland. No matter what the activity is—or whether in summer or winter, day or night, indoors or out— the event will be sure to attract a group of people ready to expend their energies as participants or spectators. Week after week, huge, fiercely partisan crowds shout themselves hoarse at college football or high-school basketball games. Heartlanders seem to welcome the region's bitter winters in order to challenge one another at the breakneck speeds of iceboat races or, with equal fortitude, to sit quietly for hours, in subzero temperatures, next to a hole in the ice waiting for a fish to nibble. They even attach their own brand of exuberance to eating corn: in a scene repeated in many places, thousands of happy, energetic munchers converge on one Illinois town every year for a four-hour-long feast.

Intensely partisan rooters watch a jump-off
in a sectional match between two Indiana
basketball teams. Reelsville and Cloverdale,
meeting in the annual state-wide tournament,
attracted a capacity crowd of more than 2,500
to the gym at Brazil, the nearby county seat.

Basketball fever starts early in Indiana—these grade-school boys have wolfed lunch to make time for practice. Local legend says that the game determines school design: "First you put two peach baskets on posts; then you build your high school around them."

"Hoosier hysteria" distorts the faces of these Cloverdale High students with uncontrolled laughter, tears of joy or the blank stares of an emotion that defies description. This attack of the mania, whose cause is high-school basketball, followed a victory.

Ravenous Heartlanders watch with hungry anticipation as a new batch of corn is dumped into the bubbling water of a mammoth vat. The scene is the two-day Sweet Corn Festival held each August in Mendota, Illinois, in the heart of the Corn Belt. One such feast in the mid-1960s attracted 30,000 happy eaters, spectators and merrymakers. The corn—20 tons of it—was donated by a local food processor; others picked up the tab for 136 pounds of butter. Everybody was welcome to eat all he could —for free—and every last ear had been stripped in four hours—a consumption rate of five tons an hour.

A random sampling of feminine corn connoisseurs at Mendota shows representatives of all age groups from infancy on up. For the under-12 set, competition enhances simple consumption in a contest to see who can put away the greatest number of ears in the least time.

166

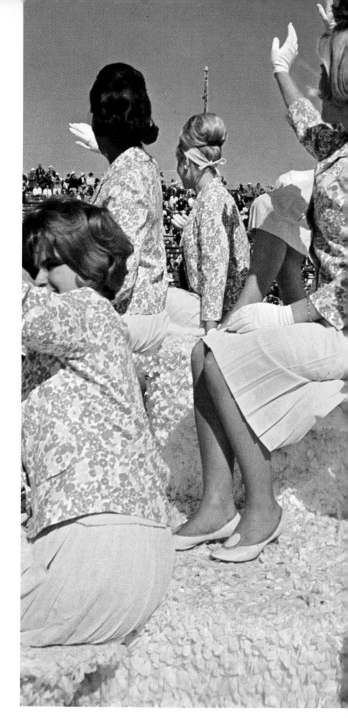

Even the most avid of auto-racing fans must relax at times, and this flower-hatted lady at the Indianapolis Speedway is doing just that, oblivious of the roaring cars. Held every Memorial Day, the Indianapolis 500 (200 grueling laps around the two-and-a-half-mile oval, lasting about three and a half hours) is America's best-known auto race.

A carnival spirit of fun and hoopla is part of the pre-race build-up
at Indianapolis. Floats draped with pretty girls parade through
the city, and "500" Festival Associates, a local booster group, keeps
enthusiasm at fever pitch through banquets and a grandly festive ball.

Some 300,000 fans—more paying customers than attend any other
U.S. sporting event—throng the grandstand and the infield grass at
the speedway. Many are drawn by love of the sport, others by morbid
expectation of crashes as the cars average 160-plus miles per hour.

Braving the intense cold, crews ready their iceboats for the start of the annual DN60-class national championship races, held in 1966 on Gull Lake, near Kalamazoo, Michigan, where driving, frigid winds push the craft at speeds up to 70 miles per hour.

Always looking for new winter sports, hardy Heartlanders race their snowmobiles through the deep snow of Michigan's Upper Peninsula. The ski-mounted vehicles, propelled by a cleated, endless track, were originally designed for use in roadless areas.

Shanties sheltering ice fishermen create hundreds of temporary towns on the region's frozen waters. At the first hard freeze the sportsmen haul their huts to favored spots. Despite the insulation of layers of clothing, it takes immense enthusiasm to endure hours of waiting for that one good bite.

171

Flinging themselves skyward in a synchronized display of youthful energy, Ohio State cheerleaders rouse fans to exultant yells as the Buckeye eleven clashes with Texas Christian University. Ohio State football games, like those of other members of the Big Ten, average larger crowds than elsewhere in the nation. But it is the quality, not just the quantity, that is pure Heartland in style: the cheers often seem louder, the victory grins wider—and the gloom that follows the home team's loss deeper—than anywhere else.

Suggested tours

On the following pages a number of maps show sections of the Heartland that are of interest to the tourist. No attempt has been made to show every road or town. Instead, scenic routes, parks and other special features have been emphasized. The text accompanying each map gives a brief description of the area. Opening dates and hours, especially of the business tours, should be confirmed locally, since these vary during the year. The areas covered are shown in the small map below, along with a key to the symbols used.

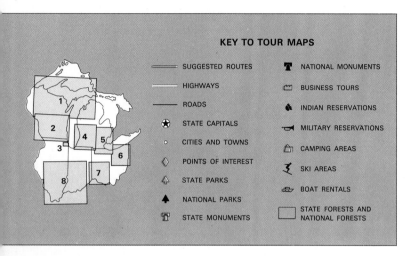

KEY TO TOUR MAPS

═══ SUGGESTED ROUTES	♆ NATIONAL MONUMENTS
──── HIGHWAYS	⌢ BUSINESS TOURS
──── ROADS	⚹ INDIAN RESERVATIONS
✪ STATE CAPITALS	➹ MILITARY RESERVATIONS
○ CITIES AND TOWNS	⌂ CAMPING AREAS
◇ POINTS OF INTEREST	⚐ SKI AREAS
△ STATE PARKS	⇔ BOAT RENTALS
▲ NATIONAL PARKS	▭ STATE FORESTS AND NATIONAL FORESTS
� STATE MONUMENTS	

1. The Northern Heartland

The vast stretches of state and national forest, lakes and rivers in the northern parts of Wisconsin and Michigan make the area the Heartland's outdoor playground. On the Upper Peninsula's northern shore is golden-tinted Tahquamenon Falls. Westward near Munising are Pictured Rocks, a series of multicolored cliffs. Two mines are open to the public in the summer: Crystal Falls Iron Mine and, to the north, Arcadian Copper Mine.

Many of the islands of the Great Lakes have unique features. In Lake Superior, north of Ashland, the wild, remote Apostle Islands contain perhaps the last great wilderness in Wisconsin. Farther out in the lake lies Isle Royale, one of the most isolated of all national parks. Lake Michigan contains Beaver Island (see pages 84-85), with an unusual historical museum. Lake Huron has Mackinac Island, a resort with an 18th Century fort.

On the western shore of Lake Michigan, northeast of Green Bay, is the Door Peninsula resort area. Here Peterson Builders' shipyards can be toured. The Chicago and North Western Railway offers tours of its Escanaba ore-shipping docks, and west, at Rhinelander, the Logging Museum shows how the men lived who helped denude the region of its original timber. On the southern side of the Straits of Mackinac, Michilimackinac State Park preserves the site of an early French fort. Sault Ste. Marie's locks are among the world's busiest. Farther south, the Big Rock Point Nuclear Plant maintains a visitors' center. The National Music Camp, at Interlochen, offers summer performances by student groups.

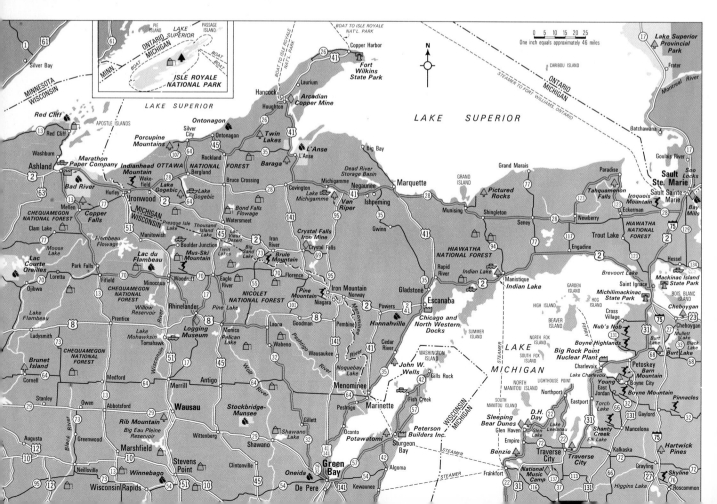

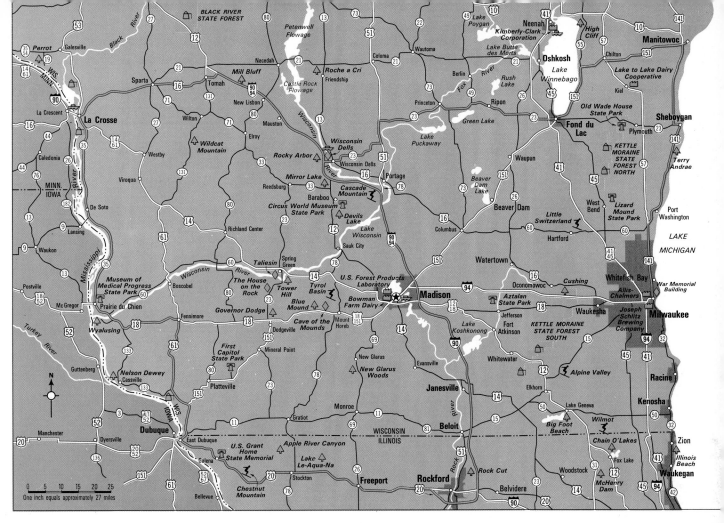

2. Southern Wisconsin

This area between Lake Michigan and the Mississippi River has some of the richest dairyland in the world, and some of the most scenic countryside in the Heartland. Much of the eastern half consists of small lakes and gently rolling hills, covered with lush fields or wooded patches. The western half contains some 20,000 square miles of land that was largely bypassed by the glaciers that leveled and smoothed so much of the region. Called the Driftless Area, the rugged countryside has bluffs that resemble those of the drier southwestern U.S.

Within the Driftless Area is Galena, Illinois, a town that briefly became rich from lead mining in the days before the California Gold Rush. Galena has many well-preserved Greek revival and mid-Victorian buildings; a home once inhabited by General Ulysses S. Grant is maintained as a museum.

The recommended route from Galena follows parts of the Great River Road, a network of highways that parallels the Mississippi from the river's source to the Gulf of Mexico. Along this section, wide flood plains alternate with high bluffs, many of them in state parks such as Wyalusing, where Indian burial mounds are preserved on Sentinel Ridge. At Prairie du Chien, on this route, is the Museum of Medical Progress.

To the northeast, at the Wisconsin Dells, is a channel up to 150 feet deep, cut by the river, which has carved the soft sandstone walls into fantastic forms (*see page 163*). Near the Dells, in Baraboo, is the Circus World Museum. Also nearby is Devils Lake, a small body surrounded by 500-foot-high cliffs of lavender quartzite. In Madison the U.S. Forest Products Laboratory, where scientists look for better ways to use wood, offers tours. Near Madison are a number of attractions, including The House on the Rock, a modern home built on the summit of a 400-foot-high chimney rock; Taliesin, the home of the late architect Frank Lloyd Wright; Cave of the Mounds, a cavern with colorful formations; and Mineral Point, a town of small stone houses built by Cornish miners during the lead-mining boom in the 1800s.

On Lake Michigan, Milwaukee is the nation's beer-brewing capital, and many of the breweries welcome visitors. The War Memorial Building incorporates the city's Art Center. The City Hall's ornate façade reflects the German influence that has marked the city since the 1840s, when many Germans settled here. Near the city the Kettle Moraine State Forest contains glacial landforms. The Old Wade House at the northern end of the Kettle Moraine Drive is a stagecoach inn of the 1850s. Aztalan State Park is named after the Aztecs of Mexico; it was once erroneously believed that they built the mounds now preserved in the park—which were actually built by tribesmen of the local Mississippian group.

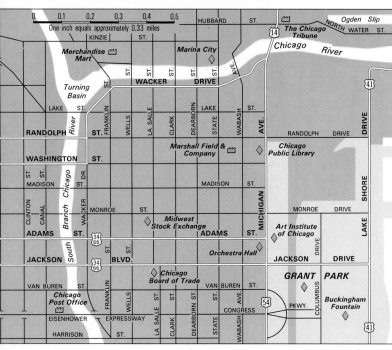

3. Chicago and the Loop

The largest city in the Heartland, Chicago presents a wealth of diversions for both visitor and resident. For sports enthusiasts, Wrigley Field, at Clark Street and Addison Avenue, in the city's northern half, is the home of the Chicago Cubs (baseball) and the Bears (football); in the southern half is Comiskey Park, home of the Chicago White Sox (baseball). Riverview Park, on Western Avenue, offers more than 100 amusement-park rides. Lincoln Park, stretching along the lakeshore for more than five miles, contains bathing beaches, yacht clubs and harbors, and tennis courts, among other facilities. It also contains Chicago's unusually fine zoo, with more than 2,600 animals and birds.

One of the few buildings to escape the 1871 Chicago fire was the pseudo-Gothic Water Tower, on Michigan Avenue. Another reminder of the fire is Grant Park, east of the city's center, built on rubble from the fire. Within or near the park today are the Field Museum of Natural History, with approximately 13 acres of exhibit halls; the Shedd Aquarium, with more than 10,000 specimens; and Soldier Field, a stadium put to diverse uses that has held as many as 200,000 spectators. Not far to the south is the world's largest exposition center, McCormick Place, which suffered an enormous fire in early 1967. In Garfield Park is a huge conservatory, with almost every conceivable type of plant exhibit. Within the downtown area the fire department shows fire fighters in training. The world-famous Union Stock Yards, no longer as active as they once were, can now be seen only through special arrangement with individual packers. On the city's South Side, about five miles from the Loop, is the Museum of Science and Industry, with a full-scale section of a coal mine, among other exhibits; the Fountain of Time, a major work by the celebrated Chicago sculptor Lorado Taft; and the 100-acre campus of the University of Chicago.

The center of shopping and business, the Loop district (*lower map*) contains most of the city's theaters, larger hotels and civic administrative offices. An unusual housing complex, the round-towered Marina City, rises on the Chicago River. The huge Merchandise Mart (*see page 116*) provides tours. Newspaper production can be observed at the offices of the *Chicago Tribune*, on North Michigan Avenue. To the south, on State Street (Chicago's main shopping boulevard), Marshall Field & Company, the world-famous department store, gives a look-before-shopping tour. The Public Library building, on Michigan Avenue, is noted for its marble and mosaic interiors. At the Midwest Stock Exchange visitors may observe securities transactions.

Nearby cultural centers are the Art Institute of Chicago, an excellent art museum, and Orchestra Hall, home of the Chicago Symphony Orchestra. In Grant Park, the large, ornamental Buckingham Fountain presents spectacular lighting displays totaling 45 million candle power. The latest in mail-processing techniques can be viewed at the Chicago Post Office. Visitors to the Board of Trade can watch the grain trading from a fifth-floor gallery.

4. Southwest Michigan

This section of Michigan has many farms and wooded patches set among small lakes and hills. It also boasts a number of good beaches on the lake. Southwest Michigan is especially beautiful in the spring, when the many fruit orchards come into bloom and the fields of flowering tulips give some areas the look of the Netherlands. Indeed, the town of Holland is in the center of an area settled by Dutch immigrants in the 1840s. Today their descendants operate the only wooden-shoe factory in the United States and a museum of Dutch life. Nearby Saugatuck still retains the flavor of an old boomtime lumber town.

Farther south is Deer Forest, where visitors may feed tame deer by hand. Benton Harbor, in the heart of Michigan's fruit-growing area, claims the world's largest non-citrus fruit market. Unusual limestone formations may be found in Bear Cave, to the south. Warren Woods, a tract of native hardwood forest, was spared by the loggers who cleared the area in the 1800s.

In South Bend, Indiana, the Council Oak, under which the French explorer La Salle negotiated a friendship pact with the Indians, still stands, supported by guy wires. Elkhart's C. G. Conn factory, the nation's first wind-instrument factory, offers tours, as does the Kellogg corn-flakes plant at Battle Creek, Michigan. The Furniture Museum at Grand Rapids displays the craftsmanship that has made the city a furniture capital.

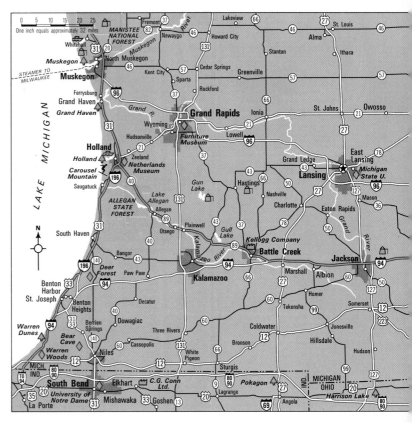

5. Southeastern Michigan and Lake Erie

Although much of this area is rural, it is dominated by the manufacturing complex centering on Detroit, auto capital of the world. Most of the automobile factories offer tours; the most varied is that of the Ford Motor Company's Rouge Plant, southwest of Detroit, where the visitor can watch every step from the unloading of iron ore to final assembly. Nearby at Dearborn is the 11-acre Ford Museum, jammed with antique automobiles, steam locomotives, airplanes and other displays of the history of American industry; next to the museum is Greenfield Village, 200 acres of buildings in which important American inventions were made, and which were moved here by Henry Ford.

Detroit has the Institute of Arts, with early American paintings, and a historical museum. The zoo, with its 3,300 species, can be toured on a miniature railroad. Southwest of Detroit is Hidden Lake Garden in the Irish Hills. On the outskirts of Detroit is Cranbrook, an educational complex with many buildings designed by Eliel Saarinen and an Orpheus fountain by Carl Milles.

South of Detroit, in Lake Erie, a number of islands present unusual sights: Kelleys Island features Glacial Grooves and Indian inscriptions; South Bass has a monument to Commodore Perry's victory and Middle Bass offers a castlelike winery. Back on the lakeshore, Blue Hole, near Sandusky, is an artesian spring that Indians thought was medicinal. The Toledo Museum of Art is noted for its ancient, European and American glass.

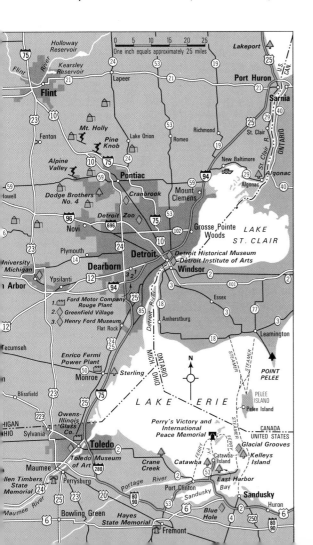

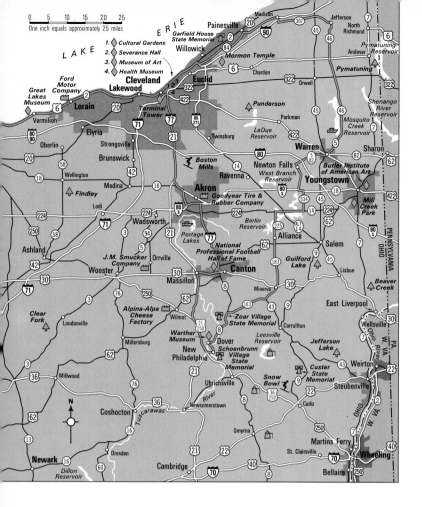

6. Northeastern Ohio

Much of the northern part of this section still retains in its town squares and white churches a hint of the New England origins of its first settlers. This can be seen in villages like Chardon and Painesville, east of Cleveland.

The larger cities, however, have a more cosmopolitan air. Some 63 peoples are represented among Cleveland's citizens; the Cultural Gardens honor 17 of the largest of these national groups. The city's skyline is dominated by the 52-story Terminal Tower, which has a visitors' observation deck on its 42nd floor. Cultural life centers around the many theater groups; the art museum; and Severance Hall, home of the top-flight Cleveland Orchestra. The Health Museum has exhibits and models revealing the workings of the human body. To the east of the city is the nation's first Mormon temple, built in the 1830s during the Mormons' brief sojourn before they continued on to the West. Also in this area, the last home of James A. Garfield, 20th President, has many of his personal effects.

South of Cleveland, the Warther Museum has hand-carved working models of locomotives. Schoenbrunn Village, built by Indian converts, was the first Christian settlement in the state, and Zoar Village once housed an experiment in communal living. The Goodyear Tire & Rubber Company in Akron offers a tour that includes historical exhibits, a lecture and a film. The J. M. Smucker Company in Orrville shows jams and jellies being made.

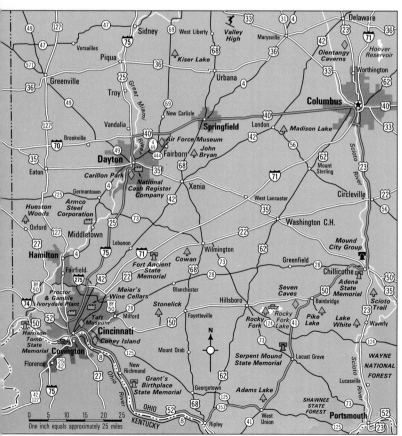

7. Historical Ohio

This section of Ohio abounds in noteworthy places dating from the days of the prehistoric Indians and later. One of the earliest settlements in the area was at Cincinnati. The tomb of William Henry Harrison, who once commanded the fort at Cincinnati and later became the ninth U.S. President, is west of the city, on the Ohio River. The birthplace of another general who became President, Ulysses S. Grant, is to the southeast.

The opulence of the 1800s can be seen in the architecture of Cincinnati's Taft Museum; the museum houses canvases by old masters. In the Dayton area, Carillon Park preserves a section of the old Miami and Erie Canal. The Air Force Museum, near Dayton, displays planes that have helped make aeronautical history. The National Cash Register Company in Dayton and the Armco Steel Corporation in Middletown present tours for visitors. From just north of Dayton to Columbus, the tour route follows U.S. 40, the old National Road. The Adena State Memorial, near Chillicothe, preserves the palatial residence of Thomas Worthington, Ohio's sixth governor.

Scattered throughout the area are remains of the pre-Columbian Hopewell Indians. They built an extensive edifice, preserved in Fort Ancient State Memorial, northeast of Cincinnati. They also built one of the world's largest earthwork effigies, Serpent Mound, on Route 73 near Locust Grove. Some of the finest pre-Columbian implements in America have been taken from a burial ground called the Mound City Group, near Chillicothe.

8. Lincoln's home country

It was in the southern part of Illinois and Indiana—and in northern Kentucky—that Abraham Lincoln grew up and lived until he became the nation's 16th President. The suggested tour route follows much of the Lincoln Heritage Trail, a tri-state route. In the middle of the area, the Lincoln Trail Monument commemorates the spot near Vincennes where the Lincoln family crossed the Wabash from Indiana to Illinois in 1830. Illinois' Lincoln Log Cabin State Park, to the north on the tour route, includes the 80-acre farm owned by Lincoln's father and part of 40 acres owned by Lincoln himself. Decatur, farther along the route, maintains the log cabin courthouse where Lincoln, in 1838, won his first big law case. In and around Springfield, Illinois' state capital, are many Lincoln memorials, including his tomb. The village of New Salem nearby has been restored to show how it appeared when Lincoln lived there as a young man.

The main Lincoln monument in Indiana is his boyhood home, near Boonville, where he grew to manhood. Vincennes, Indiana's oldest town, has the George Rogers Clark State Memorial, which honors one of the Heartland's earliest Indian fighters. Another famous Indian fighter, William Henry Harrison, lived in the town; his home, Grouseland, is open to the public. The town's Harrison Park has the restored Indiana Territorial Capitol and the first printing press in the territory.

Another section of the tour route follows the lower Ohio River Valley, starting at Cairo, Illinois, an old town filled with Southern-style homes. Cave-in-Rock, upstream, is a natural cave that once was an outlaw's hide-out. One of the river's most opulent settlements for many years was Shawneetown, today a state memorial. The New Harmony State Memorial, on the Wabash in Indiana, marks the site of utopian experiments of the 1800s (see page 55). Corydon, to the east, succeeded Vincennes as territorial capital. The original capitol still stands. The Howard National Steamboat Museum, in Jeffersonville, contains many steamboat models and relics of the ships that once plied the region's rivers. Visitors can see modern industries at work at the Allison Division of General Motors in Indianapolis, which also has permanent exhibits of aircraft engines and product development. In Evansville, Mead Johnson & Company offers tours that show the production of pharmaceutical supplies and baby foods.

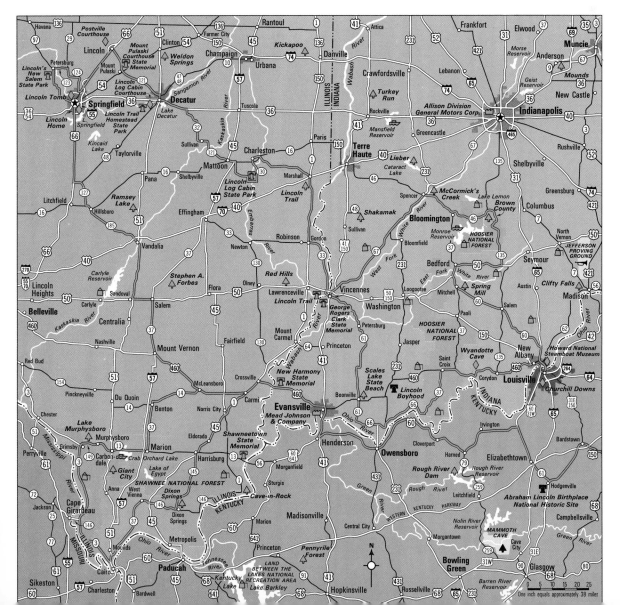

Museums and galleries

Illinois

Champaign-Urbana
Krannert Art Museum, University of Illinois. Permanent collection of old masters; shows by American artists. Mon-Sat 9-5; Sun 2-5.

Chicago
Adler Planetarium and Astronomical Museum, Grant Park. First U.S. planetarium. Daily 9:30-5; Tues and Fri (winter) and Tues-Sun (summer) to 9:30.

Art Institute of Chicago, Michigan Ave. at Adams St. Extensive Impressionist and Post-Impressionist collection; European and Oriental art. Mon-Sat 10-5; Thurs eves to 9:30; Sun and hols 12-5.

Chicago Historical Society, N. Clark St. at W. North Ave. Large collection of Lincolniana. Mon-Sat 9:30-4:30; Sun 12:30-5:30.

Field Museum of Natural History, E. Roosevelt Rd. and S. Lake Shore Dr. Exhibits in anthropology, botany, geology, zoology. Winter: generally 9-4; spring and fall: 9-5; summer: 9-6 or 9-8.

Garfield Park Conservatory, 300 N. Central Park. More than 5,000 plant species and varieties; flower shows. Daily 9-5; shows to 6.

Lincoln Park Zoological Gardens, Lincoln Park. Popular zoo. Daily 9-5.

Museum of Science and Industry, 57th St. at Lake Michigan. Exhibits on scientific and industrial processes. Fall-winter: Mon-Sat 9:30-4; spring-summer: Mon-Sat 9:30-5:30; Sun and hols 10-6.

Oriental Institute Museum, University of Chicago, 1155 E. 58th St. Ancient Near Eastern objects. Tues-Wed 10-12, 1-5; Thurs-Sun 10-5.

John G. Shedd Aquarium, Grant Park. Excellent collection of aquatic life. Hours depend on month.

Rockford
Rockford Art Association, Burpee Gallery of Art, 737 N. Main St. Contemporary American graphics, paintings, sculpture. Tues-Sat 9-12, 1-5; Sun 2-5.

Springfield
Illinois State Museum of Natural History and Art, Spring and Edward Sts. Natural science, anthropology, art. Mon-Sat 8:30-5; Sun 2-5.

Indiana

Bloomington
Indiana University Museum of Art, Indiana University. Small collections in most periods; art library. Mon-Sat 9-5; Sun 1-5.

Evansville
Evansville Museum of Arts and Sciences, 411 S.E. Riverside Dr. Exhibits in art, natural history, history; planetarium. Tues-Sat, hols 9-5; Tues eves 7-9; Sun 12-5.

Fort Wayne
Fort Wayne Art Institute— Museum of Art, 1202 W. Wayne St. Paintings, prints, sculpture. Tues 1-5; Wed 1-8; Thurs-Sun 1-5.

Indianapolis
Children's Museum of Indianapolis, 3010 N. Meridian. Exhibits aimed at children in grades 1-8. Tues-Sat 9-5; Sun 2-5. Closed Sun June-Aug.

John Herron Museum of Art, 110 E. 16th St. European and American paintings, sculpture; Chinese art. Tues-Sat 10-5; Sun 1-6.

Indianapolis Motor Speedway and Museum, 4790 W. 16th St. Exhibit of racing cars dating from 1909. Daily 9-5.

New Harmony
Workingmen's Institute, W. Tavern St. Artifacts tracing town's history as early utopian experiment. Tues-Sat 10-12, 1-4; Sun (summer only) 2-5.

South Bend
Northern Indiana Historical Society, 112 S. Lafayette Blvd. Regional artifacts. Tues-Thurs, Sat 9-5.

South Bend Art Center, 121 N. Lafayette Blvd. Contemporary American art. Tues-Sat 9-5; Sun 2-5.

University of Notre Dame Art Gallery, O'Shaughnessy Hall. Stress on 16th Century Italian, 18th Century French and English paintings; primitive art collection. Mon-Fri 12-5; Sat-Sun 1-5.

Terre Haute
Sheldon Swope Art Gallery, 25 S. Seventh St. Contemporary American paintings and sculpture; Oriental art collection. Tues-Sat 12-5; Sun 2-5. Closed Aug.

Michigan

Ann Arbor
Kelsey Museum of Archeology, 434 S. State St. Antiques, mainly Greco-Roman and Egyptian. Mon-Fri 1-4; Sun 3-5.

University of Michigan Museum of Art, Alumni Memorial Hall. Western and Oriental art from medieval times to present. Mon-Sat 9-5; Sun 2-5.

Bloomfield Hills
Cranbrook Academy of Art Galleries, 500 Lone Pine Rd. Egyptian, pre-Columbian, Oriental art; contemporary paintings and sculpture. Tues-Fri 2-5; Sat-Sun 1-5.

Dearborn
Henry Ford Museum and Greenfield Village, U.S. 12. Exhibits covering history of automobile, development of decorative and mechanical arts and industries. Daily 9-5; June 15-Labor Day 9-6:30.

Detroit
Detroit Historical Museum, 5401 Woodward. Industrial and social history exhibits; Detroit history. Tues-Sun 9-6.

Detroit Institute of Arts, 5200 Woodward. Excellent representative collection; armor collection. Tues 9-9; Wed-Sun 9-6.

Grand Rapids
Grand Rapids Art Museum, 230 E. Fulton St. German Impressionists; early and contemporary American, French, English. Mon-Sat 10-5; Sun 2-5.

Grand Rapids Public Museum, 54 Jefferson Ave., S.E. Furniture collection; planetarium. Mon-Sat 10-5; Sun 2-5.

Ishpeming
National Ski Hall of Fame and Ski Museum, Mather Ave. Displays of ski equipment, including oldest known pair in existence; memorabilia. June-Labor Day 10-4 daily; by appointment rest of the year.

Kalamazoo
Kalamazoo Institute of Arts, 314 S. Park St. Twentieth Century American art. Tues-Fri 11-4:30; Sat 9-4; Sun 1-4.

Marquette
Marquette County Historical Society, Inc., 213 N. Front St. Upper Michigan artifacts: logg[ing], mining, Indian, pioneer. Mon-F[ri] 9-12, 1-4:30.

Muskegon
Hackley Art Gallery, 296 W. Webster Ave. Old masters' etchings, engravings. Mon-Fri 9-5; Sat 9-12; Sun 2:30-5:30.

Ohio

Canton
Pro Football Hall of Fame, 212 Harrison Ave., N.W. Commemorative plaques, trophies, memorabilia. June-Sept: Mon-Sat 9-9; Oct-May: daily 10-5.

Cincinnati
Cincinnati Art Museum, Eden Park. Ancient, Oriental, Europe[an] and American art of all types. Mon-Sat 10-5; Sun, hols 2-5.

Taft Museum, 316 Pike St. Historic house of 1820s Federal architectural style; per[iod] furnishings; paintings and porcelain. Mon-Sat 10-5; Sun and hols 2-5.

Cleveland
Cleveland Health Museum, 89[0] Euclid Ave. Displays on huma[n] body, hygiene, public health. Mon-Sat 9-5; Sun 1-5.

Cleveland Museum of Art, 111[50] East Blvd. Well-balanced colle[ction] representing many periods. Tues-Fri 10-6; Wed (all year) a[nd] Fri (Oct-Jan) eves to 10; Sat 9-5; Sun 1-6.

Cleveland Natural Science Museum, 10600 East Blvd., University Circle. Natural histo[ry] displays; planetarium. Mon-Sa[t] 10-5; Sun 1-5:50.

Columbus
Columbus Gallery of Fine Arts, 480 E. Broad St. Old masters, American oils and watercolors. Daily 12-5.

Dayton
Air Force Museum, Wright-Patterson Air Force Ba[se.] Aviation displays, including aircraft and missiles. Hours var[y.]

Dayton Art Institute, Forest an[d] Riverview Aves. General collection, Renaissance to contemporary. Tues-Fri 12:30-[5;] Tues eves (Sept-May) 7-10; S[at] 10-5; Sun 1-6.

Dover
Warther Museum, 331 Karl Av[e.] Collection of hand-carved working models of railroad

motives. Daily 9-5; June-Sept
dark.

do
do Museum of Art, Monroe
nd Scottwood Ave. Excellent
s collection, American
tings, book and manuscript
ction. Tues-Sat 9-5; Sun,
, hols 1-5.

million
t Lakes Historical Society
eum, 142 Main St. Marine
ction: ship models,
uments. Summer: 10:30-9;
er: 10:30-5.

ngstown
er Institute of American Art,
Wick Ave. American
tings and prints. Tues-Sat
:30; Sun and hols 1-5.
ed June and Sept.

Wisconsin

Appleton
Dard Hunter Paper Museum, 1043
E. South River St. History of
papermaking from Sixth Century
A.D.   Mon-Fri 8-12, 1-5.

Baraboo
Circus World Museum, 426 Water
St. Fifteen acres of circus lore.
May-Sept: daily 9:30-5:30.

Green Bay
National Railroad Museum, 2300
S. Broadway. Railway engines,
cars, relics. May-Oct: daily 10-5.

Neville Public Museum, 129 S.
Jefferson St. History, art,
geology, biology, archeology.
Mon-Sat 9-5; Sun 2-5.

Madison
State Historical Society of

Wisconsin, 816 State St. Items
of social, economic and political
interest in the Midwest's
development. Mon-Sat 8-5.

Milwaukee
Milwaukee Art Center, Inc., 750
N. Lincoln Memorial Dr.
Nineteenth and 20th Century
American and European paintings.
Mon-Wed 10-5; Thurs 10-10;
Fri-Sat 10-5; Sun 1-5.

Neenah
John Nelson Bergstrom Art Center
and Museum, 165 N. Park Ave.
European and antique glass,
American paintings. Wed, Thurs,
Sat, Sun 1-5.

Oshkosh
Oshkosh Public Museum, 1331
Algoma Blvd. Historical and
natural history material related to

the surrounding area. Daily
9-12, 1-5.

Prairie du Chien
Museum of Medical Progress, 700
S. Beaumont Rd. Historical
artifacts and exhibits of medicine
from pioneer days. May-Oct: daily
9-5.

Rhinelander
Rhinelander Logging Museum,
Pioneer Park. Replica of logging
camp, with equipment and
photographs. June-Labor Day:
daily 9-8.

Wausau
Marathon County Historical
Society and Museum, 403
McIndoe St. Exhibits on
lumbering, Indians, early
occupations. Mon-Fri 9-5; Sun
2-5.

cal festivals and events

ois
rican Passion Play,
mington. Biblical drama.
days, Palm Sunday—June.

nia Festival, Highland Park.
-air performances at the
mer home of the Chicago
phony Orchestra. Late
e—August.

d Coast Art Fair, Chicago.
walk exhibitions on Rush
et, in city's night-club strip.
-August.

ois State Fair, Springfield.
stock exhibitions, harness
g, amusements. Mid-August.

Quoin State Fair, Du Quoin.
includes top horses in famed
bletonian harness races. Late
ust—Labor Day.

Lincoln in Illinois shows,
rsburg. Enactment of Robert
herwood's play. Late August
rly September.

rnational Livestock Exhibition,
ago. Animal judging, rodeo,
e show. Late November.

ana
0'' Festival, Indianapolis.
th-long celebration
inating on May 30 in the
ed 500-mile auto race.

ison Regatta, Madison. Two
s of power-boat racing on Ohio
r, preceded by week-long
val. Early July.

eer Threshermen's

Convention, Rushville.
Demonstrations of old-fashioned
steam threshing machines at
work. Early August.

Schweizer Fest, Tell City. Swiss
festival, with entertainment, beer
gardens, rides. Early August.

Indiana State Fair, Indianapolis.
Exhibits, harness racing, midway.
Late August—early September.

Little Italy Festival, Clinton.
Gondolas on the Wabash River,
boccie tourney, dancing, fishing.
Early September.

Michigan
Grayling Winter Sports Carnival,
Grayling. Winter events, beauty
contests, dances. Early February.

National Ski Jumping
Championship, Iron Mountain.
Early March.

Tulip Time Festival, Holland.
Tulip blooms, Dutch festivities.
Mid-May.

Bavarian Festival, Frankenmuth.
German celebrations. Mid-June.

International Freedom Festival,
Detroit. Sponsored by Detroit and
Windsor, Canada. Parades, nightly
fireworks, waterfront events. Late
June—early July.

National Cherry Festival, Traverse
City. Cherry harvest celebration,
with parades, beauty contests,
sideshows. Early July.

National Motorcycle Hill Climb,
Muskegon. August.

Magic Convention, Colon. Magic
shows, tours of magic-equipment
factory. Mid-August.

Mackinac Bridge Walk, Mackinaw
City-St. Ignace. On Labor Day,
the only day pedestrians
are permitted to walk the
five-mile-long span.

Old Car Festival, Greenfield
Village, Dearborn. More than 300
vintage cars, circa 1896-1927, in
parades and contests.
Mid-September.

Ohio
Maple Festival, Chardon.
Old-fashioned sugar camp,
sugar-making demonstrations,
good food. Early April.

May Show, Cleveland Museum of
Art, Cleveland. Outstanding and
sometimes controversial annual
exhibition. May.

Ohio Hills Folk Festival, Quaker
City. Songs, games, arts and
crafts of the 19th Century.
Mid-July.

Pottery Festival, Crooksville. Large
displays of antique pottery and
technique. Late July.

All-American Soap Box Derby,
Akron. Youngsters in
gravity-powered cars compete for
scholarship prizes. Mid-August.

Ohio State Fair, Columbus. One of
the Heartland's top fairs, with the
world's largest livestock exhibit.
Late August—Labor Day.

Sweet Corn Festival, Portsmouth.
Celebration featuring fresh sweet
corn, entertainment. Late August

—early September.

Ohio Swiss Festival, Sugarcreek.
Village turns into an Alpine town,
with reveling, feasting, music.
Late September.

Wisconsin
Uihlein Field polo, Milwaukee.
On Sundays from late May
through August, outstanding
polo contests.

Lakeshore Art Festival, Milwaukee.
Outdoor art fair combined with
concerts by top classical, jazz and
pop musicians. Late June.

Old Milwaukee Days, Milwaukee.
Four-day festival of top-name
music concerts culminating in big
July Fourth circus parade.

Lumberjack World Championships,
Hayward. Last weekend in July.

Peninsula Music Festival, Fish
Creek. Gathering of amateur and
professional musicians.
Mid-August.

Road America, Elkhart Lake. Week
of sports-car racing, topped by
500-mile race on tricky course.
Early September.

Wilhelm Tell Festival, New Glarus.
Opera *Wilhelm Tell* in English and
German, with other festivities.
Early September.

Oktoberfest, La Crosse. Sudsy
festival said to rival Munich's.
Early October.

Folk Fair, Milwaukee. Jamboree
of ethnic groups showing their
culture, dress, food, dances.
Late November.

Wildlife of the Heartland

A sampling of the natural life frequently found in the Heartland is given on these pages. In each case both the object's common name and its scientific name are given. For further information, specialized books on wildlife should be consulted by the reader; a number of useful reference works are listed on page 188.

Mammals

Prairie mole

With a strength belied by its size (males grow to not quite nine inches), the prairie mole *(Scalopus aquaticus machrinus)* digs its tunnels a foot below the meadows of the Heartland, building nests and seeking its food—insects, earthworms and insect larvae.

Red bat

A migratory creature, the red bat *(Lasiurus borealis)* spends the warmer half of the year in the Heartland and the Northeast, flying south for the winter. It flies at great heights at night, then spirals earthward to catch its prey.

Mearns cottontail

The leading game animal of Michigan, the Mearns cottontail *(Sylvilagus floridanus mearnsii)* defends itself from cats by leaping over the enemy's back and bowling it over with its hind legs.

Thirteen-lined ground squirrel

Distinguished by the thirteen alternating light and dark stripes that run the length of its back, the thirteen-lined ground squirrel *(Citellus tridecemlineatus)* is found on prairies and in brush country throughout the Heartland.

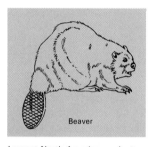
Beaver

Largest North American rodent, the beaver *(Castor canadensis)* weighs up to 70 pounds and measures more than three and one half feet, including its tail. To compensate for wear, its four incisor teeth never stop growing.

Red fox

One of the most cunning of animals, the red fox *(Vulpes fulva)* is also a fast runner and good swimmer. It prefers meat, but also eats grass and berries.

Black bear

Though virtually omnivorous, the black bear *(Ursus americanus)* subsists mainly on fruit, berries and nuts, with an occasional rodent or fish for variety. It grows to about five feet.

Raccoon

A good climber and swimmer, the raccoon *(Procyon lotor)* is curious and curious. It is clever at opening garbage pails, but is not as fastidious as legend has it: it does not always wash its food.

Least weasel

Smallest carnivore in North America, the least weasel *(Mustela rixosa alligheniensis)* is no more than nine inches long, no heavier than two and a half ounces. It lives on mice and insects.

Badger

The state animal of Wisconsin, the badger *(Taxidea taxus)* is a ferocious fighter. About 30 inches in length and up to 25 pounds in weight, it can defeat any animal its size. The badger, which feeds on rodents, is also a champion digger, tunneling as deep as six feet.

Bobcat

Like most cats, the bobcat *(Lynx rufus)* is nocturnal, seldom emerging during the day. It normally feeds on rabbits, but its speed and size (about three feet long) enable it to catch larger prey.

White-tailed deer

One of today's most popular game animals, the white-tailed deer *(Odocoileus virginianus)* was protected under America's first game law. Bucks may weigh as much as 300 pounds, but can run up to 40 miles an hour.

sh and reptiles

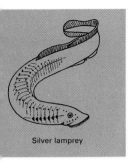

Silver lamprey

...arasite, the eel-like silver ...prey *(Ichthyomyzon unicuspis)* ...tens its mouth to other fish, ...erating them with its tongue.

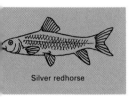

Silver redhorse

...excellent food fish, the silver ...horse *(Moxostoma anisurum)* ...erally ignores baited hooks, but ...be caught in the large nets ...d by commercial fishermen.

Blanding's turtle

...entially aquatic, Blanding's ...tle *(Emydoidea blandingi)* often ...nders on land, but never far ...m a stream or swamp.

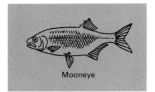

Mooneye

Although not a good food fish, the mooneye *(Hiodon tergisus)* often takes the bait—and hook—meant for other species; it is a source of food for many larger game fish.

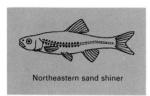

Northeastern sand shiner

The most common species of its kind in the Great Lakes area, the Northeastern sand shiner *(Notropis deliciosus stramineus)* lives mostly along the sandy bottoms of swift-running streams.

Kirtland's water snake

The harmless red-bellied, black-spotted Kirtland's water snake *(Natrix kirtlandi)* is an excellent swimmer but prefers damp meadowland. When it is frightened it can flatten itself almost to a ribbon for concealment.

Central mudminnow

A misnamed fish, the Central mudminnow *(Umbra limi)* is unrelated to the true minnow. The four-inch-long creature is fond of muddy bottoms. When endangered it quickly wriggles, tail first, into the mud.

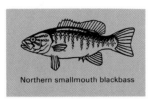

Northern smallmouth blackbass

Known as the "gamest fish that swims," the Northern smallmouth blackbass *(Micropterus dolomieui)* may reach seven pounds, but specimens of more than four pounds are seldom hooked.

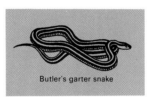

Butler's garter snake

Dark brown or black with a vivid yellow stripe running the length of its back, the innocuous Butler's garter snake *(Thamnophis butleri)* prefers open fields, where it feeds on leeches and worms.

Great Lakes muskellunge

The largest of the pike family, the Great Lakes muskellunge *(Esox masquinongy)* is a prized game fish. Catches of 40 pounds are common; the record is nearly 70.

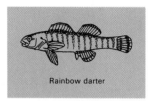

Rainbow darter

Seclusive by temperament, the rainbow darter *(Etheostoma caeruleum)* is most often found in larger streams with gravel bottoms.

Eastern massasauga

Although also known as the swamp rattler or black snapper, the poisonous Eastern massasauga *(Sistrurus catenatus catenatus)* is generally mild-mannered, rattling only when thoroughly angered.

rds

Least bittern

...enizen of marshes, the least ...tern *(Ixobrychus exilis)* reacts to ...ger not by fleeing but by ...nding stock-still so as to ...emble marshland cattails.

Mallard

The commonest North American waterfowl, the mallard *(Anas platyrhynchos)* is found in watery areas throughout the Heartland.

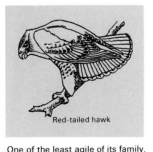

Red-tailed hawk

One of the least agile of its family, the red-tailed hawk *(Buteo jamaicensis)* is too slow to snatch any but very sluggish or sick birds on the wing. It generally uses the same bulky twig nest year after year, but redecorates it with green sprigs each spring.

Sharp-tailed grouse

Found mostly in the northern Heartland, the sharp-tailed grouse *(Pedioecetes phasianellus)* attracts its mate by inflating its neck sacs, shaking its tail and strutting about, uttering cries and squawks.

Ring-necked pheasant

Originally imported from the Far East, the ring-necked pheasant *(Phasianus colchicus torquatus)* is found in most of the Heartland.

Upland plover

Nearly hunted to extinction, the upland plover *(Bartramia longicauda)* is now protected and flourishes on the prairies of the Heartland. It is found in summer from Maine to Oklahoma but winters in South America.

Mourning dove

The young male mourning dove *(Zenaidura macroura)* leaves its flock in February, mates and thereafter raises three or four broods a year. This prolific bird is seen throughout the Eastern U.S.

Red-winged blackbird

A precision flyer, the red-winged blackbird *(Agelaius phoeniceus)* often flies in flocks of several thousand, each bird turning at same instant. The male can be distinguished by the red patches at the base of its wings.

Flowers and trees

Jack-in-the-pulpit

A familiar woodland flower, the jack-in-the-pulpit *(Arisaema triphyllum)* puts forth its tiny greenish-yellow flowers in late spring. It is partial to damp areas.

White trillium

A hillside dweller, the white trillium *(Trillium grandiflorum)* grows on wooded slopes or in ravines. Its single large flower, which is pure white when it appears in April, turns to pink or dull rose after a few weeks.

Eastern troutlily

A day-blooming plant, the Eastern troutlily *(Erythronium americanum)* takes its name from the mottled purple-brown and white of its leaves, which gives it a resemblance to the back of the brook trout. Its leaves are often so thick as to obscure the ground.

Round-leaved hepatica

Harbingers of spring, the flowers of the round-leaved hepatica *(Hepatica americana)* show themselves even before the leaves. The tiny purple, blue or pink flowers are often half-hidden by fallen leaves in rocky woodland.

Rue anemone

A cousin of the buttercup, the rue anemone *(Anemonella thalictroides)* prefers moist woodland. Its flowers, white or magenta-tinged, appear in clusters.

Butterfly violet

The state flower of both Illinois and Wisconsin, the butterfly, or common, violet *(Viola papilionacea),* with its familiar violet flowers, abounds in fields and woods. Also found near farmhouses and other dwellings, it blooms from March to June.

Common goldenrod

With its large clusters of yellow blooms, the common goldenrod *(Solidago canadensis)* brightens meadows and hillsides in late summer and early autumn.

White field daisy

Hardy and prolific, the white field daisy *(Chrysanthemum leucanthemum)* is abundant in meadows. Although popular, is considered a weed by farmers.

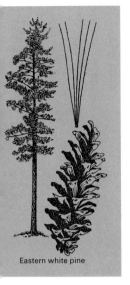

Eastern white pine

state tree of Michigan, the ern white pine *(Pinus strobus)* ages from 50 to 75 feet tall, may reach 180 feet.

Bur oak

is' state tree, the bur oak *rcus macrocarpa)* is named e rough cup around its ns. It may grow to 170 feet.

Kentucky coffeetree

a true coffeetree, the ucky coffeetree *(Gymnocladus us)* has seeds that were once as a coffee substitute.

Shagbark hickory

The shagbark hickory *(Carya ovata)* is an extremely useful tree, for its delicately flavored nuts make good eating and its heavy, tough wood is eminently suited for agricultural implements.

Tuliptree

The state tree of Indiana, the straight-trunked tuliptree *(Liriodendron tulipifera)* takes its name from the greenish-yellow tuliplike flowers that bloom in May and June.

Sugar maple

The sugar maple *(Acer saccharum)*, though common throughout the Northeast as well as the Heartland, has been chosen as Wisconsin's state tree.

Blue beech

Taking its name from its smooth, slate-blue bark, the blue beech or American hornbeam *(Carpinus caroliniana)* has a hard wood, which is often used as fuel but is also suitable for tool handles.

Buttonwood

The buttonwood *(Platanus occidentalis)*, also called the American sycamore, can grow to 175 feet—the largest deciduous tree in eastern North America.

Ohio buckeye

Named the official Ohio tree, the Ohio buckeye *(Aesculus glabra)* gave the state its nickname of the Buckeye State. It is a common tree of the woodlands and riverbanks, growing to a height of 50 feet, with a trunk a foot and a half in diameter.

Pin oak

Important for its wood, which is used in barrelmaking and for shingles and clapboard siding, the pin oak *(Quercus palustris)* is named for the short, pinlike twigs that grow on its branches.

Sweet crab apple

A small, bushy tree that rarely exceeds 30 feet in height, the sweet crab apple *(Malus coronaria)* bears tart fruit that makes fine jellies. The tree is favored for ornamental uses.

Blue ash

Although not confined to the Heartland states, the blue ash *(Fraxinus quadrangulata)* attains its greatest height—about 120 feet—in the valleys of southern Indiana and southern Illinois. The tree is named for the blue dye made from its inner bark.

185

Statistical information

State nickname, date of admission, capital

Illinois: Prairie State; admitted 1818 (the 21st state); Springfield.

Indiana: Hoosier State; admitted 1816 (the 19th state); Indianapolis.

Michigan: Wolverine State; admitted 1837 (the 26th state); Lansing.

Ohio: Buckeye State; admitted 1803 (the 17th state); Columbus.

Wisconsin: Badger State; admitted 1848 (the 30th state); Madison.

Population

By state (U.S. Census, 1960):
Illinois: 10,081,158.
Ohio: 9,706,397.
Michigan: 7,823,194.
Indiana: 4,662,498.
Wisconsin: 3,951,777.

By city (region's 10 largest cities are listed, followed by their population and rank in the U.S. according to the 1960 Census):

City	Population	Rank
Chicago	3,550,404	2
Detroit	1,670,144	5
Cleveland	876,050	8
Milwaukee	741,325	11
Cincinnati	502,550	21
Indianapolis	476,258	26
Columbus	471,316	28
Toledo	318,003	39
Akron	290,351	45
Dayton	262,332	49

U.S. center of population

The center of population has been in the Heartland since the 1860 Census. As of 1960, the center for all 50 states is a point six and one half miles northwest of Centralia, Illinois; the center of the 48 conterminous states is a point four miles east of Salem, Illinois.

Land areas

Michigan: 57,019 square miles.
Illinois: 55,930 square miles.
Wisconsin: 54,705 square miles.
Ohio: 40,972 square miles.
Indiana: 36,185 square miles.

Bodies of water

Great Lakes

Superior: 80,000 square miles; maximum depth, 1,333 feet.

Huron: 72,600 square miles; maximum depth, 750 feet.

Michigan: 67,900 square miles; maximum depth, 923 feet.

Ontario: 34,800 square miles; maximum depth, 802 feet.

Erie: 32,630 square miles; maximum depth, 120 feet.

Principal rivers (lengths in miles)

Mississippi (flows past Illinois and Wisconsin): 2,348.

Ohio (flows past Ohio, Indiana and Illinois): 981.

Wabash (flows through Ohio, Indiana and Illinois): 475.

Wisconsin (Wisconsin): 430.

Rock (Illinois and Wisconsin): 300.

Illinois (Illinois): 273.

Grand (Michigan): 260.

Scioto (Ohio): 237.

St. Joseph (Michigan): 210.

Chippewa (Wisconsin): 183.

Important engineering feats

Canalization of the Ohio River: A series of 46 locks and dams along the entire length of the 981-mile river assures a constant nine-foot depth to aid navigation, and helps curb flooding.

The Soo Canal (Michigan): Officially the St. Marys Falls Canal, this passageway, featuring four locks, opened Lake Superior to commercial shipping in 1855; in 1964 more than 90 million short tons passed through the canal.

The Mackinac Bridge (Michigan): The world's longest anchorage-to-anchorage suspension bridge (8,614 feet) connects Michigan's Upper and Lower Peninsulas.

Some U.S. superlative

Busiest commercial airport: O'Hare, Chicago.

First unemployment relief in U Wisconsin, enacted 1932.

First labor union in U.S.: Knig of Labor, formed in Illinois in 1877.

Longest fresh-water shoreline Michigan.

First coeducational college in U.S.: Oberlin (Ohio).

Largest attendance for a spor event: Indianapolis "500" au race, which attracts more tha 250,000 paying spectators each year.

Busiest rail center in U.S.: Chicago, handling 34,000 fre cars daily.

Largest college-owned footba stadium: Michigan Stadium, Ann Arbor, seating 101,001.

Agricultural statistics (1965)

	Number of farms	Acreage (in millions)	Principal commodities
Illinois	154,644	30.3	Corn, hogs, cattle, soybeans
Indiana	128,160	18.6	Hogs, corn, soybeans, cattle.
Michigan	111,817	14.8	Dairy, cattle, corn, dry beans
Ohio	140,353	18.5	Dairy, cattle, hogs, soybeans
Wisconsin	131,215	21.2	Dairy, cattle, hogs, eggs.

Manufacturing and mining statistics (1965)

	Steel and ingot production (in millions of net tons)	Principal minerals
Illinois	11.2	Petroleum, coal, stone, gravel
Indiana	17.1	Coal, cement, petroleum, stor
Michigan	9.7	Iron ore, cement, copper, san
Ohio	22.2	Coal, stone, cement, lime.
Wisconsin	—	Sand, gravel, stone, cement.

Pronunciation glossary

Auglaize (o GLAZE). County and river in Ohio.
Baraboo (BAH ruh boo). City, range and river in southern Wisconsin.
Cahokia (kuh HO kee uh). Oldest town in Illinois, near East St. Louis.
Cairo (KAY ro). City in southern Illinois.
Calumet (KA lyoo met). Region in Indiana; lake and city near South Chicago; county in eastern Wisconsin.
Champaign (sham PANE).
County and city in central Illinois; county in central Ohio.
Cheboygan (shi BOY gen). County and city in Michigan. Also **Sheboygan** (shi BOY gen). County and city in Wisconsin.
Chillicothe (chil li KOTH ee). City in Ohio; city in Illinois.
Coshocton (co SHOCK ton). County and city in central Illinois.
Cuyahoga (kai HO guh or kai yuh HO guh). County and river in Ohio.
Gogebic (go GEE bik). County and lake in Michigan; iron-ore range in Wisconsin and Michigan.
Kankakee (kang kuh KEE). County, city and river in Illinois.
Mackinac (MAK ih naw). County, village, island and straits in Michigan. Also **Mackinaw** (MAK ih naw). Village in Michigan; river and village in Illinois.
Menominee (muh NAH muh nee). County, city and iron-ore range in Michigan; river in Wisconsin and Michigan.
Moline (mo LEEN). City in northwestern Illinois.
Pekin (PEE kin). City in central Illinois.

Racine (ray SEEN). County ar city in Wisconsin; town in Oh
Sauk (SAWK). Indian tribe of Chief Black Hawk; county in Wisconsin.
Sault Ste. Marie (SOO saint REE). City in Michigan; site of canals connecting Lakes Supe and Huron.
Tahquamenon (tuk WAH mu nun). River and falls in Michig
Tecumseh (te KUM sa). Nineteenth Century chief of th Shawnee Indians; village in Michigan.
Vincennes (vin SENS). City in Indiana on the Wabash River.
Ypsilanti (IP sil an ti). City in southeastern Michigan.

edits and acknowledgments

Maps for front and back
end papers by Jeppesen
& Company, Denver,
Colorado, and for pages
74 through 179 © by The
H. M. Gousha Company,
San Jose, California.
Maps on pages 11, 52, 76
and 91 by Lothar Roth.

sources for the illustrations
appear in this book are
vn below. Credits for the
res from left to right are
rated by commas, from top
ottom by dashes.
er—John Zimmerman.
t end papers—Drawings by
ard Boland.
oter 1: 8-9—Art Sinsabaugh.
—Drawings by James Flora.
—John T. McCutcheon and
Chicago Tribune. 13—
vings by James Flora.
15—Map and drawings by
van Eersel. 17 through
—John Zimmerman. 24, 25—
Spiegel from Rapho
umette except top center
Munroe and center second
left John Zimmerman.
27—John Zimmerman.
oter 2: 29—Courtesy State
orical Society of Wisconsin.
31—Map and drawings by
van Eersel. 33—Culver
res, Inc. 35—Culver
res, Inc. 37—Drawing by
van Eersel. 39—Joe
roe. 40, 41—Top J. C. Allen
tesy Funk Brothers Seed
pany, bottom Joe Munroe.
42, 43—Joe Munroe. 44—
Peterson. 45—The Pillsbury
pany, Joe Munroe—Joe
roe, Bob Peterson. 46, 47—
Munroe.
oter 3: 48—Culver Pictures,
50, 51—Culver Pictures,
53—Illinois Historical
ety. 55—Ohio State Historical
ety. 56—Drawings by
ph Bertelli. 57—United
s International—Torkel
ng, Wide World. 59—The
ago Historical Society.

60, 61—No credit, Wide World.
62, 63—United Press
International, Wide World (2).
64, 65—Joseph Locke—Wide
World. 66, 67—No credit,
Billy Davis for the Louisville
Courier-Journal.
Chapter 4: 68, 69—Howard
Sochurek. 70—Drawing by Otto
van Eersel adapted from material
provided by St. Lawrence Seaway
Development Corporation. 71—
Drawing by Joseph Bertelli
adapted from Frontier Living by
Edwin Tunis; copyright The
World Publishing Company. 72—
Drawing by Joseph Bertelli. 73—
From the Collection of Captain
Frederick Way Jr. 74, 75—United
Press International. 77—
Drawing by Otto van Eersel
adapted from material provided
by American Shipbuilding
Company. 79—A. Y. Owen.
80 through 87—Howard
Sochurek.
Chapter 5: 88—John
Zimmerman. 92—The Ford
Motor Company Archives. 95—
Association of American
Railroads. 97 through 107—Ted
Spiegel from Rapho Guillumette.
Chapter 6: 108—Joe Munroe.
111—Trains Collection, from
The Interurban Era © Kalmbach
Publishing Company. 112—Wide
World. 113—United Press
International. 114—Courtesy
George Hoefer. 115—Wallace
Kirkland courtesy Hull Mansion,
Francis Miller. 116—Fran Byrne,
drawing by George V. Kelvin.
117—Chicago Tribune. 119—
Leonard McCombe. 120—
Chicago's American, Chicago
Sun-Times and Chicago Daily
News, Chicago's American—no
credit, Chicago Tribune, courtesy
Montgomery Ward & Co.—
Chicago's American. 121, 122,
123—Leonard McCombe. 124—
Bernard Hoffman—The Detroit
News (3)—Leonard McCombe.
125—Leonard McCombe—Fred
Schnell. 126, 127—Leonard
McCombe except extreme left
Wide World, Walter Sanders from
Black Star. 128, 129—Left

Chicago's American, Paul
Toppelstein for The Cleveland
Press—The Cleveland Press, Paul
Toppelstein for The Cleveland
Press—Leonard McCombe; right
Leonard McCombe (2). 130—
The Milwaukee Journal (3), S. L.
Stein for State Historical Society
of Wisconsin—Fred Schnell,
Leonard McCombe. 131—
Frank Scherschel for FORTUNE.
Chapter 7: 132—Laurence Lowry
from Rapho Guillumette. 134—
Michigan Historical Commission
Archives. 135—The Willard
Library, Battle Creek, Michigan.
137—No credit, The Chicago
Plan Commission. 139—George
Skadding. 141—Gordon Tenney.
142-143—Gordon Tenney
except left Richard Meek. 144
through 147—Gordon Tenney.
148, 149—Richard Meek.
150, 151—Gordon Tenney.
Chapter 8: 152—Wallace
Kirkland. 154—Michigan
Historical Commission Archives.
155—The Bettmann Archive,
no credit. 156—Chicago
Historical Society. 157—Frank
Scherschel, Alfred Eisenstaedt.
158—Culver Pictures, Inc. 159—
The Bettmann Archive except left
and second from right Culver
Pictures, Inc. 160-161—
Courtesy the University of
Chicago. 163—Henry Hamilton
Bennett, courtesy the H. H.
Bennett Studio, Wisconsin Dells,
Wis. 164 through 169—Fred
Schnell. 170, 171—Fred Schnell
(2)—A. Y. Owen. 172, 173—
Fred Schnell. 182 through 185—
Drawings by Rudolf Freund.
Back end papers—Drawings by
Richard Boland.

The editors of this book wish to
thank the following persons and
institutions for their assistance:
The American Ship Building
Company, Lorain, Ohio; Yeatman
Anderson, Curator of Rare Books,
and Clyde Bowden, Curator of
the Inland Rivers Library, Public
Library of Cincinnati and
Hamilton County, Ohio;
Association of Western Railways,
Chicago; Raymond S. Baby,
Curator of Archeology, The Ohio
Historical Society, Columbus;

Burger Brewing Company,
Cincinnati; Chicago Daily News
Library; Chicago Historical
Society; Chicago Sun-Times
Library; Chicago Tribune Library;
Chicago's American Library;
Chrysler Corporation, Press
Information Services, Public
Relations Office, Detroit; The
Cincinnati Post and Times-Star;
Dayton and Montgomery County
Public Library, Ohio; Reverend
Edward J. Dowling, S.J., Curator
of the Detroit Marine Historical
Collection, University of Detroit;
Richard Flerage, President,
Flerage Marine, Inc., Cincinnati;
Mrs. Lawrence C. Goodhue,
Executive Secretary, Chamber of
Commerce, Greencastle, Indiana;
The Grand Rapids Public Library,
Michigan; The Great Lakes
Historical Society, Cleveland;
Leonora Hass, Carnegie Public
Library, Sault Ste. Marie,
Michigan; Hazel Hopper and
Louise Wood, Indiana State
Library, Indianapolis; Sidney
Horenstein, Department of Fossil
Invertebrates, American Museum
of Natural History, New York City;
Illinois State Historical Society,
Springfield; Indiana Historical
Society, Indianapolis; Benjamin
F. Klein, Young and Klein, Inc.,
Cincinnati; Dr. Ralph E. Krenzin,
Department of Agronomy, Cornell
University, Ithaca, New York;
Donald Lynch, Lynch Fish
Company, Cincinnati; Jacob
Meckstroth, Columbus, Ohio;
James E. Miller, Chairman,
Department of Meteorology and
Oceanography, New York
University, New York City;
Museum of the American Indian,
Heye Foundation, New York City;
Saint Lawrence Seaway
Development Corporation,
Massena, New York; Janet Coe
Sanborn, Cleveland Public Library;
Anne Shepherd, Eleanor Wirmel,
The Cincinnati Historical Society
Library; State Historical Society of
Michigan, Lansing; The State
Historical Society of Wisconsin,
Madison; State of Ohio
Department of Natural Resources,
Columbus; The Summit County
Historical Society, Akron; Trains
Magazine, Milwaukee.

Bibliography

Available also in paperback.
† Available only in paperback.

General and historical reading

Angle, Paul M., *Bloody Williamson*. Alfred A. Knopf, 1952.

Bald, F. Clever, *Michigan in Four Centuries*. Harper & Brothers, 1961.

Billington, Ray Allen, *Westward Expansion*. The Macmillan Company, 1960.

Bond, Beverley W., Jr., *The Civilization of the Old Northwest*. The Macmillan Company, 1934.

Brownell, Baker, *The Other Illinois*. Duell, Sloan and Pearce, 1958.

Buley, R. Carlyle, *The Old Northwest: Pioneer Period, 1815-1840*. Indiana University Press, 1950.

Ford, Thomas, *A History of Illinois—1818-1847*, 2 vols. The Lakeside Press, 1945.

Gara, Larry, *A Short History of Wisconsin*. The State Historical Society of Wisconsin, 1962.

Goulder, Grace, *This Is Ohio*. The World Publishing Company, 1965.

Harlow, Ralph, *The Serene Cincinnatians*. E. P. Dutton and Company, 1950.

Havighurst, Walter:
The Great Lakes Reader. The Macmillan Company, 1966.
The Heartland: Ohio, Indiana, Illinois. Harper & Row Publishers, 1962.
Land of Promise. The Macmillan Company, 1946.
Land of the Long Horizons. Coward-McCann, 1960.
The Long Ships Passing.* The Macmillan Company, 1942.
Wilderness for Sale. Hastings House, 1956.

Hinsdale, B. A., *The Old Northwest*. Townsend MacCoun, 1888.

Lewis, Lloyd, and Henry Justin Smith, *Chicago: The History of Its Reputation*. Harcourt, Brace and Company, 1929.

McKee, Russell, *Great Lakes Country*. Thomas Y. Crowell Company, 1966.

Martin, John Bartlow:
Call It North Country; the Story of Upper Michigan. Alfred A. Knopf, 1944.
Indiana: An Interpretation. Alfred A. Knopf, 1947.

Masters, Edgar Lee, *The Tale of Chicago*. G. P. Putnam's Sons, 1933.

Nye, Russel B., *Midwestern Progressive Politics*.* Michigan State University Press, 1959.

Parkman, Francis, *A Half-Century of Conflict*.* Little, Brown, 1892.

Paxson, Frederic, *History of the American Frontier 1763-1893*. Houghton Mifflin Company, 1924.

Pierce, Bessie Louise, *A History of Chicago*, 3 vols. Alfred A. Knopf, 1937, 1940, 1957.

Quaife, Milo M., and Sidney Glazer, *Michigan*. Prentice-Hall, 1948.

Rose, William Ganson, *Cleveland: The Making of a City*. The World Publishing Company, 1950.

Roseboom, Eugene H., and Frances P. Weisenburger, *A History of Ohio*. The Ohio State Archaeological and Historical Society, 1953.

Turner, Frederick Jackson:
The Frontier in American History.* Holt, Rinehart & Winston, 1962.
Rise of the New West: 1819-1829.* Peter Smith, 1959.

Special topics

Baldwin, Leland D., *The Keelboat Age on Western Waters*. University of Pittsburgh Press, 1960.

Beer, Thomas, *Hanna*. Alfred A. Knopf, 1941.

Carson, Gerald, *Cornflake Crusade*. Rinehart and Company, 1957.

Condit, Carl W., *The Chicago School of Architecture*. University of Chicago Press, 1964.

David, Henry, *The History of the Haymarket Affair*.* Russell & Russell, 1936.

Doan, Edward N., *The La Follettes and the Wisconsin Idea*.* Rinehart and Company, 1947.

Duffey, Bernard, *The Chicago Renaissance in American Letters*.* Michigan State University Press, 1954.

Ginger, Ray, *The Bending Cross; A Biography of Eugene Debs*.* Rutgers University Press, 1949.

Hansen, Harry, *Midwest Portraits*. Harcourt, Brace and Company, 1923.

Hatcher, Harlan:
A Century of Iron and Men. The Bobbs-Merrill Company, 1950.
The Western Reserve. The World Publishing Company, 1966.

Hilton, George W., *The Great Lakes Car Ferries*. Howell-North Books, 1962.

Holbrook, Stewart H., *Holy Old Mackinaw*. The Macmillan Company, 1938.

Jordan, Philip Dillon, *The National Road*. The Bobbs-Merrill Company, 1948.

Klein, Benjamin F., *The Ohio River Handbook and Picture Album*. Young and Klein, 1964.

Lindsey, Almont, *The Pullman Strike*.* University of Chicago Press, 1942.

Mabee, Carleton, *The Seaway Story*. The Macmillan Company, 1961.

Middleton, William D., *The Interurban Era*. Kalmbach Publishing Company, 1961.

Nevins, Allan, and Frank Ernest Hill:
Ford: Decline and Rebirth. Charles Scribner's Sons, 1962.
Ford: Expansion and Challenge. Charles Scribner's Sons, 1957.
Ford: The Times, The Man, The Company. Charles Scribner's Sons, 1954.

Nordhoff, Charles, *The Communistic Societies of the United States*.* Harper & Bros., 1875. Schocken Books, 1965.

Price, Robert, *Johnny Appleseed, Man and Myth*. Indiana University Press, 1954.

Russell, Charles Edward, *A Rafting on the Mississippi*. The Century Company, 1928.

Sandburg, Carl, *Abraham Lincoln: The Prairie Years*.* Harcourt, Brace and Company, 1929.

Siegel, Arthur, ed., *Chicago's Famous Buildings*.* University of Chicago Press, 1965.

Tucker, Glenn, *Tecumseh, Vision of Glory*. The Bobbs-Merrill Company, 1956.

Wilson, William E., *The Angel and the Serpent; the Story of New Harmony*. Indiana University Press, 1964.

Natural setting and wildlife

Alley, Hartley, *Southern Indiana*. Indiana University Press, 1965.

Banta, R. E., *The Ohio*. Rinehart and Company, 1949.

Burt, William Henry, *Mammals of the Great Lakes Region*. University of Michigan Press, 1957.

Conant, Roger, *A Field Guide to Reptiles and Amphibians of Eastern North America*. The Peterson Field Guide Series. Houghton Mifflin Company, 1958.

Derleth, August, *The Wisconsin*. Farrar & Rinehart, 1942.

Gray, James, *The Illinois*. Farrar & Rinehart, 1940.

Hansen, Harry, *The Chicago*. Farrar & Rinehart, 1942.

Hatcher, Harlan:
The Great Lakes. Oxford University Press, 1944.
Lake Erie. The Bobbs-Merrill Company, 1945.

Hatcher, Harlan, and Erich A. W
*A Pictorial History of the Gr
Lakes*. Crown Publishers, 1

Hylander, Clarence J., and Edi
Farrington Johnston, *The
Macmillan Company Wild F
Book*. The Macmillan Comp
1954.

Landon, F., *Lake Huron*. The B
Merrill Company, 1944.

Lillard, Richard G., *The Great
Forest*. Alfred A. Knopf, 194

Masters, Edgar Lee, *The Sang
Farrar & Rinehart, 1942.

Nute, G. L., *Lake Superior*. The
Bobbs-Merrill Company, 19

Peterson, Roger Tory, *A Field
Guide to the Birds*.* Hought
Mifflin Company, 1947.

Pough, Richard H., *Audubon L
Bird Guide*. Doubleday and
Company, 1949.

Quaife, Milo M., *Lake Michiga
The Bobbs-Merrill Company

Sargent, Charles Sprague, *Mar
of the Trees of North Ameri
2 vols. Dover Publications, 1

Trautman, Milton B., *The Fishe
Ohio*. Ohio State University
Press, 1957.

Wilson, William E., *The Wabas
Farrar & Rinehart, 1940.

Guidebooks

Fodor, Eugene, ed., *Fodor Shel
Travel Guides U.S.A.;
Midwest*.* David McKay
Company, 1966.

Great Lakes Area.† Mobil Oil
Company and Simon and
Schuster, 1966.

Hepburn, Andrew:
Complete Guide to Chicago.
Doubleday & Company, 196
*Complete Guide to the Grea
Lakes*.† Doubleday &
Company, 1962.

Illinois Writers' Project, *Illinois.
A Descriptive and Historical
Guide*. A. C. McClurg &
Company, 1939; rev. 1947.

Indiana, State of Surprises.†
Indiana Department of
Commerce, 1966.

Indiana Writers' Project, *Indian
A Guide to the Hoosier Stat
Oxford University Press, 19

Michigan Writers' Project,
*Michigan: A Guide to the
Wolverine State*. Oxford
University Press, 1964.

Ohio Writers' Project:
*Cincinnati: A Guide to the
Queen City and Its Neighbor
The Wiesen-Hart Press, 194
The Ohio Guide. Oxford
University Press, 1940.

Wisconsin Writers' Project,
*Wisconsin: A Guide to the
Badger State*. Duell, Sloan a
Pearce, 1941.

PRODUCTION STAFF FOR TIME INCORPORATED
John L. Hallenbeck (Vice President and Director of Production),
Robert E. Foy, Caroline Ferri and Robert E. Fraser
Text photocomposed under the direction of Albert J. Dunn and Arthur J. Dunn

The Heartland: the works of man

Total land area of the Heartland covers 244,811 square miles, about 7 per cent of the United States. The five states comprise most of the old Northwest Territory, a region set up by the Northwest Ordinance of 1787. Early surveys created the checkerboard character of the present county lines. With more than 38 million residents, the region is the most populous of those in the TIME-LIFE Library of America series.

Economic activity throughout the region is widely diversified. Heavy industry, such as auto manufacturing and steel production, is located along the lakeshores, for the lakes enable manufacturers to transport huge quantities of raw materials cheaply by ship. Also along the lakes are most of the larger cities, located in a belt that includes dairy and truck farming. Many of the products made farther south, such as farm machinery, are closely connected with agriculture. The highly productive Corn Belt of the lower Heartland makes the region a very important farming area. In the North Woods, lumbering, recreation and mining are major pursuits.

Historical monuments in the Heartland range from Serpent Mound, a huge animal effigy built by prehistoric Indians, to the architect Frank Lloyd Wright's most notable modern structures, such as Taliesin, his home in Spring Green, Wisconsin. Many buildings associated with Abraham Lincoln, such as those reproduced in Lincoln's New Salem State Park *(above)*, are open to visitors.